K·I·S·S

The Only Guides You'll Ever Need!

THIS SERIES IS YOUR TRUSTED GUIDE through all of life's stages and situations. Want to learn how to surf the Internet or care for your new dog? Or maybe you'd like to become a wine connoisseur or an expert gardener? The solution is simple: just pick up a K.I.S.S. Guide and turn to the first page.

Expert authors will walk you through the subject from start to finish, using simple blocks of knowledge to build your skills one step at a time. Build upon these learning blocks and by the end of the book, you'll be an expert yourself! Or, if you are familiar with the topic but want to learn more, it's easy to dive in and pick up where you left off.

The K.I.S.S. Guides deliver what they promise: simple access to all the information you'll need on one subject. Other titles you might want to check out include: Playing Guitar, Living With a Dog, the Internet, Yoga, Sailing, Gambling, and many more.

GUIDE TO

DIY

MARTIN PRESTON

Foreword by Mike Lawrence
Bestselling author of over 50 DIY books

A Dorling Kindersley Book

LONDON, NEW YORK,
MUNICH, MELBOURNE, DELHI

Dorling Kindersley Limited
Project Editor Caroline Hunt
Managing Editor Maxine Lewis
Managing Art Editor Heather McCarry

Production Heather Hughes
Category Publisher Mary Thompson

DK Publishing Inc.
Editors Eve P. Steinberg, John T. Cunningham
Series Editor Jennifer Williams
Editorial Director Chuck Wills

Created and produced for Dorling Kindersley by
M-Press Publishing Ltd,
61-63, Churchfield Road, Acton, London W3 6AY

The M-Press team
Rob Bennett, Ieva Carroll, Jeff Carroll, Judy Fovargue,
Nicki Gault, Christine Heilman, Ed Herridge, Nich Hills,
Edward Horton, David Preston, Mike Trier,
Jerry Udall, and Darius Valoutis

First published in Great Britain
by Dorling Kindersley Limited
80 Strand, London WC2R 0RL
A Penguin Company

2 4 6 8 10 9 7 5 3

Copyright © 2001
Dorling Kindersley Limited
Text copyright © 2001 Martin Preston

A CIP catalogue record for this book is available from the British Library

ISBN 0 7513 3847 8

Colour reproduction by ColourScan, Singapore
Printed and bound by MOHN media and Mohndruck GmbH, Germany

For our complete catalogue visit
www.dk.com

Contents at a Glance

PART ONE

DIY Basics

Do You or Don't You?
Keeping it Simple
Don't Blame Your Tools!
Tricks of the Trade

PART TWO

Decorating

Painting Walls and Ceilings
Painting Woodwork
Wallpapering
Ceramic Tiling
Staining and Varnishing
Laying Floorcoverings

PART THREE

Indoor Improvements

Doors and Windows
Floors and Staircases
Shelves and Storage
Walls and Ceilings
Heating and Ventilation

PART FOUR

Outdoor Improvements

Fences and Gates
Paths and Patios
Walls and Roofs
Gutters and Drainage

PART FIVE

Plumbing and Electrics

Know Your Plumbing
Home Plumbing Jobs
Know Your Electrics
Home Electrical Jobs

CONTENTS

PART ONE DIY Basics

PART FOUR Outdoor Improvements

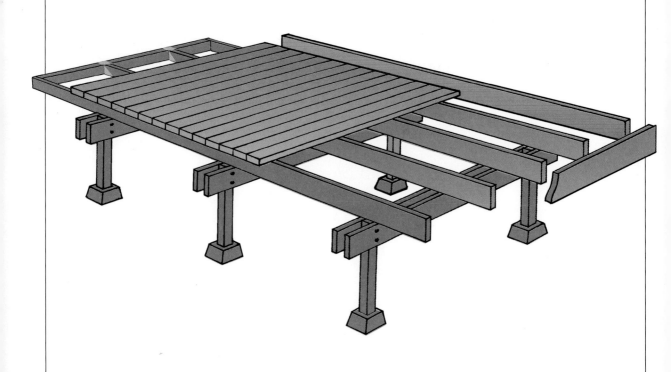

PART FIVE Plumbing and Electrics

APPENDICES

Foreword

I've been writing about DIY for almost 30 years now, and in that time it has changed almost beyond recognition. It used to be a necessary activity for people who couldn't afford the local handyman, and it involved either buying whatever the local hardware store stocked or braving the arcane world of the trade merchant whose staff sneered at the ignorant amateur trespassing on their premises. DIY wasn't easy back then, and you had to have patience and perseverance in abundance to succeed. Then two big things happened to change everything.

The first was the arrival of the sheds – huge aircraft hangers stocking the stuff of DIY dreams. Here you could buy paint that didn't drip, wallpaper with paste already on the back, shelves shrink-wrapped and ready to put on their brackets, plumbing fittings and pipework that didn't need assembling with a blowlamp, wood cut to size and ready to use, power tools that took the hard work out of all sorts of jobs… the list went on and on. Everything you needed was under one roof, and you could browse to your heart's content before making up your mind.

The second big thing was a revolution in DIY information. In the old days, Dad did the DIY and if you were interested, he'd pass on his wisdom – and eventually his old toolkit – to you. There was no other realistic way of finding out how to do things. The instructions that came with tools and materials were minimal or non-existent. Then magazines and books about DIY started to appear in ever-increasing numbers, with information about the latest products and pages of detailed instructions that made any job look clear and manageable. They contained step-by-step instructions complete with photographs, exploded illustrations, and checklists to help you shop without forgetting half the things you needed. They helped you to learn new skills and to master techniques that only the professionals used to know about. They meant you could be a builder, a carpenter, a decorator, an electrician, a plasterer, or a plumber – or all of these. All you needed was the time…

This information revolution, coupled with being able to get hold of DIY tools and materials easily, has turned DIY into a mainstream leisure activity for millions of people. They have discovered that improving their homes is fun, and that it also maximizes their investment in their home as the biggest asset they are ever likely to own. They're becoming increasingly ambitious in their aspirations, which are fuelled in particular by the growing number of home interest magazines and television programmes featuring a wide range of home and garden improvements. They're keen to master new techniques, and to tackle projects they might not have considered within their capabilities in the past. They also want to keep out of the clutches of the DIY cowboys by carrying out home improvement and repair work themselves if they can. They have become masters of their own DIY destiny.

To do all this, they need DIY information that is accessible, comprehensive and up to date, but that doesn't ignore traditional skills and techniques where these are relevant. That's where the KISS Guide to DIY kicks in. It's the new kid on the block, distilling years of DIY progress and evolution into one handy, bang up-to-date book that lives up to its name in every respect – to keep it simple, stupid. It's a book for everyone with a DIY dream. If you're a complete novice, it introduces the tools, skills and techniques you need, and holds your hand as you climb the ladder to DIY competence. If you think you know a bit about what you're tackling, it will confirm that you're on the right track and teach you new things as you proceed. And even if you're a DIY know-all, it will still surprise you with tricks of the trade and handy short-cuts that will give great results and get you out of trouble when things don't go according to plan. Keep it in your toolbox and you'll always be able to keep DIY simple.

Mike Lawrence

Introduction

WELL DONE! Okay, so you haven't done very much yet. But you have opened this book, and that's a start. It's also a good investment, because the next time something goes wrong with your home, instead of reaching in a panic for the Yellow Pages, you'll be calmly picking up your toolkit – and in all probability fixing the fault in less time than it takes a contractor to calculate the emergency call-out charges. Take that one bold step, and pretty soon you'll be walking tall. Shelves, kitchen cabinets, a new floor... easy; new taps, an extra socket, garden lights... no problem. It's a wonderfully reassuring feeling to know you can do it. And now, that knowledge is within your grasp.

Not that it will all be easy, of course. I'd be less than honest if I tried to persuade you otherwise. When I first started fixing things, which admittedly was a very, very long time ago, I found myself breaking out in a cold sweat every time I so much as picked up a screwdriver. It felt like my first driving lesson. And then it dawned on me that like car drivers, every one of those people you see confidently cruising down the aisles of your local DIY store had to start somewhere. So don't worry if you're a little nervous – you've every right to be. It's your home, after all!

Right, let's make some plans. First we'll go through the vexed question of "do you or don't you?" We'll be doing plenty, I promise, but there are some things that, as a relative newcomer to DIY, you really would be better off leaving to the experts. Like pitched roofs, for example, where the safety risks simply don't justify attempting to save money. And plastering, which takes months, even years, of practice to get right.

Still with me? Great, then we'll move on to the basic skills that all self-respecting do-it-yourselfers need to have tucked under their belt. You'll be using or adapting the information in these chapters again and again, so please give it your best shot. Decorating comes next, and on the basis that people do it more than any other form of home improvement, I've really gone to town on this section.

The next two sections cover indoor and outdoor improvements – repair jobs and home-enhancing projects that won't stretch either your skills or your budget. Then, to round things off, we'll look at plumbing and electrics. In my experience, these split do-it-yourselfers neatly into two camps: those that do (and love it) and those who would just as soon take up brain surgery. But even if you're one of the latter, it will still pay dividends to know how these essential services work – and what to do in an emergency.

Finally, a few points by way of explanation. First, I've used metric measurements throughout. That's the way most things are sold these days, and there's a real danger that you'll double the possibility of errors if you mix systems. Second, I've tried to be non-product specific as much as possible. DIY products and brands change faster than Premier League football strips, and my sincere hope is that you'll find this book useful for many years to come. And lastly, apologies for not covering everything. Can I just say in my defence that if I had, this book would have gone on. And on. And on. Anyway, I've talked the talk, so now it's time to walk the walk. Don't worry – I'll be with you every step of the way. Oh yes, and good luck!

MARTIN PRESTON

What's Inside?

THE INFORMATION IN THE KISS Guide to DIY *is arranged by the types of job you have to do, with early chapters getting you up-to-speed on some of the basic information and techniques you'll need to complete these tasks.*

PART ONE

In Part One I'll teach you the basics that you should know before tackling any DIY project. You'll be introduced to the tools you need and to the basic techniques. I'll also advise on which jobs you can do yourself, and which are best left to the professionals.

PART TWO

Part Two will cover decorating your house. You'll learn about painting, wallpapering and tiling ceilings and walls, as well as preparing and painting wood. To finish off, I'll teach you about laying floor coverings.

PART THREE

In Part Three I'll teach show you how to improve the inside of your house. We'll cover doors and windows, floors and staircases, fitting and building shelving, walls, and and dealing with heating and ventilation.

PART FOUR

Part Four deals with outdoor improvements, covering the outside of your house as well as your garden. You'll find out about fencing, laying paths and patios, repairing and maintaining walls and roofs, as well as gutters and drainage.

PART FIVE

Part Five covers perhaps the most daunting areas of do-it-yourself – plumbing and electrical jobs. I'll teach you a bit of theory on both before covering the common jobs that a do-it-yourselfer should be able to tackle.

The Extras

THROUGHOUT THE BOOK, *you will notice a number of boxes and symbols. They are there to emphasize certain points I want you to pay special attention to, because they are important to your understanding and improvement. You'll find:*

Very Important Point

This symbol points out a topic I believe deserves careful attention. You really need to know this information before continuing.

Complete No-No

This is a warning, something I want to advise you not to do or to be aware of.

Getting Technical

When the information is about to get a bit technical, I'll let you know so that you can read carefully.

Inside Scoop

These are special suggestions and tips come from my own personal experience, which I've found useful over the years.

You'll also find some little boxes that include information I think is important, useful, or just plain fun.

Trivia...
These are interesting DIY facts that will give you an extra appreciation for the history and background of some techniques.

DEFINITION
*Here I'll **define** words and terms for you in an easy-to-understand style. You'll also find a Glossary at the back of the book with DIY terms and phrases.*

INTERNET
www.dk.com

The Internet can be a useful resource for DIYers, so I've scouted out some web sites that will help source materials and give useful tips and advice.

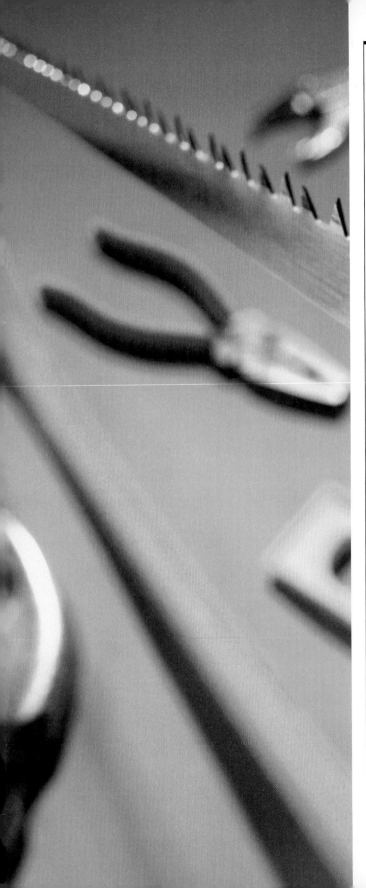

PART ONE

START WITH THE BASICS

Chapter 1

Do You or Don't You?

SOME DO-IT-YOURSELF JOBS ARE EASY. Others aren't. Sometimes it's because they require a host of expensive tools. More often, it's because they require practice – the kind of practice that comes from doing them day in, day out. As a beginner, it will pay you to know the difference, and to steer clear of the jobs that are likely to land you in trouble. Rest assured, it's not defeatist; it's just plain common sense.

In this chapter...

✓ Know your limitations

✓ Be prepared!

✓ Calling in the professionals

Know your limitations

IT'S AMAZING how many do-it-yourselfers leap right in without really knowing what they're doing. You wouldn't attempt to do brain surgery without a little practice – and the same thing applies to some areas of home improvement!

Is it worth it?

Before you set out to do any DIY, ask yourself the following questions:

1. **Do I know what I'm doing?** This applies especially to alterations or additions to plumbing and electrical systems, and to any kind of structural modifications. If you're in any doubt about the safety of a job, don't do it.

   Some jobs are nearly always best left to the professionals, including anything to do with gas appliances, pressurized water heating systems, and work on roofs (even if you're not scared of heights, actually working at a height is very different from simply being high up).

2. **Do I have enough practice?** Some home improvement skills, such as plastering, simply cannot be learned out of books alone: you need to have a natural talent for them, and to practise – sometimes for years. If the job you're planning falls into this category, do the smart thing and call in a professional; otherwise, you could spend twice as much making good your mistakes.

3. **Am I equipped?** Without the right equipment, your chances of successfully carrying out certain jobs will be severely limited. Also, buying or hiring what you need may well turn out to be more expensive than getting the job done professionally. The way to beat this trap is to build up a network of like-minded friends with whom you can swap tools and equipment.

4. **Do I have the time?** As an enthusiastic amateur, you'll almost certainly take longer to do things than an expert. This may not matter if you have time on your hands – but there again, you could be better off earning money doing something you're really good at and leaving the home improvements to a professional.

5. **Is it allowed?** In the UK you need building permission (from your local authority's Building Control Office) for some jobs. I'll be pointing out in this book where such regulations may apply. Major additions or alterations may need Planning Permission.

Be prepared!

THERE'S A TIME *and a place for everything, so they say – and that includes home improvements. Pick your time carefully, and be prepared for anything!*

When to do it

Unless there's an emergency, it's a good idea to "store up" DIY jobs – particularly those in a single room or area – until you've enough of them to justify the time and trouble of preparing the house. And prepare the house you must do, for even simple tasks can create clouds of plaster dust that get everywhere. Another great enemy of DIY is clutter, so organize things so that the area you're working in is as clear as possible.

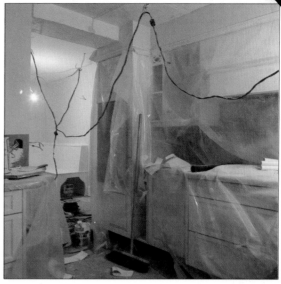

■ **Clear up, cover up:** *it may be a chore, but time spent clearing away clutter, masking fixtures, and laying dust sheets will be rewarded.*

Old bed-linen makes a far better dust protector than plastic disposable sheets, which tend to slip out of place and be slippery underfoot. Tape the sheets to skirtings, and run lengths of tape along the gaps around doors.

And some more points to remember…

- Those in the know do their DIY when the stores are open: no matter how well organized you are, there's bound to be something you've forgotten or need to hire in a hurry.

- Children and DIY don't mix. Kids have a fascination for tools, which could get them into a lot of trouble if they hang around while you're working.

- Keep the phone numbers of local tradespeople handy in case the worst does happen and you need to get hold of an expert urgently.

- Make certain you know how and where to turn off essential services, such as water, gas, and electricity.

ng in the professionals

O HAVE TO *call in a*
you want to be sure that
he or she does a good job for a fair
price. But as we all know, there are
plenty of cowboys out there, just
waiting to rope you in…

How to find contractors

By far the best way to hire a builder or
other trade professional is by personal
recommendation from someone you
trust. Failing that, always get at least two
quotations for the job. Choose firms that
are affiliated to a reputable trade
organization, and if they seem at all
reluctant to take on the job, move on
to the next one.

■ **Someone has to do it!** *Contractors in the*
building trade are notoriously unreliable, but if you
do your homework you should be able to ensure
you get one of the good guys.

Be aware that you'll nearly always pay more for work done
outside normal working hours. Even in an emergency, it may work
out cheaper to make a stop-gap repair until you can get the job
fixed properly by a professional.

Six steps to making a deal

1 Be sure both you and the contractor know the difference
between an *estimate*, the price of which isn't binding, and
a *quotation*, which contains a guaranteed fixed price for
the job. On larger jobs, if the contractor prepares a
specification, any later deviation from it – for example, to
fit better-grade windows – will be costed as an "extra". The
same goes if you later insist on a specific brand on which
the contractor is unable to get a trade discount.

2 Get contractors to explain what they propose to do and
what problems they anticipate. If it doesn't make sense, go
elsewhere; if it does, get it in writing.

> **DEFINITION**
>
> An **estimate** *is the*
> *contractor's opinion of what a*
> *job will cost, but it cannot be*
> *taken as binding. A*
> **quotation** *is a written*
> *specification and price, and*
> *as long as the specification*
> *doesn't change, it is binding.*

3 Be realistic about timescales. Good contractors tend to stay busy, so they may not be able to start immediately. Likewise, on jobs that must be done in good weather, both you and the contractor may be at the mercy of Mother Nature. Either way, aim never to be rushed into employing someone.

4 On larger jobs, it's perfectly normal for the contractor to ask for an advance to cover the cost of materials, or even for a "scale" of payments to be made at key stages of the job. But be sure to get a receipt, and don't pay more money if the job falls behind schedule. Oh, and never ever pay for the entire cost of a job in advance.

Trivia...

In 1948, President Harry S. Truman decided to call in the professionals when he noticed that the bath was sinking into the floor of his White House bathroom. It soon became clear that the whole building needed extensive refurbishment – and the builders were in for almost 4 years.

5 If you plan to be out, make sure your contractor takes adequate security precautions and tidies ladders away before leaving work. It's also worth checking if the contractor is covered for site theft, which is becoming an increasingly common form of burglary.

6 Arrange a time and a place to discuss the job and to run through faults – but don't stand over people's shoulders nitpicking or you'll arouse resentment. Don't settle the final bill until all faults have been put right. Having said all that, it is obvious sense to have a friendly, cooperative relationship with those you employ.

A simple summary

✔ Be realistic about what you can and can't do, taking into account the time and equipment you have available. And don't attempt to work on plumbing and electrical systems or the structure of the house unless you're sure you know what you're doing.

✔ Save up small jobs until you have enough to justify clearing the area in which you intend to work and sending children out for the day.

✔ If you find you have to call in a contractor, try to get one through personal recommendation. Failing that, choose firms that belong to a reputable trade organization and get at least two quotations for the job.

Chapter 2

Keeping It Simple

WHERE DOING THINGS YOURSELF IS CONCERNED, the simpler the better. A simple job is less likely to go wrong, is more likely to yield significant savings, and stands a better chance of being finished. So put those attic conversion plans on hold and try some of the ideas in this chapter instead. They promise results – fast.

In this chapter...

✓ Indoor decorating

✓ Outdoor decorating

✓ Kitchen and bathroom facelifts

✓ Better storage

✓ Securing your home

✓ Selling your home

SIMPLE CHANGES CAN MAKE A BIG DIFFERENCE

Indoor decorating

THANKS TO THE USER-FRIENDLINESS of modern decorating materials, you can accomplish in a weekend what would once have taken weeks of planning. So pick up your paintbrush and roller and try out some of the no-hassle facelifts described here.

1 Stuck for a colour scheme? Then start at the end! Go out and buy an attractive blind, curtain fabric, or bedspread and then pick out two or more colours from these. Alternatively, if a piece of packaging catches your eye, try combining the same colours, safe in the knowledge that they've been chosen by professionals. This is also the ideal time to take advantage of the paint-mixing service offered by many DIY stores – simply take a sample of the material with you and match it up.

2 Not sure about that colour you like? Buy one or more sampler pots, paint a whole wall, and see how it looks under different lighting conditions. Paler colours, particularly blues, often look much more intense on the wall than they do on the paint card, and pale yellows can change dramatically depending on whether they're in sunlight or artificial light. Better to be safe than sorry!

3 Frustrated by those lumpy, uneven walls that show their worst side every time you switch on a light? If you don't want to go to the lengths of having them replastered, resurface them with ready-mixed skimming plaster. You paint this on straight from the tub using a large wall brush, and smooth it out with the plastic spatula provided. After the plaster dries (about 24 hours), simply sand off any remaining blemishes. An even easier option is to repaint the wall (see pp. 78–79 for paint effects). The broken colour will disguise any blemishes, as well as giving the room a fresh new look.

4 Decent lighting will transform even the dowdiest room. Banish all overhead pendant lights and replace them with recessed, low-voltage downlighters, spots hung from a tensioned wire, or wall lights. For even quicker results, try positioning one or two free-standing uplighters in the corners. Many come with their own dimmer switch, giving you even more control.

■ **These strikingly** *vivid curtains and cushions are perfectly set off by the cool beige tones that predominate in the remainder of the room.*

Outdoor decorating

WHAT GOES FOR INDOORS *goes for the outside, too, especially during the summer months when you don't want your spirits dampened by a tired-looking house and garden. Aside from regular maintenance tasks, there are plenty of quick ways to brighten up your immediate surroundings.*

1 Repaint your old wooden garden furniture in Mediterranean-style pastels or bright primary colours. Make cushions to match, with an inner waterproof lining and washable outer cover. Checks and stripes look good in the garden.

2 Use interesting containers for pot plants. This is one area where plastic imitations of classic designs and materials really can win the day.

3 Give your plain concrete patio a new look. Engineering bricks laid in a herringbone pattern is a low-cost option, as is timber decking, which is available in kits from DIY superstores. Alternatively, to "bring the inside out", consider continuing a quarry tile or slate floor out onto the patio; it may be costly, but you'll find that in summer it turns the patio into an extra "room".

4 Replace old fencing or revive it with freshly painted trellis and plant bamboo in front of it to create a natural-looking screen.

5 Window boxes instantly brighten any home. For a clean, minimalist look, use plants of all one colour. Terracotta is the classic window box material, but wooden planters – such as those shaped like like mini picket fences – can also look very effective.

6 In a small garden, create the illusion of space and light by strategically placing a large mirror to catch the reflections from a brighter area. Carefully positioned, the mirror may even look as if it is a doorway to another part of the garden.

7 If you don't want to go to the trouble of properly wired outdoor lighting, try illuminating the garden with candles on sticks, lanterns, or flares, all of which are widely available from garden centres.

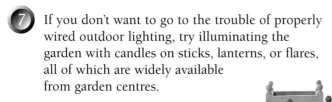

■ **There is** *a huge variety of containers for pot plants that will brighten up a patio or terrace.*

Kitchen and bathroom facelifts

THE KITCHEN IS THE HEART *of many homes, which often means it takes more of a battering than other parts of the house. The bathroom is likely to be a morning battleground for the entire family. In both cases, however, there's plenty you can do to give these rooms a new lease of life – short of a total refit.*

Simple ideas for the kitchen

1 Fitted kitchen cabinets look dowdy after a while, but if the cabinets themselves are structurally sound, consider replacing just the doors. Replacement door specialists advertise in decorating magazines, and because most cabinets are modular, there's seldom any problem with sizes. A cheaper option is to make your own doors from 15mm or 18mm MDF (medium density fibreboard) and paint them to match the rest of the kitchen. Bear in mind that a small kitchen will look much larger if the cabinets and walls are painted the same colour.

■ **Centre-island** *worksurfaces (with so much to hand directly overhead) form the heart of this traditional-looking but high-tech kitchen.*

2 Give tired old "white goods" such as a refrigerator or cooker, a new lease of life by repainting them with a metallic-effect paint such as Hammerite. Give the existing surface a light sanding first to provide a key for the new paint.

3 Fit a new worksurface. These days, the most popular materials are wood, which looks smart but is vulnerable to damage, and marble-effect resin, which looks uncannily like the real thing. This may also be the time to think about installing a new hob and cooker.

4 Fit a new floor. Popular materials include terracotta tiles, woodstrip flooring, or – simplest of all – sheet vinyl. Avoid hard ceramic tiles, as they tend to be cold and slippery underfoot and will show no mercy if you drop something on them.

5 Install or replace a tiled splashback. Old ones often consist of just a single row of plain tiles and accumulate layers of grime along the join with the worktop. Instead, consider carrying the new tiles up to the height of your wall cabinets, or finish them off with decorative moulded border tiles.

6. Consider revising your cooking arrangements and fitting one of the latest-generation "professional"-style freestanding cookers. These tend to be finished in stainless steel and come complete with matching extractor hood and splashback. Prices are tumbling all the time, and you'll definitely recoup the cost when you come to sell your home. Free-standing "walk-in" refrigerators are also making a big comeback, and are stylish enough to be treated as pieces of furniture in their own right. It could be worth sacrificing a couple of kitchen cabinets to make the space, and then "cannibalizing" them to fit out the areas where the old fridge and cooker used to be.

Don't attempt to fit a new gas appliance yourself, even if the connections are already there. Quite apart from the safety aspect, modern gas cookers tend to be highly pressure-sensitive and may need expert adjustment after installation.

7. Think about fitting new taps – and perhaps some matching new accessories such as a utensil rack, towel rail, or wine rack.

8. Banish worktop clutter by fitting an industrial-style, wall-mounted grid system. Hang utensils from butcher's hooks and fit wire baskets to take odds and ends.

9. Take a long, hard look at the lighting – especially if you also eat in the kitchen. Overhead lighting can be toned down by fitting low-voltage downlighters operated from a dimmer switch. You can also buy fluorescent "skeleton" striplights for illuminating worktops and providing atmospheric sidelighting. Simply screw them to the underside of your wall cabinets and connect to a power socket.

10. If you find that your wall cabinets encroach too much on working space, consider replacing them with industrial-style, open, stainless steel shelving. Having items on display is also a good way to avoid hoarding.

■ **Fluorescent downlighters** *softly illuminating natural materials like wood and brick can provide a kitchen with a warm, inviting atmosphere.*

Simple ideas for the bathroom

1 No matter how often – or how well – you clean tiled surfaces, the gaps between tiles will become grimy after a while. Clean the grouting using household bleach and an old toothbrush. Alternatively, you can buy a proprietary grout whitener. If the grouting is beyond a facelift, scraping it out and regrouting is not a big job. At the same time, replace any worn sealant around the bath, sink, and so on. Gouge the old sealant out with a screwdriver and clean off any residue with paintbrush cleaner, then reseal.

2 There's only so much that a bath mat can hide. If your bathroom carpet is worn or stained, a replacement will improve the look of the room instantly – look for cheap offcuts in carpet stores. But first, is carpet really your best option? The inevitable spills of bathwater, toothpaste, toiletries, and talcum powder won't do a carpet any good. Sheet vinyl or resilient vinyl tiles are two economical, easily cleaned, and much harder-wearing alternatives.

■ **Choose a new bath mat** *and a few matching accessories to give your bathroom an instant boost without spending a lot of money.*

3 Even though bath and basin taps can be cleaned until they gleam, consider buying new taps to give a fresh look to your bathroom without the expense of replacing the entire suite. Reinforce the effect with matching accessories in chrome or brass. And, if space is at a premium, an all-in-one chrome or brass towel rail and radiator is a smart, practical addition to any bathroom.

■ **New taps** *will brighten up your existing bathroom suite.*

4 Give the shower curtain a facelift. Shower curtains can be bleached and most are machine-washable – just hang them back up on the rail to dry. But splashing out on a new shower curtain, perhaps with a new bath mat and matching towels, certainly won't break the bank. A transparent plastic one with built-in pockets is a good buy. You can use the pockets for decorative items or to store everyday toiletries. Curtains are made in different thicknesses: the thin ones dry more quickly but may cling to your body.

5 Getting rid of the clutter will make you feel better. If you can, keep toiletries in a cupboard. If you can't, buy a couple of matching baskets to store bottles and tubes. It'll make your life easier when it comes to cleaning, and even giving the bottles a clean will brighten things up.

6 Tired of that plastic bath panel? Get modern and replace it with tongue-and-groove panelling. Continue the panelling around the walls up to chest height to give the room a more unified feel. Use low-cost medium density fibreboard, available in a tongue-and-groove effect.

Tongue-and-groove panelling needs to waterproofed, otherwise it will swell. To prevent damage, paint the panelling and seal it around the edges. Or apply a preservative wood stain – intended for outdoor use but equally suitable indoors.

7 If there are separate splashbacks around the bath and basin, consider unifying them with matching tiles up to chest height to give the room a smarter, more streamlined appearance. Finish the tiles off with a row of decorative border tiles or with painted or varnished wooden dado rail moulding.

8 Give your bathroom window a new look. You could replace outdated patterned or textured glass with frosted glass. Consider replacing curtains with a smart Roman or slatted blind, or with louvred shutters.

9 Get rid of that old-fashioned lighting. Wall lights or recessed downlighters will create a much cosier atmosphere. (But make sure all bathroom lighting is approved for bathroom use and is operated via a pull-cord switch.)

10 Stained ceramics can spoil your makeover. Use limescale remover to give them a new lease of life. The same cleaner will also add renewed sparkle to taps, watermarked tiles, and mirrors.

■ **The soft glow** *of wall-mounted lights lends a warmer feel to a tiled bathroom. For extra calm and relaxation, light a few candles, too.*

Better storage

WHY DO OTHER PEOPLE'S HOMES *always seem to have more cupboard space? Well, perhaps they haven't. They could be storing just the things they really need, or making better use of the space they've got.*

1. Before you reorganize your storage space, rationalize the things you are hoarding. Anything you haven't looked at, worn, or used in the past year can probably go, unless it is a valued memento. Check all foodstuffs for use-by dates and discard out-of-date spices and tins. Remember that make-up and toiletries have shelf-lives, too. Do you need to keep all your books and magazines? If you save magazines for inspiration, don't keep whole issues – just cut out the pictures you like and stick them in a scrapbook.

2. Items that you feel you must keep but which you're unlikely to use regularly, such as out-of-season clothes, holiday gear, decorations, and documents can be stored in less accessible places. Use boxes under beds, on tops of wardrobes, or in a cellar or attic.

3. Do you tend to throw things in an understairs cupboard, one layer upon another? You can store more under the stairs by building shelves. And lighting the area will help you find things more easily.

4. If you work at home, a simple box file unit – and a little self-discipline when it comes to using it – will enable you to keep on top of the paperwork.

5. Knowing what's in a cupboard or drawer helps. Label the doors or drawer fronts so you don't have to search through everything every time. Luggage labels with neat lettering look good. Or you could stick a Polaroid photo of a box's contents on the front.

6. Subdivide spaces in cupboards and wardrobes with hanging fabric shelves or clear plastic boxes. Multiple hangers will help you arrange your clothes much more easily and they save acres of wardrobe space.

■ **A wooden box file** *unit, neatly stacked, can take the panic out of paperwork.*

7 Even when they are neatly arranged, you don't always want to look at your stored belongings. For an uncluttered look, hide walls of shelving behind louvre doors (which have angled slats fitted in a wooden frame) or narrow double doors. Where space is at a premium, roller blinds or muslin curtains can be as effective.

8 Often the ideal solution is to use one room just for storage. Attic or cellar conversions are ideal, as are dark spare bedrooms; if you do it right, there's no reason why the room should look a mess. Line the walls with strong shelves and organize them by subject. Make sure the room is well lit, ventilated, and free of damp. Also ensure that all shelving is accessible, or the room may become a dumping ground that you never dare set foot in.

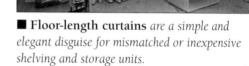

■ **Floor-length curtains** *are a simple and elegant disguise for mismatched or inexpensive shelving and storage units.*

Craft shops are full of beautiful boxes in a wide variety of styles, colours, and materials. You're bound to find some that would look just right in your room. But if space is short, it's best to avoid gimmicky, over-specialized storage items: even if they look fantastic, they're usually expensive and take up too much room.

■ **A built-in storage space** *like the base of this window seat provides a spot to stash magazines and other clutter. For more flexibility, look for a coffee table with a hinged top.*

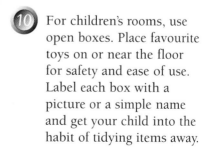

9 If space is tight consider that old favourite, the window seat, or items with unusual storage spaces, such as footstools and coffee tables with hinged lids and beds with drawers underneath.

10 For children's rooms, use open boxes. Place favourite toys on or near the floor for safety and ease of use. Label each box with a picture or a simple name and get your child into the habit of tidying items away.

Securing your home

MOST BURGLARS ARE OPPORTUNISTS, *on the look-out for a house or flat that seems like an easy target. Don't let them choose your home. You can do a great deal to put off all but the most determined intruder by following the basic precautions described here.*

1 Use lighting to fool a burglar into thinking that the house is occupied. Leave a light on in a living room or bedroom while you are out, preferably attached to a timer switch so lights aren't on at an unlikely time of the day or night. It's not a good idea to keep curtains and blinds drawn while you are away.

2 Don't bother fitting a good lock to a weak door; someone trying to force an entry will only kick down the door. It's vital to replace a front or back door that has a hollow core by a solid hardwood door. The same applies to windows – it doesn't matter how many locks you fit if the wood in your windows is rotten; a burglar will simply force the frame.

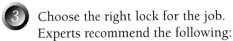

Don't leave windows and external doors open when you're not around to keep an eye on them. In about a quarter of all domestic break-ins, the burglar gains access through a window or door left open by careless householders who think it can't happen to them.

3 Choose the right lock for the job. Experts recommend the following:
- **Front door:** a five-lever mortise deadlock (British Standard BS 3621) plus an automatic deadlocking rim lock.
- **Back door:** a mortise sash lock (BS 3621) and mortise rack bolts or surface-mounted key locks.
- **Sliding glass doors:** key-operated surface-mounted locks at the top and bottom, plus an anti-lift device to keep doors in their tracks.
- **Windows:** key-operated locks or sash stops.
- **French windows:** fit mortise rack bolts or security pressbolts at the top and bottom of each door.

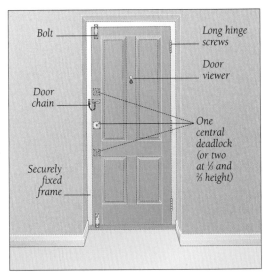

Bolt

Long hinge screws

Door viewer

Door chain

One central deadlock (or two at ⅓ and ⅔ height)

Securely fixed frame

■ **The front door** *is the point of entry for over a third of burglaries – make sure that yours is secure.*

Spotlight illuminates passage to back garden

Windows accessible from roof securely locked

Alarm box visible from front and side of house

Low fence offers intruders minimal cover

Security light over front door

Ground floor windows securely locked

■ **Guard against intruders** *by checking each of the watchpoints listed above. Security lighting and an alarm system are useful deterrents, but there's no substitute for good locks on windows and external doors.*

④ Security lights fitted to the outside of the building make it difficult for a burglar to break in unseen at night. Passive infrared (PIR) units that work on body heat, rather than movement, will automatically operate lighting when anyone approaches your home. Key areas to spotlight are over the front door, garage, outbuildings, passages, and any other obvious entry point.

A break-in is not the only threat to your home – take the risk of fire just as seriously. Smoke detectors can be life-savers. Fit ones that include automatic emergency lighting on hall and landing ceilings. A detector with a press-button that allows you to switch off the sound is handy near the kitchen, where cooking may trigger it.

⑤ Lock away garden and DIY tools in a garage or shed; a burglar may use them to break into your house. For the same reason, never leave ladders lying around. If you don't have a shed or garage to put them in, lay them on their side and chain and padlock them to a secure fitting on the side of the house.

⑥ People living in homes fitted with burglar alarms make far fewer insurance claims than those without – in other words, housebreakers avoid them. An alarm that has been fitted by an approved security firm will cost more than the DIY kind, but will be more effective and reliable. You should be able to recoup part of the cost by earning a discount on your house insurance premium.

Selling your home

WHEN YOU'RE SELLING A HOME, *remember that appearances count for everything. Hide what can be hidden, clean what can be cleaned, and make your home as welcoming as you can. It's also wise to fix what can be fixed. A home that looks well maintained will be more favourably viewed by surveyors.*

Renew and replace

It could be worth replacing anything that is not up to scratch. A new carpet, a new fitted kitchen, or even a new bathroom suite won't be cheap, but the outlay will be worth it if it helps to sell your home – and is almost certain to be reflected in a higher asking price. There will be features that you cannot change, but make the most of what you do have. If a room is particularly small, make it look larger with some strategically positioned mirrors – they reflect what light there is back into the room, giving the illusion of increased space. If the house is fairly dark overall, arrange viewings for the morning when it will be looking its brightest.

Repair any holes or cracks – indoors and out. They may only be superficial, but they will raise worries in buyers' minds. Repair or replace any loose doorknobs, and make sure the lights work. Clean windows also make a house look cared-for.

First impressions

Make sure that your home looks like somewhere strangers might like to live. Fitted bathrooms and large cupboards may help to sell it once viewers are inside, but if the garden is overgrown, then most buyers will switch off before they cross the threshold.

■ **If you have an open fire,** *light it – even in summer! There is no more welcoming sight.*

■ **Bathrooms sell houses,** *so consider making improvements and renew accessories.*

■ **Flowering plants** *placed in interesting containers will cheer up even the dullest back garden.*

Cut the grass, add some cheap props of flowering plants, and give the front door a fresh lick of paint. These small jobs will make the house look more inviting, and inspire would-be buyers to think of what they could do with the garden if it was their own. If there is any old junk in the drive, clear it away to make the garden look more spacious. Although it is important that viewers feel they can make your home theirs, too many personal effects can work against a seller. Remove items such as family photographs, and if you own any pets (especially a barking dog), keep them out of the way until the appointment is over

Keep them interested

Mess is a big turn-off, and once viewers are inside, make sure that they don't see any kitchen clutter or unmade beds. Tidy rooms also make a home seem bigger. Similarly, since buyers will want to feel their new home has plenty of storage, try to avoid bulging wardrobes and piles of paperwork. Bathrooms and kitchens sell houses, so fix any leaking taps and make sure that towels are fresh and clean. Use every good accessory you have. Dimmed lighting can make your living space look more cosy, but make sure that it isn't so dark that viewers think you've got something to hide. If you have to redecorate, choose a neutral colour like white or magnolia, which gives viewers a blank canvas on which to visualize their new home. When you get them inside, bombard their senses with fresh flowers, jars of pot pourri, and the smell of brewing coffee and freshly baked bread. Believe me, it works!

INTERNET

www.assertahome.co.uk

This site covers a wide range of information about the legal and practical aspects of buying or selling a home, and also offers a searchable database of properties.

A simple summary

✔ Give the inside of your home a rejuvenating facelift.

✔ Brighten up the outside of the house to get the most from the garden in summer months.

✔ Kitchens and bathrooms are too important to life's comforts to simply take them for granted.

✔ Banish clutter by sorting out sensible storage.

✔ Give your home an immediate security survey and strengthen any weak points.

✔ When selling your home make sure it's clean, tidy, and welcoming to potential buyers.

Chapter 3

Don't Blame Your Tools!

T HERE ARE VERY FEW JOBS YOU CAN DO YOURSELF without a decent set of tools. But that doesn't mean you have to spend a fortune on all the latest gadgets. The trick is to know what tools you'll use again and again, buy the best-quality ones you can afford, and then borrow or hire the rest. Oh, and you need to look after your tools, too. Blunt, rusty, or damaged tools are a liability – and if they cause things to go wrong, you really do have only yourself to blame!

In this chapter...

✓ Hand tools it pays to buy

✓ Acquiring power tools

✓ Somewhere to work

✓ Playing it safe

WELL-MAINTAINED TOOLS MAKE DIY JOBS EASIER

Hand tools it pays to buy

THE TOOLS LISTED HERE *are all worth buying if you do DIY on a regular basis. I can't guarantee that they'll cover you for everything, but they are almost certain to pay their way within a short space of time.*

Hand tool buying do's and don'ts

- Buy the highest-quality cutting tools you can afford – and then look after them. At best, cheap cutting tools quickly deteriorate; at worst, they are dangerous to use.
- Don't skimp on sharpening tools for chisels and plane blades; blunt tools are dangerous! Have larger saws professionally sharpened. Stock up on replacement blades for pad saws, hacksaws, and so on.
- You can never have too many screwdrivers, drill bits, or clamps! Keep a look-out for "bargain" sets in DIY stores.
- Ratchet or pump-action screwdrivers are costly, but they do save a lot of arm ache.

■ **Kitted out** – *a carefully chosen set of hand tools will make any job easier. But the tools listed here should get you off to a flying start.*

A basic toolkit

The tools shown below are must-haves for anyone who owns a home. All have a variety of uses and at a pinch can often be used as substitutes when you don't have the correct tool for the job. So don't skimp: investing in a basic toolkit is a lot easier and cheaper than calling in a professional at emergency call-out rates!

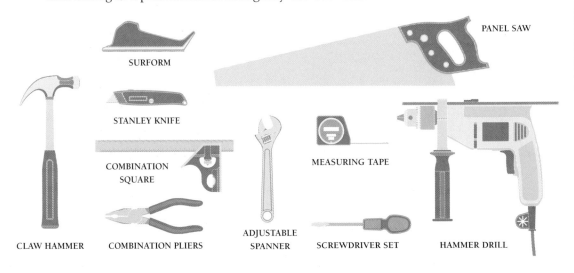

PANEL SAW

SURFORM

STANLEY KNIFE

COMBINATION SQUARE

MEASURING TAPE

CLAW HAMMER

COMBINATION PLIERS

ADJUSTABLE SPANNER

SCREWDRIVER SET

HAMMER DRILL

GENERAL PURPOSE HAND TOOLS

Cutting and shaping

Panel saw	(crosscut blade) for general cutting of wood and boards.
Tenon saw	for mouldings and joints; used with a mitre box.
Pad saw	(a saw blade with a handle on one end) for cutting holes in boards.
Junior hacksaw	for cutting pipes and other metal objects.
Utility knife	with replaceable blades.
Bolster chisel	for cutting holes in solid plaster and masonry.
Set of wood chisels	for cutting hinge recesses, joints, and mortises.
Block plane	for shaping and shaving wood and boards.
Surform	for shaping wood and filler.
Oil stone	for sharpening chisels and plane blades.
Sanding block	for general sanding.
Half-round metalwork file	for removing the burr from sawn metal.

Marking and measuring

Steel tape	for general measuring.
Steel rule	for accurate measuring.
Combination square	for marking out wood at 90° and 45° (alternatively buy a separate try square and sliding bevel).
Spirit level	for checking that something is level or plumb.
Marking gauge	for accurate marking out of wood and boards.

Drill and hammering

Bradawl or gimlet	for making pilot holes for small screws (No.6 or less).
Pump action hand drill	(with a selection of twist and wood bits) for drilling accurate holes in wood.
Countersink	for countersunk screws.
Claw hammer	(450g) for general nailing and removing nail heads.
Pin hammer	(140g) for fine nailing.
Mallet	for driving chisels.
Club hammer	heavyweight hammer for driving a bolster.
Nail punch	for sinking lost head nails beneath the surface.

Extracting and clamping

Tack lifter	for lifting tacks and pins.
Pincers	for lifting larger nails.
Crowbar	for general levering and prying jobs.
Pliers	for general gripping tasks.
Wire strippers	for cutting and stripping electrical cable.
Locking pliers	(e.g. mole wrench) for general-purpose clamping.
Adjustable spanner	for tightening plumbing joints, nuts, and bolts.
Set of G-clamps	for clamping woodworking joints and boards. A **web cramp** and **sashcramps** may also be useful if you do a lot of woodworking.
Portable workbench	(e.g. Workmate™) for clamping larger items and as a support for sawing.
Screwdrivers	buy sets of slot-head and cross-head screwdrivers with various head sizes and blade lengths. Shorter sizes give good accessibility; larger handles give more turning force.

Acquiring power tools

SOME PEOPLE LOVE POWER TOOLS, *other people love giving them as presents! But before you rush out to buy a power tool, think about how often you'll use it: if the answer is every few months, you may well be better off hiring a professional quality model that's bang up to date.*

Power tool do's and don'ts

- With power tools, you generally get what you pay for. The better-quality tools are more powerful and more robust – but this may not matter if you rarely use them.
- Tempting as they are, drills with multiple attachments for sawing and sanding never work as well as their dedicated cousins; they are best avoided
- It's worth paying extra for a secure case for each power tool that you buy.
- As with hand tools, blunt power saws are dangerous – only more so. Make sure you get a stock of replaceable blades when you buy.
- Check hired power tools carefully for damage, especially the power cords. Make sure you understand how to use them before leaving the store.
- Tie back long hair, avoid loose clothing, and wear appropriate safety gear.

Power tools to buy

A mains-operated electric drill (right) is indispensable if you plan to do DIY on any kind of regular basis. Choose one with multiple speeds and a hammer action for drilling into masonry. If you do a lot of woodwork, consider buying a drill stand as well. Wire brush and circular sander attachments are inexpensive and useful for jobs such as removing rust – but a circular sander is no good for sanding wood.

You might also consider buying a portable rechargeable drill (right), which also doubles as a power screwdriver. Today's models hold their charge much better than older ones, and are powerful enough to cope with most indoor jobs. Once you get the knack of using them, the power screwdriver attachments are among the best labour-saving devices you can buy.

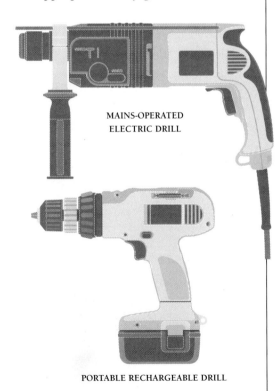

MAINS-OPERATED
ELECTRIC DRILL

PORTABLE RECHARGEABLE DRILL

POWER TOOLS TO BUY OR HIRE

It's great to own a power tool for every occasion, but consider how much you will actually use one before buying – you might be better off hiring.

Circular saw

Makes short work of cutting all but the heaviest wood and is the first choice for sheet materials such as MDF or plywood. Great for trimming doors. Even easier to use in conjunction with a saw table, which enables foolproof cutting of straight lines.

Jigsaw

Not as versatile or as powerful as a circular saw, but essential for cutting holes in panels – for example, when installing a worktop-mounted cooker hob or sink.

Band saw

Hired out with an integral saw table for cutting really heavy timber such as floor joists or other structural members. Not really worth buying unless you're into heavy building work.

Power planer

A very easy and accurate way to plane planks of wood, but rarely needed for do-it-yourself work. A must-buy for keen woodworkers.

Router

A fantastically versatile power tool supplied with a set of different cutters for making grooves, recesses, and mortises, or for turning and shaping mouldings. The spring-loaded "plunge" type, in which the tool can be brought to the workpiece, is generally more useful than the older bench-mounted type, which works the other way round. For general DIY you can get by without one, but if you do a lot of woodworking, a router is a must-buy.

Sander

Orbital sanders are better at smoothing flat surfaces than circular drill attachments, but are only worth buying if you have a lot of sanding to do. For larger projects, consider hiring a belt sander.

Angle grinder

Another superbly versatile power tool, capable of cutting thick ceramic tiles, metal bars and pipes, paving slabs, and roof tiles; also makes short work of cutting grooves or chases in masonry. Rarely worth buying, but a must-hire for jobs involving any of the materials above. An angle grinder is potentially dangerous: be sure to read and follow the maker's safety instructions.

Somewhere to work

IF YOU DON'T HAVE THE LUXURY *of a garage or workshop in which to work and store tools and materials, it will pay you to get organized before you tackle jobs of any size. There's nothing more frustrating than having to search for a tin of paint, only to find it spilt in the back of some dark store cupboard.*

A DIY home from home

In the absence of somewhere permanent to work, you can't beat a portable folding workbench. The best types have a split work surface with a built-in vice and plastic inserts for holding larger pieces of wood and boards. They also double as a step, which is useful if you're wallpapering or working at ceiling height.

Fatigue brought about by working in discomfort is one of the most common causes of DIY accidents. Wherever you work, make sure it is warm and well ventilated. If you find yourself stretching or having to apply excessive force, stop and re-evaluate your working situation.

Even if space is at an absolute premium, allocate somewhere in the house where you can store your DIY tools and materials. Not being able to find what you need will inhibit you from doing anything at all. Do-it-yourself stores also do a roaring trade in replacing lost or damaged tools and materials that have been improperly stored. It may not seem much of an outlay compared with the cost of calling in a professional, but it all adds up.

■ **From holding boards steady** *while sawing, to providing a sturdy surface for measuring and marking, an adjustable workbench is an invaluable tool.*

STORING TOOLS AND MATERIALS

Keep your tools easily accessible and you'll overcome one of the biggest hurdles to starting a job. Put them away clean, sharp, and ready for use. Likewise, store left-over materials methodically and you'll be able to use them for future projects; for example, colour-code the ends of cut timber to show at a glance what usable lengths you have left. There are countless tool storage racks and fittings on the market, but the arrangements shown here can be custom-made to fit the space available and are likely to work out cheaper. Power tools are best stored in their cases and in a locked cupboard, especially if children might have access.

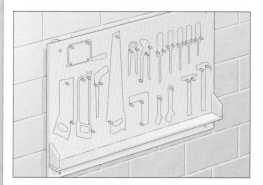

a Tool storage board with outlines

Mark the outlines of tools on a wall-mounted storage board so that you can see instantly where to replace them – or what's missing.

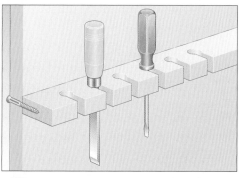

b Batten with keyhole slots/clips

Drill and cut keyhole slots in a 25 x 50mm batten to store screwdrivers, chisels, and files. Alternatively, secure the handles in spring clips.

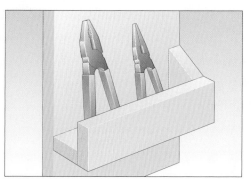

c Shelf with front rail

Screw together a batten shelf and front rail to store two-handled tools like pliers and cutters. Alternatively, hang them from screw-in hooks.

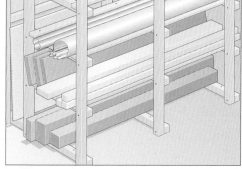

d Storage rack for materials

Store timber, boards, mouldings, and pipes on an open rack system. Lay timber on edge, and fit dowels into pre-drilled holes to stop it sliding.

Playing it safe

THE NUMBER OF ACCIDENTS in the home would surely be dramatically reduced if people were as cautious when carrying out DIY tasks as they are when, say, crossing the road. So make sure you wear the right protective gear and never take unnecessary risks.

Goggles with side air vents will cover spectacles

Ear defenders

Hard hat to BS 5240

Face mask covering nose and mouth

Cotton overalls will not melt, unlike synthetic fibres

Builder's gloves made from leather and canvas

Knee pads protect knees and prevent fatigue

Heavy duty boots protect toes and feet

■ **Wear the right protective clothing** *for the task at hand.*

Personal safety and power tools

- Take care to remove any loose clothing or dangling jewellery when using a power tool, and remember to tie back long hair.
- Keep the flex out of the line of a power tool and never use the tool with the flex stretched tight.
- Never put a tool down while it's still running.
- Unplug tools before fitting new attachments.
- Don't ever be tempted to remove a safety guard from a circular saw or angle grinder.
- Plug power tools into a socket protected by a residual current device (RCD), especially outdoors.
- Always uncurl power cables fully and, if you must use an extension cable with a power tool, be sure to use only a heavy-duty cable – never a lamp extension cable.

Treat flammable liquids with respect. Never use them near a naked flame, or close to flammable materials such as paper or sawdust. Store them away from the floor – preferably on a high shelf – and in a well-ventilated area.

Working with chemicals

- Keep the area you are working in well ventilated. This will allow any toxic or flammable fumes to disperse more easily. If fumes are noxious, wear a respirator.
- Wear rubber or PVC gloves when dealing with caustic fluids of any kind.
- Dispose of unused chemicals safely. Don't pour unwanted fluids down the drain.
- Have water close by to wash off any splashes.
- Always store chemicals in their original containers, and keep the labels readable.

Safety do's and don'ts

- Always switch off the power at the mains before working on an electrical circuit.
- Don't work in a poor light. Ensure your workspace is well lit, so that you can see exactly what you are doing.
- Don't trail power leads across your work area; someone (including you) could trip over them.
- Do keep tools sharp: less force is needed, resulting in greater accuracy and less chance of accidents.
- Do take care that pieces of work are securely clamped to a bench when cutting with a power saw.
- Don't place your free hand near a blade when sawing. When using a knife, keep to one side of the cutting line.

Never work at a height unless you are confident and your ladder is secure. Settle the base on firm, level ground and ensure the ladder extends four or five rungs above the landing place. Pull the ladder out from the wall no more than one-quarter of its length.

A simple summary

✔ You can't hope to do any DIY without a reasonably complete set of tools. Buy the best-quality hand tools you can afford and look after them. Never work with blunt or rusty tools – they're dangerous.

✔ Power tools can save a great deal of hard work, but you won't recoup the cost unless you use them a lot. Before you buy, consider whether it might be better to hire them.

✔ Store tools and partly used DIY materials in an organized way so that you can find them easily the next time; not being able to find something will give you an excuse to put off the job.

✔ Take your safety and that of others very seriously. In particular, take steps to protect your eyes, hands, and ears when working with power tools, and keep leads and fingers out of the way of blades.

Simple to fix wi
Blue Hawk Cove Adhe
2431809

Chapter 4

Tricks of the Trade

THE BASIC SKILLS DESCRIBED IN THIS CHAPTER will cover you for a multitude of jobs, large and small. I won't pretend that they'll turn you into an expert overnight, but I guarantee they'll make things easier.

In this chapter...

✓ Measuring and marking

✓ Cutting wood and boards

✓ Gluing and joining

✓ Nailing, drilling, and screwing

✓ Fixing things to walls

✓ Curtains and pictures

✓ Concrete and mortar

✓ Working with plasterboard

EXPERT TECHNIQUES HELP CREATE PROFESSIONAL-LOOKING RESULTS

Measuring and marking

MEASURING AND MARKING *pieces of wood is a bit like boiling an egg: it's not as easy as it looks. Wood is a natural material, which means that your measuring and marking techniques have to account for variations in size between one piece and another. The golden rule is "measure twice; cut once".*

Marking out components

The big risk with measuring and marking wood is that you'll introduce cumulative errors by measuring from a side or edge that isn't straight, by forgetting to allow for the width of your saw cut, or simply by marking in the wrong place. So get into the habit of always applying the following rules:

- Never assume that a piece of wood or board is square.
- Allow a margin of waste at both ends of a piece of timber – the workpiece – and always cut to the waste side of the cutting line.
- For fine work, choose a face side and face edge for the workpiece – and, if needed, plane them flat (see below). Take all other measurements from here.

The best tip for measuring is: avoid it if at all possible. For example, when cutting components of the same size, measure one and then use this as a template to mark the rest. Similarly, if you can, mark individual components directly against the space they have to fit.

SQUARING UP TIMBER

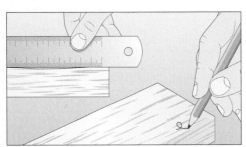

a Choosing the face side

Lay a ruler along the best-looking side of the workpiece to check for undulations and, if necessary, plane it flat. Mark it with a loop.

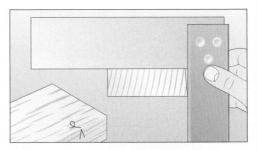

b Choosing the face edge

Lay the blade of a try square flat across the face side of the timber and sight along the edge. If necessary, plane it to 90° and mark it with a V.

TIPS FOR MEASURING AND MARKING

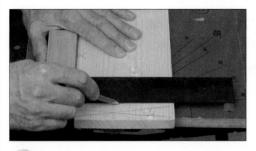

a **Squaring the end of a workpiece**

Take all length measurements from a mark squared across the end with a try square. Draw a cross on the waste timber outside the mark.

b **Measuring the length**

Set the end of a rule or measuring tape on the squared mark. At the dimension, mark an angled line each side of the point on the scale.

c **Measuring a mitred component**

Measure the outside length of the piece to be mitred (i.e., cut to 45°) and mark this distance on the face side and edge. Double-check it.

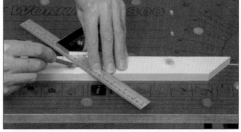

d **Marking the mitred end**

Set the handle of a combination square on the edge mark, with the blade sloping inwards, and mark the mitre on the face side.

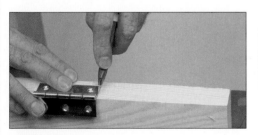

e **Marking a hinge recess**

Lay the hinge squarely on the edge of the door with the knuckle projecting. Mark round the hinge leaf with a sharp knife.

f **Marking the hinge depth**

Set a marking gauge to half the thickness of the closed hinge. Hold the gauge against the edge of the door and score the depth on the face.

Cutting wood and boards

THERE'S NOTHING MAGICAL *about sawing timber straight, although it can be hard work unless you use power tools. Simply make sure that you use the right saw, that its blade is sharp, and that the workpiece is well supported.*

Sawing by hand

Cut timber by hand with a panel saw, preferably one fitted with a medium-toothed "crosscut" blade. Take extra care if cutting with the grain, as the blade tends to wander off-line. To saw across the grain, clamp the workpiece or support it against a firm edge with your free hand. Then, holding the saw at 30°, position the blade to the waste side of the cutting line with your fingers, and lightly draw it back and forth to start the cut. Once the blade "bites" you can increase the length of your stroke – but don't force it; let it find its own way. To keep the saw on-line, sight down the length of the blade keeping the cutting line just visible. As you approach the end of the cut, increase the angle of the saw up to 90° to stop the last few fibres tearing.

If a panel saw starts to stick, check how the workpiece is supported – it could be that the cut is closing up and pinching the blade. Failing that, remove the blade and rub it with an ordinary household candle. You should find it cuts more freely.

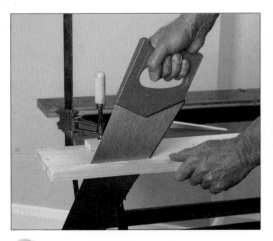

a **Sawing by hand with the grain**

If you have to saw with the grain, clamp the timber so that the waste hangs free. Hold the saw at about 45° and sight down the blade.

b **Power sawing with a circular saw**

Clamp a piece of timber parallel with the cutting line to act as a guide. Use the same technique to make straight cuts with a jigsaw.

Power sawing

A power circular saw is better for making straight cuts in large boards, but should always be used with a cutting guide, or the saw "fence" near the edges. Align the blade on the waste side of the cutting line, then clamp a straight piece of timber parallel to the line so that it just touches the sole plate of the saw. Double-check that the board is secure and that there's nothing underneath it to get in the way of the blade. Start the cut from the edge of the board, holding the saw against the guide as you go.

Fine cutting

To cut woodworking joints and to join lengths of moulding in a 45° mitre, use a tenon saw and a mitre box (see below). Clamp the box in your bench, insert the workpiece, and place the saw in the slots so that the blade is just to the waste side of the cutting line. Then, guiding the saw with your fingers, draw it back and forth.

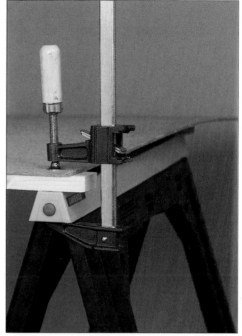

■ **Support a large board** *on pieces of timber and clamp it to a pair of trestles or low tables so that it doesn't slip or bow when you start sawing.*

CUTTING ACROSS THE GRAIN

a **Using a mitre box**

Position the workpiece so the waste side of the cutting line aligns with the slot. Press the timber against the back of the box when cutting.

b **Using a chop saw**

Set the saw to the required cutting angle and hold the workpiece against the backstop. Lower the saw slowly to make the cut.

Gluing and joining

TODAY, YOU CAN BUY ADHESIVES *to stick just about anything – and very efficient they are, too. But no adhesive will stick unless the mating surfaces are clean, dry, and free from grease. It's also vital to stop the parts from moving and to apply pressure while the adhesive dries, which may test your ingenuity.*

Holding and clamping

Most adhesives should be applied only in a very thin film – an excess will weaken the joint. Glued joints in wood can usually be held in place temporarily by pinning, and permanently by screwing or dowelling. Otherwise, clamp the joint in your workbench or with individual G-clamps, which are sold in a range of sizes. Bind timber frameworks with a string or rope tourniquet, wrapped around a piece of wooden dowel. Wrap irregularly shaped objects with masking tape, or else bed them into a bowl of sand.

If you're joining two pieces of wood and you find yourself left with unsightly gaps after the adhesive has dried, make a filler by mixing more of the adhesive with sawdust and force it into the joint.

What glue to use where

Although there are many special-purpose adhesives, the following will cover you for most DIY jobs and are worth having in the home at all times.

- **Clear adhesive** is flexible and sticks leather, cloth, cork, and laminates. Apply it to both surfaces and allow it to dry before pressing them together.
- **PVA adhesive** is the first choice for wood, but it will also glue paper, canvas, and leather and is often used as a bonding additive in cement mortar. It comes in standard and waterproof forms, and will also bond ceramics. Apply to one surface, or to both if one of them is absorbent.
- **Contact adhesive** forms a very strong, immediate bond with sheet materials and laminates. Some types allow for adjustment. Coat both surfaces and allow to dry.
- **Epoxy resin** is a two-part resin/hardener adhesive. It is water- and heat-resistant and will also fill small gaps. Use it for metals, ceramics, and hard plastics.
- **Building adhesive** is gap-filling and is applied using a cartridge gun. Use it to bond sheet building materials and slab insulation to walls and floors.
- **Glass adhesive** bonds glass to glass and metal.
- **Superglue**, also known as cyanocrylate, gains full strength after 24 hours. It's ideal for an instant repair to most non-absorbent materials.

WAYS TO JOIN PIECES OF WOOD

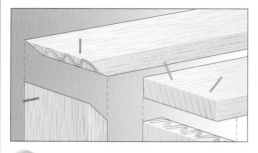

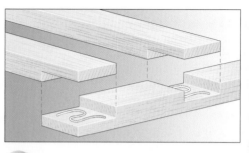

a Butt and mitre joints

Use a glued butt joint, reinforced with nails or screws, for basic frameworks. Mitre the joint for decorative frameworks and mouldings.

b Halving joints

For strong frameworks, a halving joint will resist distortion. Cut to a depth of half the thickness of the thinner piece of timber.

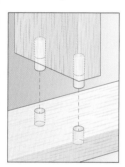

c Dowel joint

A strong joint with hidden reinforcement for frameworks. Use a dowel jig to drill the holes accurately. The dowels should have grooves to let excess adhesive escape.

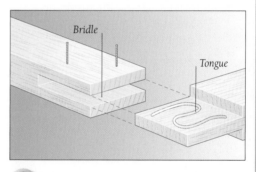

d Bridle joint

Stronger than halving joints, bridle joints resist distortion in two directions. Cut the tongue to one-third of the wood's thickness, then the bridle.

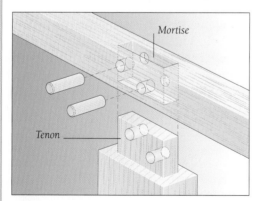

e Mortise-and-tenon joint

A strong joint for furniture and structural frames. Cut the tenon, then mark the mortise from it. Drill and chisel out the mortise.

f Housing joint

Mechanically very strong for vertical loadbearing. Cut the housing to a maximum of half the timber thickness. The joint can be reinforced by nailing or screwing.

Nailing, drilling, and screwing

NAILS AND SCREWS come in all shapes and sizes, and many are designed for specific purposes. Get to know what these are, and you'll always have the right fixing for the job at hand.

Nails

Wire nails are the all-purpose option for general, heavier carpentry and joining. Oval wire nails can be punched in and concealed. Among the special purpose nails you may come across are annular nails, which have a ridged shank for extra grip when fixing boards, and floor brads, which should be aligned with the grain to stop floorboards from splitting. Plasterboard nails have a jagged shank for extra grip; always drive the head flush with the surface of the board. Use panel pins for cabinet work, for nailing wooden moulding, and for reinforcing glued joints. Choose hardboard pins (the heads of which disappear completely) to secure hardboard, plywood, and other thin sheet materials.

Drive nails in at opposing angles – called "skew-nailing" – for extra strength. Tap small pins in with the back of a pin hammer. To save your thumb, hold them in a strip of cardboard or long-nosed pliers.

Drilling and screwing

Drilling successfully is 90 per cent about choosing the right drill and the right diameter for the screw or wallplug. When screwing into wood, you're supposed to drill at least twice – a pilot hole for the thread and a larger clearance hole for the plain shank, plus a countersink, too, if the head is countersunk. In practice, though, you can get away with

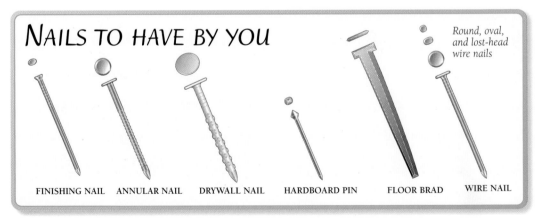

NAILS TO HAVE BY YOU

Round, oval, and lost-head wire nails

FINISHING NAIL   ANNULAR NAIL   DRYWALL NAIL   HARDBOARD PIN   FLOOR BRAD   WIRE NAIL

just a pilot hole for screws size 6 or under. In ordinary softwood, you can do this quickly by hand, using a bradawl or gimlet. For masonry and ceramics, set your drill to slow, with the hammer action on for masonry and off for ceramics. Use the size of drill recommended for the fixing.

Safety do's and don'ts

- Always screw thin to thick. For maximum strength, the screw length should be around three times the thickness of the thinner piece of wood.
- Use the handle grip supplied with an electric drill for greater control. Fix a scrap of tape over the marked hole if the drill bit slips on the surface.
- Always try to match the tip of your screwdriver to the slot size of the screw, or it may slip and hurt you. If using brass or chrome screws, drive in an equivalent-size steel one first to avoid chewing up the vulnerable heads.
- Keep the faces of your hammers clean and smooth to stop them accidentally skidding off nails.

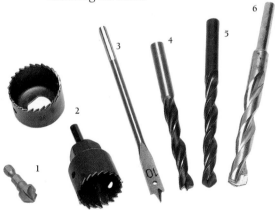

■ **Basic drill set:** *(1) countersink; (2) hole saw; (3) flat wood bit; (4) wood bit; (5) HSS bit for metal; (6) masonry bit.*

SCREW SENSE

Knowing at a glance what type and size of screw to use is a key skill to master for any do-it-yourselfer. The descriptions below refer to items from left to right and top to bottom.

■ **Screw head profiles** *Countersunk head sits flush with surface; raised head is for architectural fittings; round head sits proud of surface; pan head is found on machine and self-tapping screws.*

■ **Screw head recesses** *Slotted head is mainly for driving by hand; phillips cross-recess is found mainly on machine screws; Pozidrive is good for use with power drivers, as is hexagonal recess.*

■ **Screw shanks** *Woodscrew; chipboard screw; carcass screw (grips in end grain and minimizes splitting); twin-thread screw (reduces driving time and effort in timber and boards).*

■ **Screw sizes** *Common screws; the gauges (and clearance hole diameters) are: No. 4 (3mm); No. 6 (3.5mm); No. 8 (4.5mm); No. 10 (5mm); No. 12 (6mm); and No. 14 (6.5mm).*

■ **Screw materials** *Steel for general work; brass for cabinet work; zinc-plated and galvanized to resist corrosion; japanned for black iron fittings. Use stainless steel screws (not shown) in oak.*

Fixing things to walls

THERE ARE SEVERAL GOLDEN RULES *for fixing to walls. Always choose a fixing substantial enough for the load it is taking; always use the recommended size screw; and always check that the wall is sound before you fix anything onto it. On plasterboard walls, it's wise to screw anything heavy directly into the supporting frame. On masonry walls, try to avoid fixing into the mortar joints between the bricks or blocks, and keep heavy-duty fixings well away from the ends of walls.*

FIXINGS FOR SOLID AND HOLLOW WALLS

Wall fixings come in all shapes and sizes, but are sure to fall into one of the categories shown here.

KEY

 Wall material: solid masonry; cellular block; frame wall.

 Vertical load supported: light; medium; heavy.

 Insertion tool: drill; hammer; screwdriver; spanner.

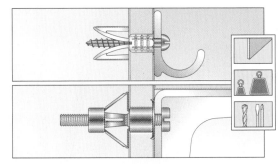

a **Masonry nail and screw**

These easy-to-use wall fixings are mainly suitable for temporary and light vertical loads.

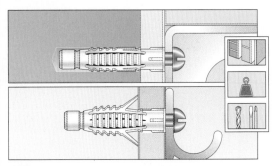

d Universal wall plug

A general-purpose plug for use in both solid and frame walls. The fins give the fixing strength.

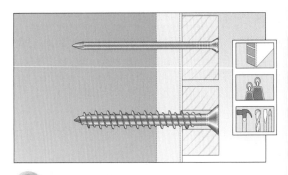

e Hollow wall fixings

Plastic cavity fixings (top) can't take much weight; the metal type (bottom) is more robust.

The right stuff

Remember that whatever the load-carrying capacity of a wall fixing, it will only ever be as strong as the material around it. Avoid fixing heavy things to plasterboard, and repair crumbling masonry before fixing to it. If you suspect there may be pipes or cables buried in the wall (e.g., above or around fixtures and fittings), or you're trying to locate frame studs, an ultrasonic detector is a good buy, although not 100 per cent reliable.

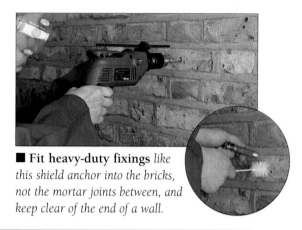

■ **Fit heavy-duty fixings** *like this shield anchor into the bricks, not the mortar joints between, and keep clear of the end of a wall.*

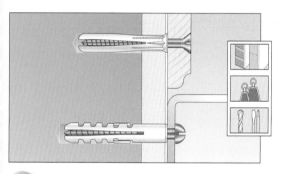

b **Wallplugs**

General-purpose (top) and nylon plugs. Use nylon plugs in cellular blocks (grey dust when drilled).

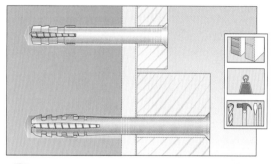

c **Frame fixings**

Hammer-in (top) and screw-in (bottom) frame fixings. Only use the screw-in type in blocks.

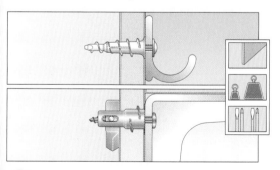

f **Drive-in hollow wall fixings**

Drive-in fixings require no pre-drilling. Metal toggle types (bottom) can take heavier loads.

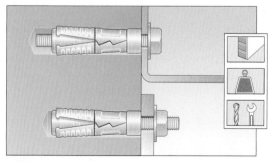

g **Shield anchors (masonry bolts)**

These heavy-duty fixings create great pressure. Don't fit more than one per brick or block.

Curtains and pictures

ALWAYS CONSIDER THE IMPLICATIONS *when hanging things on your walls. Curtains and pictures can be quite heavy and need to be properly attached if you don't want your world to start falling down around you.*

WOODEN POLE

Curtain fixings

You can screw a curtain rail to the wall, to the floor joists above, or to the window frame. Both poles and tracks can be hung from the ceiling joists above, either directly or on a supporting batten. For fixings either side of a lintel, poles can be screwed directly to the wall, while tracks need a batten to support the intermediate brackets. Tracks can also be fitted to the timber frame of the window. If the curtains are to be hung within the window recess, choose a pole. Both tracks and poles can be fixed to the face of the lintel, but only tracks are for hanging from the underside.

PLASTIC TRACK

Plastic curtain rails can be bent to fit a bay window. Bear in mind that you'll need more brackets in a bay than you would with a straight stretch of fixing.

TRACK ON BATTEN
WITH PELMET

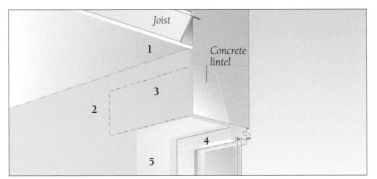

Joist

Concrete lintel

1
2
3
4
5

■ **Fixing options:** *(1) to the joists, directly or on a batten; (2) to each side of the lintel; (3) to the face or underside of the lintel; (4) to the timber window frame; (5) to the sides of window recess.*

CURTAIN CORDSET

Pictures and mirrors

There's a right and a wrong way to hang framed mirrors and pictures. It doesn't pay to experiment!

Don't improvise fixings when you hang mirrors and pictures. A wire nail and a piece of string may be out of sight, but they certainly won't be out of mind when the nail pops out, bringing a chunk of the wall with it, and smashing the picture frame in the process. Use the hooks and frame fixings made for the job and you can be sure your pictures will stay up. Always use wallplugs for very heavy items.

Think about artificial and natural light when you position pictures and mirrors. Reflections and glare on a picture may make it difficult to see. But remember that with mirrors, reflected light is an advantage. Carefully positioned mirrors brighten a dark corner with "borrowed light" and can be used to make a small room seem bigger.

■ **Trial run:** *test out how an arrangement of pictures will look by laying them out on the floor before you hang them on the wall.*

PICTURE FIXINGS

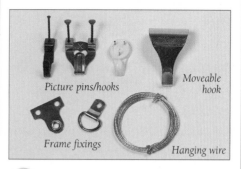

Picture pins/hooks

Moveable hook

Frame fixings

Hanging wire

a **Hardware for hanging**

Self-nailing hooks are for light loads only. Always drive in pins at a downward angle.

b **Moveable fixings**

When hung from a picture rail, these will support heavier weights than standard hooks.

c **Fitting picture wire**

Thread a length of picture wire through the D-ring, loop it back over itself, and feed the end through the loop.

Concrete and mortar

PORTLAND CEMENT AND SAND *are the two dry constituents of concrete and mortar. You'll find it more convenient to buy them pre-mixed in bags labelled "general purpose concrete" or "bricklaying mortar" for most small masonry jobs around the home. Only if you're tackling a patio or driveway will you need to order them separately from a builders' supplier.*

Know your materials

Portland cement is sold in 25kg or 50kg bags. Sharp sand for concreting and soft sand for mortar mixes are sold in "bags" that vary in size between suppliers. You can also buy a mix of sand and gravel called ballast. Mix five parts ballast with one part cement for a general-purpose concrete.

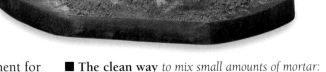

■ **The clean way** *to mix small amounts of mortar: on a special plastic tray or dustbin lid.*

MIXING BY HAND

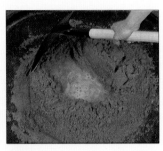

1 **Create a cavity**

Mix the sand and cement thoroughly. Form the pile into a "volcano" with the shovel.

2 **Add water**

Pour water into the "crater" you have made and gradually turn in the sides.

3 **Cut and test**

Chop the mixture through. It is ready to use when it slips easily off the shovel.

Working with plasterboard

FOR YEARS THE *most popular way to surface walls and ceilings has been to use plasterboard, since it's easy to cut and fix, provides good insulation, and is fire-resistant.*

Know your plasterboard

Standard plasterboard has a grey paper covering on one side and an ivory-coloured surface, suitable for decorating, on the other. Plasterboard is made in a range of thicknesses and sizes. All-purpose wallboard – for lining walls and ceilings – comes in various sheet sizes. Square-edged baseboard is mainly used for ceilings; lath board is similar but has rounded edges. Thermal-insulation plasterboard, which is backed with expanded polystyrene or foamed polyurethane, is thicker than standard plasterboard. Vapour-check plasterboard prevents condensation above ceilings or inside walls. Thermal-insulation board has tapered edges, which are practically invisible under a coat of paint. Standard plasterboard and vapour-check board have either square or tapered edges.

TAPER-EDGED PLASTERBOARD

SQUARE-EDGED BASEBOARD

SQUARE-EDGED PLASTERBOARD

A full sheet of plasterboard is not strong but it is surprisingly heavy; don't attempt to carry one by yourself.

When moving plasterboard, always carry sheets vertically so that they won't crack or snap. Always store sheets of plasterboard on edge.

WEBBED TAPE

PAPER TAPE

PLASTERBOARD SCREWS   PLASTERBOARD NAILS

■ **Materials:** *cover joins between taper-edge boards with webbed or paper tape (above) and filler. Fix plasterboard with galvanized plasterboard nails (far right), or plasterboard screws (right).*

Fixing and cutting plasterboard

When fitting plasterboard – for example, on a partition wall with a timber frame – start in one corner and work across the wall to the other end. When using full sheets, nail or screw the edges of the board at 100mm intervals; then fix to intermediate timbers at intervals of 150–200mm. After you've covered as large an area as possible with full sheets, measure and cut smaller pieces to fit the gaps. Nails or screws can be used on a wooden frame, but always use screws for fixing to metal laths.

When fixing sheets, don't butt them tightly together or they may crack. Leave a nail's gap between them that can be plugged with filler.

HANGING AND TAPING BOARDS

1 **Lever the sheet into position**

To free your hands while you insert the fixings, use a wooden foot lifter – made from an offcut of wood – to lever the sheet into place.

2 **Apply self-adhesive joint tape**

After fixing the sheets, apply self-adhesive joint tape to cover the gaps between them. Press the tape firmly into the gap.

3 **Cover tape with joint filler**

Apply joint filler over the tape to mask the joints and any indentations. Use a flexible plasterboard spatula and repeat if necessary.

4 **Feather the edges**

To disguise the joints, "feather" the edges of the filler while still wet by lightly dabbing with a sponge. Any other imperfections can be sanded.

Joining at corners

Coat internal corners with a thin layer of filler, then press a length of joint tape into the corner. Cover the tape with more filler, doing one wall first and then the other. Strengthen external corners with metal corner beads nailed at 150mm intervals. Fill one side, scraping the filler downwards towards the corner. Then repeat this process on the other side.

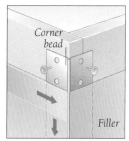

INTERNAL CORNER   EXTERNAL CORNER

1 **Cutting plasterboard**

Mark the cutting line in pencil, then cut with a utility knife held against a metal straightedge.

2 **Snapping boards**

After cutting, turn the sheet on edge and snap it against your knee.

A simple summary

✔ Don't forget the golden rule: "measure twice; cut once".

✔ When sawing, use the right saw and support the workpiece.

✔ Surfaces to be glued should be clean, dry, and grease-free.

✔ Know which nails or screws you should use for a particular job.

✔ Check a wall is sound before fixing anything to it.

✔ There's more than one way to hang a curtain.

✔ Concrete and mortar can be bought ready-mixed.

✔ Plasterboard is easy to work with and gives a smooth surface.

PART TWO

Chapter 5

Painting Walls and Ceilings

FOR FAST RESULTS, PAINT IS STILL THE number one choice – and modern paints are easier to use than ever. But no paint will disguise a rough or poorly prepared surface; you get out what you put in.

In this chapter...

✓ Paint for walls and ceiling

✓ Before you start

✓ Using rollers and pads

✓ Spray painting

✓ Texturing and stencilling

✓ Creating paint effects

✓ Access to awkward areas

✓ Outdoor decorating

Paint for walls and ceilings

NOT SURE WHAT TYPE of paint to buy? Your choice depends chiefly on what surface you're covering, the finish – gloss or matt? smooth or textured? – and on how much wear and tear the newly painted surface will have to take.

Paints for inside the house

For interiors, water-based emulsion paint is by far the easiest and most popular option. Think twice before painting walls in oil-based gloss paint, as they will be much harder to decorate next time around; if you need a shinier surface, choose silk emulsion instead.

1 **Vinyl-based emulsion:** this is the most common type of paint. Although water based, it is durable, washable and comes in matt, satin (eggshell), and silk finishes. Most ranges are coordinated with matching colours for woodwork. Use a silk finish for wall-mounted radiators and other metalwork. "Heritage" ranges of traditional colours are becoming increasingly popular, but these paints are thinner and will almost certainly require an extra coat.

As a rough guide to estimating quantities, measure the areas of the surfaces to be covered (width x height) and add them up. One litre of emulsion covers about 10–14 sq m, but bear in mind that covering a dark colour with a light one will require at least two coats.

2 **Non-vinyl emulsion:** available only in a matt finish, this is a better choice for newly plastered walls that need to be given a few months to dry out.

3 **Non-drip or solid emulsion:** worth considering if the area you are painting is vulnerable to drips – or, heaven forbid, you can't be bothered to clear the room – but the range of colours is limited.

4 **Bathroom paint:** emulsion with an insulant added to resist condensation.

5 **Ceiling paint:** a very thick form of white emulsion that's ideal for covering up hairline cracks and bumps in old ceilings. Texture paint is similar, but better at disguising faults. Both can be covered with coloured emulsion afterwards.

6 **Special-purpose paints:** these include solvent-based water-resistant paint for masonry walls that are prone to damp and aluminium-based emulsion for covering very heavily stained surfaces.

Paints for outside the house

1 **Exterior masonry paint**: available in two grades, rough, which is longer-lasting but quickly gets dirty in urban areas, and smooth, which is less durable but resists dust and pollution better. Use masonry paint on stone, concrete, render, and stucco (smooth render). Coverage varies considerably according to the absorbency of the surface, but one litre covers about 8 sq m of wall per coat. Coat very porous or powdery surfaces with masonry stabilizer before painting.

2 **Exterior texture paint**: a cheap way of covering up old render and stucco that is full of hairline cracks. Patented texture paint systems are normally sprayed on by the relevant contractor.

3 **Brick paint**: specially for painting bare brickwork – if you really must; far better to leave bricks in their natural state!

4 **Bituminous paint**: for protecting low-level masonry that is constantly getting wet. It should be re-applied at yearly intervals.

5 **Floor paint**: used to finish the bare concrete floors of a garage, shed, or outhouse, providing the surface is oil-free.

6 **Anti-climb paint**: a non-drying paint for use on the top of garden walls, or on drainpipes, as a deterrent to burglars.

> **INTERNET**
>
> **www.dulux.co.uk**
>
> *Check out Dulux's excellent paint finder site, or experiment with different combinations at their colour-scheme testing site: http://mousepainter.dulux.co.uk*

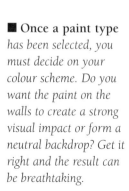

■ **Once a paint type** *has been selected, you must decide on your colour scheme. Do you want the paint on the walls to create a strong visual impact or form a neutral backdrop? Get it right and the result can be breathtaking.*

Before you start

A PROFESSIONAL-LOOKING PAINT JOB *starts with thorough planning. An empty room is far easier to paint than one full of furniture and if you can clear the room completely, so much the better.*

Pointers for getting the room ready

- Take down all mirrors, pictures, curtains, and blinds, and remove them from the room. Clear the room of everything else that is portable.
- Cover the floor with dust sheets, taped to each other and to the skirtings. Use cloth sheets if possible as they don't slip. If you have to use plastic sheets, use only a single layer, and cover with newspaper.
- Move heavy furniture away from the walls and cover with dust sheets.
- Wrap light fittings in plastic bags secured with elastic bands. If you can, unscrew switches and ceiling roses to paint behind them; if you can't, mask them.

Turn off the electricity supply at the mains before loosening the faceplates of light switches and electrical outlets to paint behind them – they may not all be on the same fused circuit. Make sure there's no danger of anyone else reinstating the supply while you are still working.

Masking fittings

Professionals tend not to bother with masking tape – often to the chagrin of the people employing them! But unless you're extra-confident of your ability to paint a steady line, it's worth masking any fixtures and fittings that you can't remove. When applying masking tape, smooth down the edge of the tape that's doing the masking and leave the other edge unstuck. This will make it easier to remove the tape, which you should do as soon as the paint is dry to the touch. If you leave the tape on any longer, it may not come away cleanly.

Suggestions for lighting and ventilation

- Arrange for some portable lighting so that you don't overlook drips and runs, or miss any areas. If you are working on a wall, bounce the light off the ceiling to throw as even a light as possible onto the surface, and vice versa.
- Before doing any sanding or scraping that will raise a lot of dust, consider sealing the edges of doors with masking tape to stop the dust spreading.
- Reverse the above procedure and keep windows and doors open when working with paint or solvents that might give off harmful fumes.

Preparing surfaces

Surfaces for painting should be as smooth and blemish-free as you can get them. They need to be clean, too. Bear in mind that textured or woodchip wallpaper may be hiding a multitude of sins in the plaster beneath. You'll need to scrape flaking paint, too. Take it back to a sound edge using a stripping knife. If the paint is gloss, you should sand it lightly to provide a key for the new paint.

Strip that wallpaper

It's not a good idea to paint over ordinary wallpaper. Even if the seams look stuck down, they will almost certainly curl after painting – and you'll never get them to stay stuck down. Painted-over wallpaper is also very difficult to strip. Below are two methods for stripping wallpaper.

1. **Soaking and stripping by hand:** this is generally easiest for ordinary wallpaper. Score through the paper before soaking. If the paper doesn't scrape off easily, score and soak again. Remove any remaining paste with clean, warm water.

2. **Steam stripping:** this method is best for heavy or textured papers, and essential for painted-over paper of any description. Score the paper before you start.
   - Fill the machine with water and let it heat up. Put on gloves and overalls.
   - When steam starts seeping from the plate, apply it to the wall in short bursts until the paper starts to loosen. Ideally, you should have someone following with a stripping knife before the paper dries out. Again, clean off any residue with warm water and a nylon kitchen scourer.

STRIPPING OLD WALLPAPER

1 Score

Score paper with the edge of a stripping knife, but be careful not to dig into plaster beneath.

2 Soak

Use a sponge to soak the paper with water. Leave for about 15 minutes before scraping.

3 Scrape

Scrape away the paper, keeping the knife at a shallow angle to avoid damaging the plaster.

Repair those cracks and holes

Inspect the surface and ring any dents, cracks, peeling paint, bumps, or nail holes in pencil so that you don't miss them. Also look out for mould and mildew stains and old water stains – especially on ceilings. Now assess your repair strategy.

To cover up a wall with lots of small blemishes, consider lining the walls with lining paper and then emulsion-painting over them. Although some professionals hang lining paper horizontally, there's little to be lost by hanging it in the same way as other wallpaper. Be sure to soak lengths in a bucket of water before you hang them. Alternatively, smooth the walls with ready-mixed fine surface filler or skimming plaster. Apply the filler and smooth it with the plastic spatula provided, then sand off any remaining marks when dry.

Patch general wear and tear with all-purpose filler. For holes more than about 4mm deep, apply the filler in layers and let each one dry before applying the next. This may seem time-consuming, but it's worth it in the long run. It's also worth making the effort to repair all minor cracks and chips, because even the smallest flaw will show through your finished work. In particular, look out for nail holes. Force filler into a nail hole with the edge of a narrow filling knife or the end of your finger. Then smooth over with the filling knife and rub down once the filler is completely dry. Use the same procedure for filling dents in plasterboard.

To fill a hole in solid plaster or lath-and-plaster, first dampen the area with water, then patch it a layer at a time using ready-mixed repair plaster or all-purpose filler. Finish the repair with fine surface filler. If the wooden laths are broken, staple a piece of zinc mesh

FILLING CRACKS

 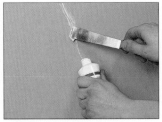 

1 **Locate cracks**

Rake out the loose material with the corner of a filling knife, then brush out the dust with a paintbrush.

2 **Apply the filler**

Press the filler well into the crack with the knife, leaving it smooth, but slightly proud of the surface.

3 **Rub down**

When dry, rub down until smooth and level with a sanding block and fine-grade abrasive paper.

across them to act as a base for the repair. Patch small holes in plasterboard with plaster patch as shown below. Cut larger holes back to the nearest studs using a utility knife and straightedge, then cut a plasterboard patch to the same size and nail it in place using galvanized nails. Finish the repair with fine surface filler.

Fill any gaps around woodwork and other movable fittings with gap filler, applied from a cartridge gun – unless the gaps are very wide, in which case you should pack them out first with an aerosol foam filler. Smooth down the filler with a dampened cloth wrapped around the end of your finger – there should be no need to sand it down afterwards.

Dealing with stains and cleaning

Mould and mildew can occur anywhere the ventilation is poor, and often point to condensation problems. Treat affected areas with a dilute bleach solution, leave for a few minutes, then scrub off and leave to dry for several days before painting. Treat old water stains with a stain-resistant primer. For very badly stained areas use an alkali-resistant primer or a spirit-based sealant to stop stains coming back through after you've repainted. Having said all that, it is best to sort out the cause of the mould and mildew before dealing with its symptoms.

Whatever the surface, even on sound painted walls, give the whole area a final wash-down with sugar soap, applied using a paint roller. Sugar soap is strong enough to get rid of grease, but won't leave walls coated in soapy suds like ordinary household cleaners.

FILLING SMALL HOLES

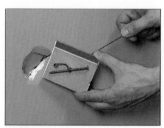

1 Measure hole

Cut a plasterboard patch to fit behind the hole. Attach string to the patch with a nail so you can pull it towards you.

2 Stick with filler

Spread filler around the edges of the patch before feeding it through the hole. Pull the patch back to stick it.

3 Hide the repair

Cut the string, fill the recess with repair plaster, then level off with fine surface filler. Sand smooth and level once dry.

Using rollers and pads

ROLLERS ARE THE FIRST CHOICE *for emulsioning large areas of wall and ceiling – although you still have to brush-paint around the edges. Not so with the paint pads. These are an increasingly popular alternative to rollers, and are especially good for dealing with awkward areas. They come in a range of different sizes and special shapes.*

Types of paint roller

Standard paint roller frames take sleeves 225mm long. Choose a frame with a handle that will take an extension pole for painting ceilings and hard-to-reach places. You may also want a more compact roller with a wire extension handle for reaching down the backs of radiators and other awkward areas. Similar, but with a special fine textured sleeve, are rollers for gloss-painting large areas.

Before filling a roller tray or paint kettle, line it with a plastic bag so that you don't have to clean it when changing colours. Even handier are moulded disposable plastic inserts for roller trays, which you can buy at most DIY stores.

■ **When loading,** *don't overfill either the tray or the roller. Dip the sleeve in the paint, then roll back and forth across the tray a few times to distribute it evenly.*

■ **For most rooms,** *a 225mm roller with tray and extension handle and a compact mini-roller are all you need.*

Picking the right roller sleeve

Roller sleeves come in foam (cheaper) or fabric (better), and in different densities to suit the job in hand. Pick a medium-density sleeve with a short pile for surfaces that are smooth and in good condition, or a medium pile if there are minor bumps and flaws. Textured surfaces need a long-piled sleeve to get into all the nooks and crannies. As for materials, a synthetic roller sleeve is fine for emulsion paint, but a mohair or lambswool sleeve is best for gloss.

When using a roller, a key tip is to remember not to lift the roller off the surface between strokes. If you do, the roller may spin and send paint in all directions. Guard against patchy painting by consciously monitoring how evenly the paint is going, adjusting pressure on the roller accordingly.

ROLLER-PAINTING A WALL

Ironically, the secret of successful roller painting is knowing how to cut in with a brush to leave a clean line along adjoining surfaces. Use a 50mm or 75mm brush, not too heavily loaded with paint. Hold it on edge, apply just enough pressure to get some spring in the bristles so that they fan out, and draw the brush along in a single, smooth stroke. It may take some time to get the knack, but persevere – it's much quicker than masking.

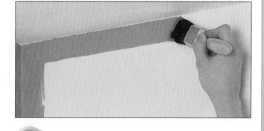

1 **Cut in with a brush around edges**

Successful cutting in comes with practice. If you make a mistake, simply sponge off the paint and start again.

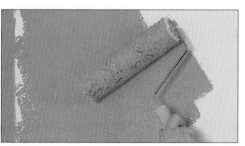

2 **Apply the paint**

Begin roller-painting about 1 metre below the wet edge, taking the paint towards the ceiling and down again in zig-zag fashion.

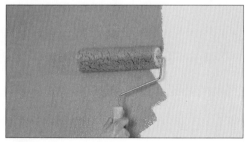

3 **Smooth out the paint**

Even out the paint with horizontal or vertical strokes, blending into the wet edges. Double-check you haven't missed anywhere.

Using paint pads

Often overlooked, paint pads are a handy alternative to rollers for difficult areas, panelled surfaces, and areas that can't be easily protected from drips. The pads themselves come in a variety of shapes and sizes, with special shapes for painting mouldings and architraves.

Paint pad techniques

Larger pads tend to be limited in their use. They hold less paint than a roller, so they take longer, and on large areas it can be tricky to get an even coverage of paint. Paint pads really come into their own when working on edges, where they can be used instead of cutting in with a brush, and for panels and smoother surfaces, where a roller can splatter the paint.

You can apply the paint from an ordinary roller tray, but a paint pad tray with a wheel is a better bet because it avoids overloading. Work the pad steadily across the surface and blend wet edges in much the same way as you would with a roller.

■ **A paint pad kit,** *with a selection of pads and a loading tray, would be a good starting point for your decorating equipment.*

APPLYING PAINT WITH A PAINT PAD

1 **Loading paint**

Load the pad from the wheel of its paint tray, scraping off the excess as you go to avoid drips.

2 **Using a pad**

Grasp the handle firmly and draw the pad in a single direction with smooth strokes.

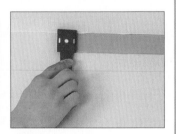

3 **Painting corners**

Use a small pad to get into corners instead of cutting in with a paint brush.

Spray painting

IF YOU'RE DECORATING a number of rooms at once, and aren't particularly worried about the overspray, hiring a spray painting gun could be a worthwhile option. Otherwise, you'll have to mask everything first, which will probably take longer than using a roller. Make sure your gun is suitable for emulsion painting – not all of them are.

Using a spray gun

For safety's sake, always wear a face mask when using a spray gun and keep the room well ventilated. For best results, move the gun gently from side to side as you spray, keeping the nozzle perpendicular to the wall or ceiling at all times. Start in the middle of the wall so that you can get used to the spray range. You can cut down on overspray by adjusting the nozzle, but it's wiser to protect the surrounding woodwork even if you're going to paint over it afterwards. Be aware that a draught might also blow the paint spray where it's not wanted.

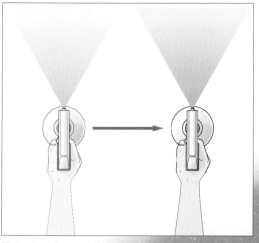

■ **Swing from side** *to side as you spray, but keep the nozzle perpendicular to the surface. Avoid spraying in an arc.*

Texturing and stencilling

IT ISN'T TO EVERYONE'S TASTE, but there's no easier way to disguise an uneven plastered ceiling, or even a wall, than texture paint. Stencilling is a fun and easy way to brighten up plain walls.

Using texture paint

Texture paint contains grains of sand or tiny foam beads that hold whatever texture you give it. You can also give the paint an embossed look by treating it with any one of a number of special texturing tools while it is still wet. Most people use a sponge, a texturing comb, or even their fingers to add texture, but you can also buy texture rollers that create a fine, even texture over large areas. Another popular tool is a wire egg whisk! On a wall, blunt the peaks of the texture while the paint is wet, or people will hurt themselves rubbing against it when it dries.

■ **Texture paint** *can be satisfying to apply on poor walls. However, once in place, the only way to get rid of it is to replaster the area.*

TEXTURE PAINTING

ⓐ **Random swirls**

Twist a damp sponge to make overlapping swirls.

ⓑ **Graceful arcs**

Work a toothed spatula over the paint in arcs.

ⓒ **Regular patterns**

A textured roller creates a far finer, more regular texture.

Stencilling

Stencilling decorative patterns on painted walls is a quick, inexpensive way to add a highly personal and unique touch to your decorative scheme. You can use it to pick out interesting features or for your own custom border design. And unlike most decorating, it's great fun!

Getting in shape

You can buy many different types of stencil in DIY shops and art shops. Some paint manufacturers also sell themed stencils to go with with their special colour ranges for children's rooms. You can make your own stencils, using stencil card bought from craft shops. When cutting repeat patterns, leave enough card between each cut-out so the stencil will be able to withstand repeated use. Stick the stencil to the wall with low-tack spray adhesive to prevent paint from seeping behind it. You can paint large patterns with a spray can, but a stencil brush or sponge will give more control. Load them lightly with paint and dab on to scrap paper until you have the colour density you want.

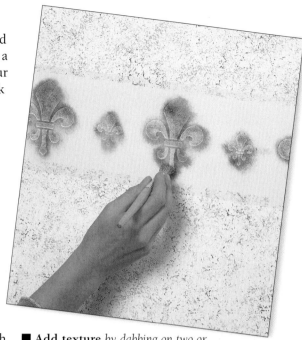

■ **Add texture** *by dabbing on two or three colours with a short-bristled stencil brush.*

STENCILLING A DECORATIVE BORDER

1 **Paint base colour**

Apply the first colour by dabbing the brush, keeping it perpendicular to the surface.

2 **Add details**

Apply a second colour when the first is dry, to give a more three-dimensional effect.

3 **Finish**

Gently peel off the stencil as soon as the paint is touch-dry to avoid smudging.

Creating paint effects

PERSONALIZE YOUR DECORATIONS *or disguise blemishes with a broken-colour paint finish. Generally this involves painting on a base coat of solid colour – usually satin emulsion – then applying a textured coat of emulsion or a glaze of coloured varnish over the top.*

Rag-rolling

This can be done in two ways: ragging off and ragging on. To rag off, brush a diluted second colour over your dry base coat, then use a twisted, rolled-up cloth to lift some of the paint off again before it starts to dry. To rag on, roll a paint-soaked rag up from the base of the wall in parallel vertical stripes, taking care to overlap them slightly. For a less regular pattern, change direction constantly, and refold the rag from time to time. Alternatively, cover the surface with random dabs from a rag crumpled up in your hand. Make sure your rags are lint-free cotton or linen, and change them frequently, before they become saturated in paint.

■ **Ragging on with a cloth soaked in paint:** *twist the rag into a "sausage", coat with paint (inset), and apply, varying the direction for a random effect.*

Sponging

Sponging, as its name implies, involves dabbing irregular patches of paint onto a dry emulsion base coat with a sponge. For best results, invest in a natural sponge about 200mm across. Soak the sponge in water until it swells to its full size, then wring it out again before dipping it in paint. Dab the paint on with a light, twisting jerk of the hand, ensuring each dab merges with the last. When the first coat is dry, repeat with a second colour. Alternatively for a deeper, more

■ **Set out your colours** *for sponging in a paint tray – there's no reason to limit yourself to two. But don't apply the first colour too densely and be careful not to overload the sponge.*

subtle effect, sponge on a second coat of a lighter version of the first colour. You can achieve an entirely different, much denser sponging effect by dabbing a damp sponge into the emulsion base coat while it is still wet. If necessary, practise first on an unobtrusive area of wall or on a spare sheet of hardboard.

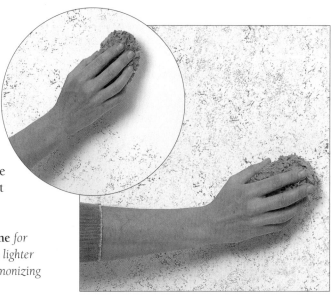

■ **Two colours are better than one** *for sponging. Make the second colour a lighter version of the first, or choose a harmonizing colour for a brighter effect.*

Colourwashing

Colourwashing is an attractive and effective way to disguise a less-than-perfect wall surface. The technique involves brushing streaks of concentrated second colour over a dry or still-wet base coat so that the underlying colour – and the brushstrokes – show through. You can enrich the effect still further with a third colour. The base and topcoats can be emulsion on emulsion or a glaze of coloured varnish over a base coat of oil-based satin-finish paint. Apply both with a wide, soft-haired wall brush – preferably natural hogshair.

APPLYING A COLOURWASH

1 **Base coat**

Satin emulsion makes a good base coat. Brush the paint on and allow to dry.

2 **Second colour**

The second colour should be stronger. Dab on and brush out over the surface quickly.

3 **Brush out**

Sweep the brush lightly over the topcoat at random so that the brushstrokes are visible.

Access to awkward areas

FALLING FROM A HEIGHT can be fatal, so if you have any doubts at all about working above ground level from a ladder or platform – don't: call in a professional. If you do decide to go ahead, take care to use the right equipment and follow the safety precautions outlined here.

Building a platform for a stairwell

Gaining access to the upper reaches of a stairwell takes thought and planning. Hire or borrow scaffold boards to make a platform and make sure that the supporting ladders can't slip by nailing wooden battens in front of the feet.

- Make sure the ladder is not raked too steeply.
- Make sure the platform ends overlap ladder rungs by 300mm or more.
- Use G-clamps to attach the boards to the ladders and to each other. Or lash them together with rope wrapped around nails part-hammered into the boards.
- Check the braces on stepladders regularly to ensure they are locked and tight.

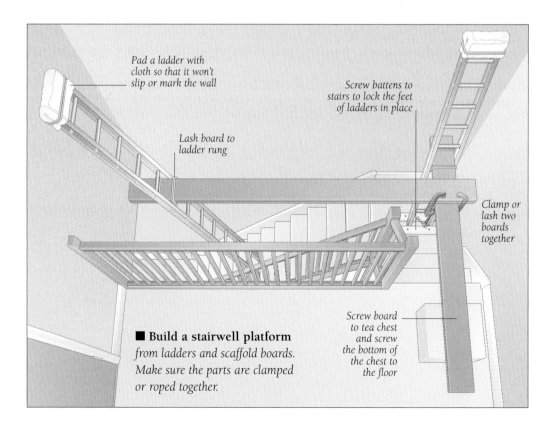

Pad a ladder with cloth so that it won't slip or mark the wall

Screw battens to stairs to lock the feet of ladders in place

Lash board to ladder rung

Clamp or lash two boards together

Screw board to tea chest and screw the bottom of the chest to the floor

■ **Build a stairwell platform** *from ladders and scaffold boards. Make sure the parts are clamped or roped together.*

Ladder safety

Falls from ladders and stepladders are the most common cause of DIY accidents, so be careful. For outdoor work, consider hiring an aluminium scaffold tower instead. These are built up in sections on adjustable feet and are much more stable. Remember the following safety rules:

● Always place a ladder on a firm, level base. If it has to go on an uneven surface, build a stable platform for it to stand on – it's much safer than propping up one leg with timber.

● When climbing a ladder, keep your hands free to grasp both sides. Carry tools in a bag or apron and keep one hand on the ladder at all times.

● If you stand higher than the third rung from the top, your chances of losing your balance are greatly increased. Likewise, "walking" a ladder along a wall is asking for a fall. Never be tempted to over-reach – the easiest way to make a ladder tip over.

● Don't stand on the top shelf of a stepladder – it is only designed to take the weight of tools.

Don't mess around with a defective ladder. Throw it away and replace it with a new one rather than risk repairing it.

● Try not to position a ladder in front of a closed door. If you must, ensure it can't be opened by unwary passers-by.

● If the top of the ladder has to rest against a window, lash a timber beam across the ladder so that the beam can straddle the width of the opening.

● Wear shoes with non-slip soles.

■ **A hired scaffold tower** *can be built up in sections. Always lock the wheels and climb up the inside or use a separate ladder for access.*

Outdoor decorating

KEEP ALL EXTERIOR PAINTWORK *in tip-top condition by sticking to a 4-year repair and redecorating cycle. You could begin with woodwork in year one, then tackle metalwork the following year, masonry or weatherboards the year after that, and fences and garden timber in the fourth year.*

Exterior woodwork

Exterior woodwork is highly vulnerable to the effects of weathering. So make a point of checking for deterioration at least once a year and patch it up quickly, before it gets any worse. Cut out and replace any rotten timber or boards. Scrape away flaking paint, then rub down the surface with abrasive paper. Coat any new or bare timber with primer and patch cracks in the wood itself with an exterior-grade wood filler. Give the patch one or two coats of undercoat, then a coat of exterior-grade gloss paint. Fill gaps between woodwork and masonry with exterior-grade flexible sealant, applied with a cartridge gun.

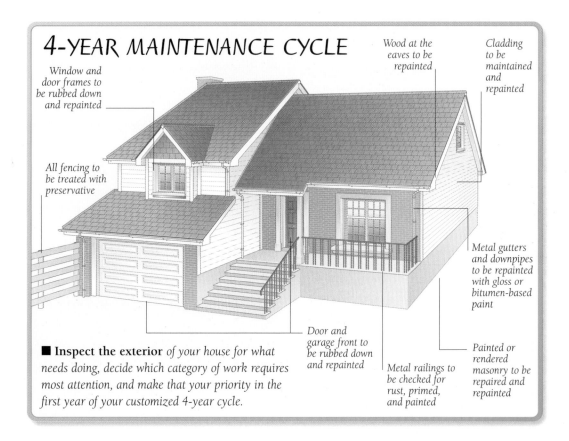

4-YEAR MAINTENANCE CYCLE

Window and door frames to be rubbed down and repainted

Wood at the eaves to be repainted

Cladding to be maintained and repainted

All fencing to be treated with preservative

Metal gutters and downpipes to be repainted with gloss or bitumen-based paint

Door and garage front to be rubbed down and repainted

Painted or rendered masonry to be repaired and repainted

Metal railings to be checked for rust, primed, and painted

■ **Inspect the exterior** *of your house for what needs doing, decide which category of work requires most attention, and make that your priority in the first year of your customized 4-year cycle.*

Metalwork

Metal begins to rust as soon as its protective layer of paint cracks. In most cases, it can be retouched with oil-based paint. But gutters and downpipes are often painted with bituminous paint, so the same type of paint must be used again. Coat bare metal with metal primer or rust inhibitor. Apply an oil-based undercoat, then two coats of gloss.

Masonry and fencing

Follow the following points for painting masonry and fencing:

- Repoint crumbling mortar joints flush with the brickwork using repair mortar.
- Hack off bubbles of "blown" render back to a sound edge and patch with a rendering mortar mix incorporating a little PVA adhesive in the mixing water. Any remaining small holes and cracks can be patched with exterior-grade filler.
- Treat algae with fungicide solution and flaking paint with stabilizing solution.
- Use a roller to apply masonry paint to smooth surfaces, use a brush on textures.
- Fences, decks, sheds, and any other exposed timber needs repainting every 4 years with two coats of creosote or outdoor timber preservative. Apply it generously, working it into the vulnerable crevices. Add the second coat before the first dries.

A simple summary

✓ Select paint not just on the basis of colour, but on the punishment it's going to take.

✓ The more time you spend on preparation, the better the result will be. At the very least, ensure surfaces are sound and clean.

✓ The fastest way to paint walls and ceilings is with a roller, plus a brush or selection of paint pads for the corners and edges.

✓ Spray painting can be the most efficient way of decorating.

✓ Stencilling is a quick and easy way to add a personal touch to your room's decor.

✓ Special paint effects can disguise blemishes on your walls.

✓ More accidents are caused by falls from ladders than anything else. Take extreme care whenever you're working off the ground.

✓ Try and keep the outside of your house looking its best by following a 4-year repair and repainting cycle.

Chapter 6

Painting Woodwork

LET'S FACE IT: PAINTING WOODWORK is a chore. But it has to be done, so the least you can do is make life easy for yourself next time around by preparing the surface properly. If you don't, the paint will flake off and you'll be right back where you started. It's important to paint doors and windows in the right order, too.

In this chapter...

✓ Paints and tools for woodwork

✓ Preparing painted wood

✓ Preparing bare wood

✓ Painting mouldings and doors

✓ Painting windows

PAINTING WOODWORK FREEHAND TAKES PRACTICE: IT'S OFTEN EASIER TO MASK AREAS WITH TAPE

Paints and tools for woodwork

THERE ARE PLENTY OF PAINTING *tools, but you don't need many for woodwork. The same goes for paint: basically the choice is between oil-based silk or gloss, which lasts longer, and water-based acrylic, which is easier to use.*

Choosing the right equipment

Invest in some quality basics. Three sizes of paintbrush should cover you: a 25mm brush for tackling window panes, raised mouldings, and the edges of skirting boards; a 50mm brush for painting door and window frames and rails; and a 75mm or 100mm brush for covering large, flat areas like door panels and flush doors. For applying traditional-style gloss paint, which is on the thin side, consider using paint pads to combat drips and runs. Shaped paint pads are also very good for complex mouldings where runs are a problem. Use a plastic paint shield to protect adjacent surfaces – it's much quicker than masking with tape.

One specialist piece of equipment that is worth buying is a decorator's cutting-in brush. This has its bristles shaped at an angle, so that they fan out to a much finer line when pressure is applied. It takes practice, but cutting-in is definitely the fastest way to paint woodwork.

FINISHES FOR WOODWORK

	Oil-based paint	Acrylic paint	Wood dye	Coloured preservative	Varnish	Oil	French polish (shellac)
Suitable for:							
Softwoods	Yes	Yes	Yes	Yes	Yes	Yes	No
Hardwoods	Yes	Yes	Yes	Yes	Yes	Yes	Yes
Interior use	Yes	Yes	Yes	Yes	Yes	Yes	Yes
Exterior use	Yes	Yes	No	Yes	Yes	Yes	No
Apply with:							
Brush	Yes	Yes	Yes	Yes	Yes	Yes	Yes
Paint pad	Yes	Yes	Yes	No	Yes	No	No
Cloth pad	No	No	Yes	No	Yes	Yes	Yes
Spray gun	Yes	Yes	No	Yes	Yes	No	No

Coverage guide for 1 litre:
general-purpose primer 10–12 sq m; undercoat 16 sq m; gloss 15 sq m; one-coat gloss 10 sq m

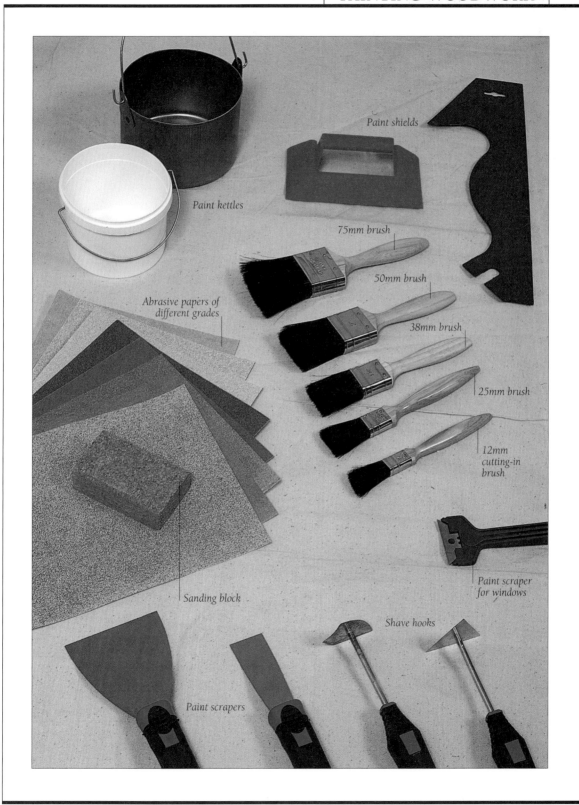

Paint shields

Paint kettles

75mm brush

50mm brush

38mm brush

Abrasive papers of
different grades

25mm brush

12mm
cutting-in
brush

Paint scraper
for windows

Sanding block

Shave hooks

Paint scrapers

Preparing painted wood

AS LONG AS THE OLD PAINT remains soundly stuck to the woodwork, there should be no need to strip it. But use your judgment: on windows especially, there comes a time when the accumulated layers of paint make surfaces look lumpy and cause edges to lose their sharpness. If you experience problems with sticking as well, it might be time to get out the heat stripper…

Assessing what to do

In most cases, paint simply needs washing down with sugar soap to remove any dirt and grease. The dirtiest areas will be those that get touched, such as around handles. But before you wash down, check for any blemishes. Fill shallow patches with fine surface filler and deeper holes with wood filler. Sand smooth, and brush or vacuum away the dust before you start painting.

Rubbing down painted woodwork with abrasive paper can generate a surprising amount of heat, so take care not to burn your fingers. As a rule it's best not to use power tools, as they can burn the paint.

Old, damp paintwork may show a green growth of mildew, which will ruin the new finish if it is not removed before you paint. Wash the woodwork down with a dilute solution of household bleach or refrigerator cleaner, let it dry, then wash again with soapy water and rinse thoroughly. Work from the top down, to avoid dribbles of dirty water.

Flaking paint should be scraped back to a sound edge. If this leaves you with bare wood, make sure you prime before repainting. If you're left with shallow indentations, fill them with fine surface filler and sand smooth.

Keep an eye out for knots that have swelled. These will need rubbing down and priming. If you find a knot is "live" and is bleeding resin, treat it with knotting primer.

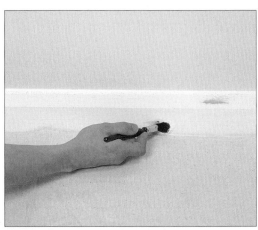

■ **Prevent the latest** *coat of paint from sinking into any patches of bare wood by applying primer. This will hold the paint at the surface.*

PREPARATION ROUTINE

1 Fill any chips

Use fine surface filler to cover blemishes in the existing paintwork. Use the corner of a filling knife to fill hard-to-reach places.

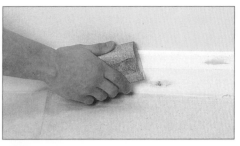

2 Rub down

Rub down the filler with abrasive paper wrapped around a cork block. In tight corners, fold the paper into a pad and use the edge.

3 Wipe away dust

Remove dust from intricate mouldings with a cloth soaked in white spirit. Leave the surface to dry before painting.

4 Wash down

Finally, wash the paintwork down with a warm sugar soap solution to remove grease and to key the surface for the new paint.

Fill any gaps around the woodwork with the appropriate type of flexible sealant, applied from a cartridge gun. You should use exterior-grade sealant around the outside of doors and windows, then paint over the sealant when you come to paint the frames to provide a totally watertight seal.

If you come across crumbling putty on window panes, this should be scraped out and filled with flexible filler – unless the pane is loose, in which case you'd be well advised to reglaze it entirely before you start painting. It's not a difficult job and well worth doing. Be sure to deal with any mould growth, which may be a problem if the old paint seal has been broken.

Preparing bare wood

FOR ALL ITS VERSATILITY AND BEAUTY, *bare wood is not without its drawbacks. The softwood used for general joinery is often peppered with knots, cracks, and other blemishes that will stick out like a sore thumb if you simply paint over them.*

Choosing a primer for painting

Primer both seals the wood and provides a key for further coats. Which type you use depends on your topcoat: use water-based acrylic primer under water-based paints; apply solvent-based primer under oil-based paints. If you really want to paint an oily hardwood such as teak, use a special aluminium-based primer to seal it.

Undercoat is largely optional these days. Modern non-drip topcoats have the bulk and covering power to do without it, but you'll save money if you undercoat before using thinner, traditional-style oil paints, or if the wood grain is very open. Apply one or two coats, and watch that you don't leave ugly brushmarks.

PREPARING BARE WOOD FOR PAINT

1 **Seal knots and fill any blemishes**

Rub down dead knots and fill. Seal any resinous knots with knotting compound. Using a filling knife, fill any gaps with flexible wood filler or general purpose filler.

2 **Prime**

Very open-grained wood can be smoothed with a thin coat of surface filler. Once the surface is smooth and level, apply the primer, making sure it is well worked into any joints.

Better left bare?

With wood that's going to be left bare for oiling or varnishing, you have to take a little more care over how you treat any gaps and blemishes. Flexible wood filler, also known as "plastic wood" and "wood stopping" comes in various shades, so make sure you get a good colour match or the effect will be ruined. On outdoor woodwork, be sure to use a solvent-based exterior grade filler. Fill and paint over any gaps with adjoining surfaces before varnishing the wood.

If you run into colour matching problems, improvise a filler by mixing sawdust from an offcut of the same wood with your chosen varnish or PVA woodworking glue.

If the wood is very open-grained, rub it down with a pad of medium grade wire wool. Brush or vacuum away the dust, then seal the surface with a mixture of half varnish, half solvent.

There's no need to treat resinous knots before varnishing, but it's worth checking that any dead knots won't fall out: if they're loose, simply stick them back with woodworking adhesive and rub down when dry. As a final precaution against dust, wipe the entire surface down with a cloth soaked in white spirit and leave to dry before varnishing. Pay particular attention to corners and crevices, where dust may have accumulated over the years.

PREPARING BARE WOOD FOR VARNISH

1 Fill holes and cracks

Fill blemishes with flexible wood filler, smoothing it with your filling knife so that it is just proud of the surface.

2 Push stopping into angles

Use your finger or the edge of a filling knife to force the filler into the tight corners found around wooden mouldings.

3 Rub down

Leave the filler to dry completely, then rub down level with the surface using abrasive paper mounted on a block.

Painting mouldings and doors

CLEANLY PAINTED WOODWORK *with crisp, firm lines puts a finishing touch to your interior decor. Your biggest enemies are drips, runs, stray lines, and the fluff from adjoining carpets.*

Painting skirtings and mouldings

Unless you're really confident of your ability to cut in with a steady hand, masking the lines of mouldings and skirtings with tape will save you time in the long run. Masking is also virtually essential for the join between a skirting and a carpeted floor – not only to protect the carpet, but also to stop stray hairs working their way into the wet paint. If you're pressed for time, use a plastic paint shield instead – but make sure that you force it hard into the join and wipe it down regularly. On narrow mouldings, use a narrower brush size, to avoid splashing paint. If your paint is the traditional thinner oil-based type, it's better to apply the first coat thinly, let it dry, then apply another coat, rather than risk a lot of drips and runs.

Always apply paint to mouldings along the grain of the wood. Paint the raised parts of decorative mouldings first, so that any runs can be dispersed when you come to paint the wider parts.

PAINTING ADJOINING SURFACES

a **Cover with tape**

Masking tape guarantees a clean line along mouldings. Peel off before the paint dries.

b **Cutting in**

A cutting-in brush gives a reasonably clean line – but only if your hand is steady.

c **Shielding lines**

Move a paint shield as you paint and wipe frequently to prevent seepage behind it.

Painting doors

There are as many ways of painting a door as there are door types, but in all cases your aim is to paint from the top down to avoid runs. Before you start painting, remove as much of the door furniture as possible and wedge or prop the door open. If you're working outside, choose a dull, still day to avoid the risk of dust or insects getting caught in the paint.

Speed is of the essence on doors, and you should aim to complete one side in a single session. Apply the paint in sections, starting with any panels, followed by the frame, and then the

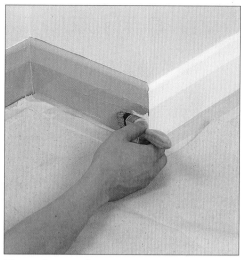

■ **Brush away from corners** *and edges to prevent paint build-ups.*

edges. Finish each section with light, vertical strokes and blend the wet edges into the adjoining sections. If the sides of the door are different colours, the parts of the door that face you from each room should be the same colour.

Glazed doors

Paint French windows and glazed doors in roughly the same order as solid panelled doors, having first masked the glazing bars if desired. Mask just slightly in from the edge of the glass so that the paint will form a seal over the glazing bars or putty.

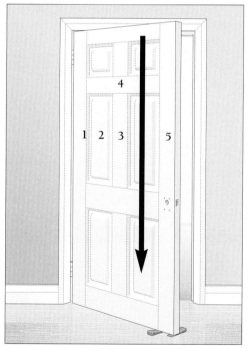

■ **The order for painting** *a panelled door is as follows: inner mouldings (1) first, followed by the panels (2), centre stile (3), rails (4), outer stiles (5), and then edges. Always work from top to bottom between sections to avoid runs.*

Unless you catch them straight away, leave stray bristles in the paint to dry, then sand smooth. Also, leave drips on the glass to dry, then scrape off with a blade.

Painting windows

KEEP THE EDGES *of window frames sharp and unstuck by painting them in sequence. This will stop pools of paint gathering in the crevices and also leave you with enough dry edges to close the window at night.*

Keeping unstuck

As with doors, paint window frames from top to bottom to avoid runs and take care not to let paint build up along the edges. Remove any hardware first. Mask glazing bars 2mm or so in from the edge of the glass so that the paint forms a watertight seal against the weather or condensation. Alternatively, use a paint shield to achieve the same effect.

On sash windows, apply the paint as thinly as possible and don't allow it to gather in the recesses of the runners. Keep it away from the sash cords, too, or they will go brittle and snap. Open casement windows are vulnerable to dust and flying insects, so choose a still day for painting. Watch the lower edge of the bottom rail for paint build-ups that could cause the window to stick.

Don't leave open windows and doors unattended while the paint dries. Make sure you're around to keep an eye on them. Burglars are opportunists and may view an open window or door as an opportunity to break into your home.

KEEPING PAINT OFF THE GLASS

a **Use a paint shield**

Paint against a plastic shield – but wipe the shield frequently to avoid accidental drips.

b **Remove paint spatters**

Leave stray flicks of paint on the glass. Remove when dry with a blade or scraper.

Order of painting

Follow the procedure described below to make painting windows easier.

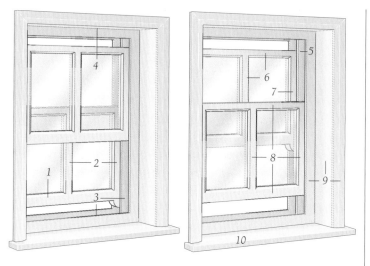

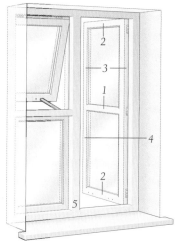

■ **With sash windows** *start by raising the inner sash and lowering the outer one. Paint the bottom of the outer sash (**1**), then the glazing bars (**2**) as high as possible. Then paint the lower part of the runners (**3**) and the top recess (**4**). Reverse the position of the sashes and paint the top part of the runners (**5**), followed by the remaining parts in numerical order.*

■ **With casement windows** *paint the glazing bar (**1**), then the horizontal rails and vertical (**2** and **3**). Finish by painting the opening edges (**4**), and finally paint the window frame (**5**).*

A simple summary

✔ A basic set of good quality brushes and the correct primer and top coat is essential when painting woodwork.

✔ If the existing paint is sound and smooth, there's no need to strip it before painting – simply wash down with sugar soap to remove dirt and grease.

✔ Fix knots, cracks, and other blemishes before painting.

✔ Unless you are good at painting straight lines, you'll save time by masking wooden mouldings.

✔ Painting windows in the right sequence will make the job a whole lot easier.

Chapter 7

Wallpapering

NOTHING BRIGHTENS UP A ROOM more than a fresh covering of wallpaper. More decorative than painting and generally cheaper than tiling, hanging wallpaper is also within the capabilities of even the most inexperienced DIYer. So long as you prepare correctly and hang the first length of paper properly, you will find the job becomes easier and easier as you go on.

In this chapter...

✓ Preparing and lining walls

✓ Choosing wallpaper

✓ Wallpapering equipment

✓ How to hang wallpaper

✓ Papering problem areas

✓ Wallpaper borders

DECORATING WITH TODAY'S WALLPAPERING MATERIALS IS NEARLY AS EASY AS PAINTING

Preparing and lining walls

BEFORE HANGING WALLPAPER, *you'll need to strip off any old paper or textured lining paper and make sure that the underlying surface is reasonably smooth. Some wallpaper manufacturers recommend that you line the walls, too. Ideally, repaint the ceiling and any woodwork before papering.*

Off with the old

Soak and scrape off old wallpaper by hand – or hire a steam stripper if the paper is thick and/or painted-over. It used to be said that you could peel off the outer layer of vinyl papers and paper over the backing. That may be so, but it's safer in the long run to strip the backing off. You can't paper over textured lining or woodchip paper – strip it off. Repair any large cracks and holes before continuing.

Lining walls with paper

Lining paper comes in various forms for covering up less-than-perfect walls. It also absorbs wallpaper paste evenly, which can be a key factor in ensuring that heavier papers stay stuck to the wall.

Ordinary lining paper is sold in standard sized rolls and in four weights. Use one of the two lighter grades if you're hanging paper on top, or choose the heavier grades for

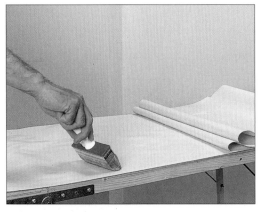

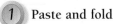

1 Paste and fold

Brush paste over the soaked strip of paper, taking care not to tear it. Then fold the strip concertina-style, pasted sides together.

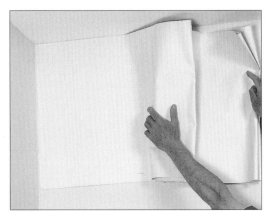

2 Lining up for corners

Hang the lining paper with a 2mm gap at the corners so that the wallpaper can be pushed fully into the corners later.

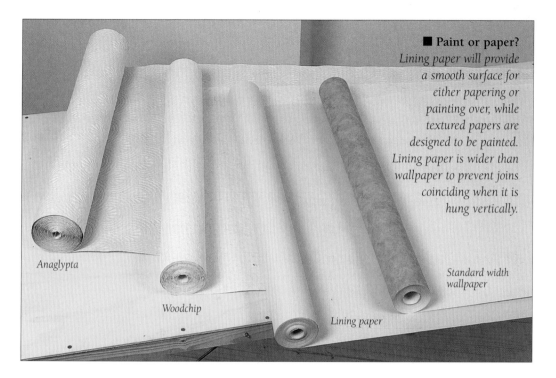

■ Paint or paper?
Lining paper will provide a smooth surface for either papering or painting over, while textured papers are designed to be painted. Lining paper is wider than wallpaper to prevent joins coinciding when it is hung vertically.

Anaglypta

Woodchip

Lining paper

Standard width wallpaper

painting over. Hang lining paper in the usual way if you're painting over it. For wallpapering, you can hang it vertically – providing the joints don't coincide – but horizontal lining is quicker. Try, if possible, to use the same adhesive for both the lining paper and wallpaper. When hanging, butt strips together. Leave for 48 hours before papering over.

Dampen lining paper with water before pasting, to ensure they dry out at an even rate when on the wall and don't blister. Take care not to tear the paper when pasting or moving.

Textured lining papers

Aside from ordinary lining paper, there are heavier textured and plaster-reinforced embossed papers that can be hung for their decorative effect or – more cynically – because the plaster underneath is falling apart. The ubiquitous woodchip – beloved of builders, hated by new homeowners – is the best known textured lining paper.

Plaster-reinforced embossed papers are extremely tough and are popular for traditional-style decorative schemes that involve lining the walls below dado rail height. They are hung in the usual way, but may require sticking with their own special adhesive.

Choosing wallpaper

STEP INTO ANY DIY STORE, *and a quick glance at the mountains of swatch books on show will give you some idea of the vast choice of wallcoverings around. Wallpaper can be good value, but be careful – as with fabrics, the cost of some designs and materials is astronomical.*

I'd like to buy some wallpaper, please!

Terms such as ready-pasted and washable are fairly self-explanatory when applied to wallpaper, but other descriptions may be a little more confusing.

- **Vinyl** is a paper with a PVC pattern or layer bonded onto it. Washable and durable, vinyl is ideal for kitchens and bathrooms.
- **Duplex** is a thin paper with a raised (embossed) pattern, backed by another layer of paper. The two are bonded together to form one sheet. Easy to hang.
- **Flock** is a paper with a velvet pile bonded onto it. One of the most expensive wallcoverings available.
- **Novamura** is a paper that feels like fabric. Wipes clean and is easy to hang, although the paste must be applied to the walls, not the paper.
- **Foil coated paper** can look spectacular in a small, dingy room. Strips are normally hung with a special vinyl-based adhesive that you apply to the wall. The same usually applies to cloth-backed papers.
- **Damp-resistant paper** is foil-backed for lining masonry walls that are inherently damp. It's better to fix the fault if at all possible.

WALLPAPER ESTIMATOR CHART (IN ROLLS)

Height/Distance	9m	10m	12m	13m	14m	15m	16m	17m	19m	20m	21m	22m	23m	25m	26m	27m
2.15–2.30m	4	5	5	6	6	7	7	8	8	9	9	10	10	11	12	12
2.30–2.45m	5	5	6	6	7	7	8	8	9	9	10	10	11	11	12	13
2.45–2.60m	5	5	6	7	7	8	9	9	10	10	11	12	12	13	14	14
2.60–2.75m	5	5	6	7	7	8	9	9	10	10	11	12	12	13	14	14
2.75–2.90m	6	6	7	7	8	9	9	10	10	11	12	12	13	14	14	15
2.90–3.05m	6	6	7	8	8	9	10	10	11	12	12	13	14	14	15	16
3.05–3.20m	6	7	8	8	9	10	10	11	12	13	13	14	15	16	16	17

Numbers are based on a standard roll size of 10.05m long and 520mm wide

ORDER OF WORK

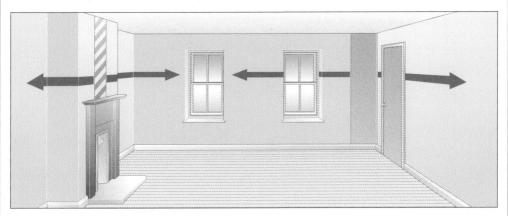

Where you start papering is largely a matter of preference. Generally it's best to start in a corner, and work clockwise round the room if you are right-handed and anticlockwise if you are left-handed (above right). By working away from the window, any less-than-perfect joins will not be emphasized by casting shadows. With a large-patterned paper, centre the first length (or lengths) on a dominant feature, such as a chimney breast, and paper outwards from there (above left).

Add a little extra

Use the chart opposite to work out how many rolls you need. Add on a couple of extra rolls if you are using a complex "step-and-repeat" pattern that's difficult to match. Most suppliers don't mind if you over-order as long as you take unused rolls back undamaged and before too long. It also makes sense to have some spare paper in case you need to make repairs in the future.

If you're hanging paper with a step-and-repeat pattern, there will be far less wastage if you cut alternate strips from two different rolls. It makes the job easier, too.

All wallpaper has a code on its back to identify when it was printed. Due to quirks in the production process, paper that seems identical can look disturbingly different once it is on the wall if it comes from different batches. Check when you buy. At the same time, don't forget to buy the paste, which comes ready-mixed, or in powder form for mixing with water. Fungicidal paste is best in today's draught-proof homes, where condensation often encourages mould growth. You might also find it handy to buy a tube of vinyl-based overlap adhesive to stick down any joins that curl up annoyingly after the paper has dried out.

Wallpapering equipment

THERE'S NO SENSE IN SKIMPING on wallpapering tools. None of them costs very much and they make the job a great deal easier. If you're only covering a small area, consider postponing the job until you have enough papering to justify the cost of getting the right gear.

Tools of the trade

The most important item in any wallpapering toolkit is a good sharp pair of papering shears. Ordinary scissors won't do, and a craft knife will tear all but the heaviest papers. Use the backs of the shears to crease the paper into corners prior to trimming.

A pasting table is also worth buying; you could improvise, but it's not really worth it. While you're about it, buy a cheap plastic seam roller for flattening the joins between strips and a decent pasting brush – smoothing the paper with your hands or with a cloth could easily damage it. You also need a plastic bucket for mixing the paste. Always clean and dry tools at the end of a session before the wallpaper paste dries hard or causes the tools to rust.

Stretch a length of string across the rim of your paste bucket and tie it to the handle anchor points. You can then rest your pasting brush over the bucket, not in it, and use the string to scrape off excess paste.

You must have some means of plumbing vertical lines on the wall. The traditional way to do this is to chalk your plumbline and snap it against the wall, but at a pinch you could get away with pencilling the lines against a spirit level.

Optional extras

Depending on the wallcovering, you may also need a trimming knife and a metal straightedge for trimming. A small pair of scissors is useful for dealing with awkward areas. And of course, if the room is carpeted, you'll need some means of protecting the floor – either dust sheets or disposable plastic sheets and newspaper. Don't forget that you may need access equipment if you're papering a ceiling or a stairwell, where it's even more important to have a secure platform than for painting. Otherwise you can probably get by with a stepladder, although a 3-step folding hop-up is much more convenient for normal height rooms.

■ The full wallpapering toolkit *doesn't amount to very much, so it's worth buying. Don't forget that you may have to hire access equipment if you're papering a stairwell or ceiling.*

Stepladder

Pasting brush

Bucket

Dust sheets

Sponge

Wallpapering shears

Chalkline

Small scissors

Seam roller

Trimming knife

Straightedge

Plumbline

Pasting table

Wallpaper brush

How to hang wallpaper

YOU'VE BOUGHT THE WALLPAPER and all the tools; now you just have to get the stuff on the wall! Hanging paper is not difficult if you take your time. Get the first length right and everything else should follow smoothly.

Pasting and folding

Cut a strip of paper to length allowing 25mm overlap top and bottom. Lay it on the pasting table so that one long and one short edge overlap the edges of the table. To apply the paste, brush out from the middle of the strip in a criss-cross pattern towards the overlapping edges so that you don't get paste on the table. Then adjust the strip and paste over the other two edges.

Hanging the strips

On every wall, always hang the first strip less than a roll's length away from a corner, door, window frame, or fireplace so that you have a decent amount of waste at each end. It's very important to align the first strip against a vertical line drawn on the wall with a plumbline or, failing that, a spirit level. That way, you know that the joins and pattern will look right; corners themselves are rarely as true as they seem, and any errors will be compounded.

HANGING THE STRIPS

1 **Plumb a line**

Use a plumbline to mark a vertical guideline for the first strip. Add 50mm to the length of drop to allow for trimming, not including pattern repeats.

2 **Align the first strip**

Use your fingertips to ease the edge of the pasted and folded strip against the line. Brush back to the far edge to remove air bubbles, and trim.

The art of cornering

Don't panic when you come to your first corner. Follow the simple tips below.

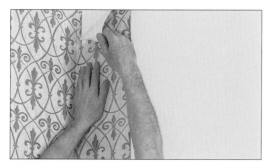

a **Internal corners**

Cut the end strip to turn the corner by no more than 10–20mm. Hang the overlapping strip to a plumbed line, trim vertically, and smooth down.

b **External corners**

Turn 25mm around the corner. If the wall is badly out of true, leave a generous overlap on the second strip and trim to the corner.

It's always a good idea to lightly fold wallpaper (paste-side in on itself) before hanging. It not only makes the strip easier to handle; it also ensures that the paste is distributed evenly. On ceilings and stairwells, fold very long strips concertina-style as you would with lining paper.

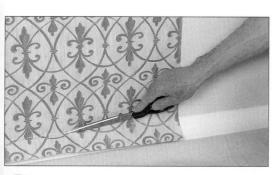

3 **Crease and trim**

Crease the wallpaper with the back of your shears to mark the trimming line, then pull away and cut along the crease. Smooth back the flap.

4 **Subsequent strips**

If the first strip hangs vertically, so will all the others on that wall. But don't forget to match the pattern when butting the strips together.

Papering problem areas

A GOOD RULE *for papering problem areas is: don't! Paint them instead. But even the boxiest rooms have their obstructions and window recesses, in which case the tips shown here will help save your sanity.*

Reducing problems

Plan ahead to reduce headaches. For example, move the starting point of your first drop of paper to avoid having to hang nasty narrow strips around doors and windows. Remove everything you can from the walls, save for radiators and electrical fittings. And make sure the walls themselves are free of dust. If you've made repairs, coat the surface with paste to stop the wallpaper drying out too fast while you wrestle to trim it round those awkward corners.

If you have to overlap strips vertically – as in a window recess – make sure the exposed edge faces the window so that it doesn't cast a shadow. If the strips start to peel back, let them dry and then coat them with PVA adhesive so that they stick firmly.

Arches and radiators

Arches are best papered with a plain or random-patterned paper, as pattern-matching is impossible between the curved and flat surfaces. Paper the walls either side of the arch first, trimming to leave a 25mm overlap all round. Then make "V" cuts every 50mm and stick down the flaps. Finally, cut the inside strips to width, pattern-match them to the walls at the bottom, and butt-join them at the crown of the arch. Around a wall-mounted radiator, hang full lengths of paper as far as possible to each side of, and between, the brackets. Then slit the remaining strips to fit over the brackets.

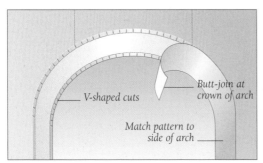

V-shaped cuts

Butt-join at crown of arch

Match pattern to side of arch

■ **To paper neatly** *around an arch, trim the inside strips exactly to the wall thickness.*

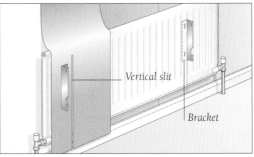

Vertical slit

Bracket

■ **Cut vertical slits** *in the wallpaper so you can fit it around the brackets behind a radiator.*

DEALING WITH WINDOWS

■ **Paper a reveal**
(side of the window
recess) in the order
shown here. For a
shallow reveal, make
release cuts in the
last length of paper,
fold it round and trim
to the frame. For a
deep reveal fit top
corner and side
pieces, and turn the
paper over the edge.

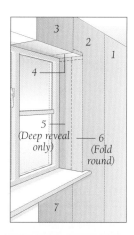

(1) **Making release cuts**

*Brush the paper against the the door frame or
windowsill to mark the projection. Cut into the
angle with the wall so the paper lies flat.*

(2) **Trimming to the sill**

*Make further release cuts into each part
of the moulding, then press the paper into
the projection and trim it to fit.*

(3) **Brushing into position**

*Add more paste if it has dried out, then brush
the paper back into place, using the tips of the
bristles to push it into the angles.*

Switches and fittings

Having turned off the supply for safety, loosen
the faceplate of an electrical fitting just before
you paper around it. Then paste up the strip,
let it hang loosely over the fitting, and press
gently on the paper to mark the four corners
of the faceplate. Now make four release cuts
from the centre of the fitting back to the marks
and tear off the waste to leave 6mm wide flaps.
Brush these under the faceplate and screw
back down. Simple!

■ **Dealing with light**
*switches is much easier
than you might think.*

Wallpaper borders

PAPER BORDERS *are a quick way to revamp tired-looking decorations or draw attention to features. The self-adhesive type are convenient, but you only get one chance to position them; most people find borders you paste yourself easier to use. Tape up an offcut of your chosen border before committing yourself; borders can easily overpower a room.*

HANGING WALLPAPER BORDERS

1 **Paste and fold**

Cut the desired length of border, allowing for plenty of overlap at corners and joins. Paste the back, then fold it concertina-fashion.

2 **Hang to a guideline**

Draw a horizontal guideline on the wall, align the edge of the strip against it, and unfurl, smoothing out any air bubbles as you go.

3 **Overlap at joins**

Allow enough overlap on any subsequent strips to match the pattern. Smooth down, then trim through both strips at once to remove the waste.

4 **Seam-roll edges and joins**

Run over all joins and edges with a seam roller to make sure they are firmly stuck to the wall. Sponge off any excess paste before it dries.

Hanging techniques

Make sure the walls are smooth and clean, then pencil a horizontal guideline around the room. Use a spirit level to ensure the line is level, unless the border is going close to the ceiling, in which case make the line parallel with the ceiling instead.

When pasting borders, lay lining paper over the table to protect the surface, and paste from the middle of the strip outwards over the edges. Align the pasted and folded border with the guideline and smooth into place.

Matching the pattern on a corner join can be tricky, so practise first. Fold two spare strips of border so that they form the desired angle, making sure the pattern is symmetrical along the join.

Along joins, overlap the strips so that the pattern matches and cut through both layers at once. To form corners, adjust the overlap to the desired angle and cut through both layers. To form a strip of border around a curve, cut V-shapes halfway into the inside edge and smooth down.

A simple summary

✔ Surfaces need to be clean, sound, and non-absorbent. For best results, or if the surface is a little uneven, hang lining paper first.

✔ Always order more rolls than you think you need – if you take them back before too long your supplier should refund you for any unused rolls.

✔ Make sure you have all the necessary equipment to hand, including extra ladders and scaffold boards for access.

✔ Always hang the first strip on each wall against a vertical line, having checked how much waste this leaves at either end.

✔ Plan ahead to make papering problems areas less of a problem. Always turn off electricity before loosening switch and socket faceplates so that you can trim the paper behind them.

✔ Wallpaper borders are an easy and cost-effective way to revamp a room's decoration.

Chapter 8

Ceramic Tiling

FOR PERMANENCE, DURABILITY, AND EASE OF CLEANING, ceramic tiles are still the number one choice for walls and floors. But tiles will only be as good as the surface they go on – so preparation is the key.

In this chapter...

✓ Choosing tiles and estimating

✓ Tiling tools and materials

✓ Preparing surfaces

✓ Splashbacks and surrounds

✓ Cutting ceramic tiles

✓ Laying ceramic floor tiles

✓ Sealing and grouting

✓ Whole walls

CERAMIC TILES: HARDWEARING, EASY TO CLEAN, AND THERE FOR KEEPS!

Choosing tiles and estimating

CERAMIC WALL AND FLOOR TILES REPRESENT *a sizeable investment, and once fixed they are there to stay. So take your time over choosing and be sure to order enough to complete the job.*

Buying tiles

A specialist tile store is the place to buy tiles, not least because it will have tiled panels on display that make it easier to judge the final effect. Specialists also buy in bulk, so there are bargains to be had, as well as a wide choice.

When it comes to choosing, there is a world of difference in price between machine-made mass-produced tiles and imported hand-made ranges; if you're on a budget, reserve these for small areas, or for decorative borders or panels.

Ceramic tiles come in all shapes and sizes, the most popular being 100mm square, 150mm square, and 200 x 150mm. Glazed tiles are non-porous and are therefore suitable for bathrooms and other wet areas. Unglazed tiles, such as terracotta, have a more subtle natural look, but are mostly decorative. Moulded border tiles are available for finishing the edges, as are round edged tiles (which are rarer than they used to be). You can also get smaller mosaic tiles, which come in panels attached to backing sheets. As a rule, small tiles look better in small areas and are much easier to cut and fit around awkward corners. On the other hand, the larger sizes give a cleaner, less cluttered look. Thicknesses vary too, especially on hand-made tiles; wall tiles are generally around 4mm thick and floor tiles 6mm or more, but your supplier will advise on both suitability and availability.

Avoid garishly patterned tiles: you may like them, but they could adversely affect the value of your home.

> ### DEFINITION
> *Ceramic tiles come either **glazed** or **unglazed**. Glazed tiles are non-porous and have a gloss or matt finish. Unglazed tiles absorb water and grease and so are harder to clean and are unsuitable for wet areas.*

Estimating quantities

The best way to estimate quantities is to mark a wooden batten in whole tile widths (use two for rectangular tiles) and run this around the area to be tiled. Count the whole tiles, then estimate the number needed to fill the gaps and add on an extra 5 per cent to cover accidental breakages. If you're tiling a whole wall with inset panels, it might be safer to draw a scale plan of the wall on graph paper – making each square one whole tile – and then count the tiles individually.

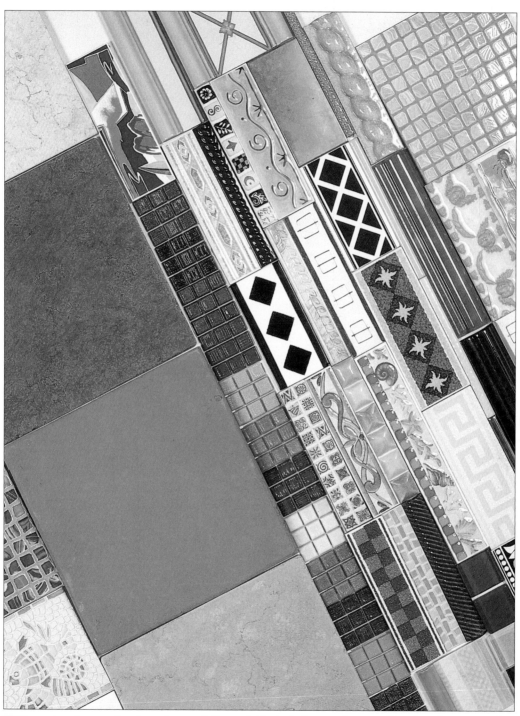

■ **There is a huge selection** *of types of tile available, including machine- and hand-made ceramic tiles (both glazed and unglazed), mosaic tile panels, and plain and moulded edging tiles.*

Tiling tools and materials

YOU SHOULD BE ABLE TO BUY or hire all the tools and obtain the other materials you need where you buy the tiles. Most specialist tiling tools are inexpensive enough to be used on a one-off basis, but a lever-operated tile cutter is a good investment if you have a large area to cover or if the tiles themselves are especially thick.

SPECIALIST TILING TOOLS

A "score-and-snap" tile cutter: this is fine for the smaller sizes of wall tiles, but is hard work on tiles measuring over 150 x 200mm or more than 4mm thick. Inexpensive "all-in-one" gadgets do the same job, but are not all that much easier than snapping tiles over a piece of wood.

A lever-operated tile cutter: this makes short work of larger wall tiles and floor tiles, and can be hired from tiles stores and hire shops. For cutting and shaping very thick glazed quarry tiles, you'll need to hire an angle grinder.

Tile nibblers: these can be used with a cutter to remove small pieces of tile for cut-outs. Alternatively, use a tile saw, which is time-consuming but reduces the risk of breakages. Use a tungsten-tipped masonry bit for drilling holes in tiles, taking care to avoid the edges.

A profile gauge: this useful tool moulds itself to the shape of awkward gaps, allowing you to trace the shape of the cut-out on the tile in felt-tip pen. In some places it is easier to make a card template of the gap.

A rubber squeegee: you'll need this and a plastic grouting tool to apply and smooth the grout between the tile joints. Tile adhesive is usually sold with its own plastic notched spreader, but if not, buy a notched tiling trowel.

TILING MATERIALS

Wall tile adhesive: this is generally sold ready mixed in tubs, and in two grades: regular and water-resistant, for baths and showers. Some types double as grout, which is handy for small areas. Floor tile adhesive is bulkier and is often sold dry for mixing with water.

Grout: buy this ready mixed or in powder form for mixing with water. Again, there are two grades – regular and water-resistant – and you can also buy grout colourant in powder form. Special grout is available for floor tiles.

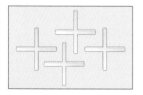

Plastic X-shaped tile spacers: these are sold in various thicknesses; generally speaking, the smaller the tile, the narrower the gap. Plastic edging strips are sold for finishing edges and external corners but can look tacky.

On a surface like a tiled worktop, which needs to be both hygienic and waterproof, fill the gaps with two-part epoxy grout. This is applied like resin filler with a spatula, and then smoothed with a cloth dipped in solvent. It dries to a hard, impervious finish.

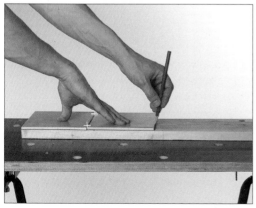

■ **Make your own tile gauge** *using a wooden batten marked in whole tile widths. Don't forget the grout gaps between the tiles.*

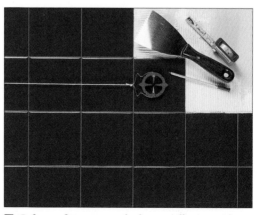

■ **Coloured grout** *can look very effective with dark tiles. The colour comes in powder form, for use with white grouting powder.*

Preparing surfaces

AS WITH ALL DECORATION JOBS, thorough preparation will avoid problems later and ensure that the tiles stay firmly stuck. Tile adhesive is a pretty forgiving material, so there's no need for surfaces to be absolutely flat. But make sure that the underlying surface can't move or flex, otherwise the grout will start falling out in no time at all.

Playing smart with surfaces

Tiles are a fairly permanent fixture, so install them to last. Any semi-permanent fixtures are better removed than tiled around, and if you're thinking of installing a new bathroom suite or fitted kitchen, now's the time to do so: if you postpone it until later, you may be faced with unsightly gaps in the tiling.

Don't make the mistake of thinking that tiles will cover up damp. Eventually, the dampness seeps through the joints and creates a mouldy, musty smell. On plasterboard walls, make sure there is no way that water can seep under the edges of the tiles.

Tiling doesn't suit areas full of nooks and crannies or plumbing and cabling. Box in service pipes and augment built-in features such as pillars so that they become more regular in shape; it not only makes the job easier, but looks better, too. Build the boxing-in with a wooden frame, screwed to the wall, and surface it with water-resistant (marine grade) plywood or cement fibreboard. You can build a recess for a luxurious semi-sunken bath in the same way.

Tile bath panels and other wall access panels separately. Fix the panels to their backing framework with domehead screws – the type with screw-on chromed caps to cover the heads. For access to underfloor services, cut out individual panels in the plywood overlay and tile separately.

Think how you're going to handle the joins with adjacent surfaces. Wherever tiles join a surface that might move – a bath, for example – fill the join with flexible sealant. If the gap is too wide, close it with quadrant tiles bedded in sealant. On a tiled floor, the chances are that the surface will be raised at door thresholds. The best way to deal with this is to screw down strips of hardwood, planed to a ramp shape. Special skirting tiles are available for quarry tiles. Fill the gaps around skirtings with flexible sealant. Finish the edges above a half-tiled wall with wooden moulding (use flexible sealant along the joint) or decorative moulded border tiles.

WHICH METHOD FOR WHICH SURFACE?

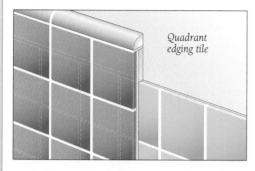

Quadrant edging tile

(a) Existing tiles

You can tile over existing tiles, providing they are firmly fixed and the surface is clean and dry. But consider the implications of doing so around fixtures and fittings first. Double edges can be hidden with rounded quadrant tiles.

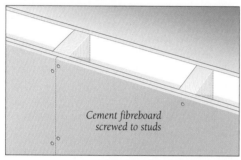

Cement fibreboard screwed to studs

(b) Plasterboard walls

Plasterboard should be fine to tile on, but around baths and shower cubicles you may want to take extra precautions. Either coat the area with waterproof paint first, or (better) line the area with cement fibreboard sheet.

Skimming plaster

(c) Masonry walls

Make sure the plaster is sound and free of dust or flaking paint. Strip any wallpaper and patch all holes. If the surface is slightly uneven, giving it a coat of ready mixed skimming plaster will make it easier to fix the tiles.

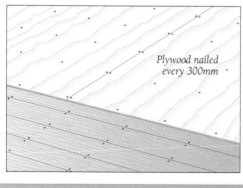

Plywood nailed every 300mm

(d) Floors

Level uneven concrete floors with self-levelling compound. On boarded floors, fix any loose boards and then nail sheets of 12mm plywood over the top. Be sure to allow access for stopcocks and other services.

Splashbacks and surrounds

A TILED SURROUND behind a basin or sink is the ideal place to practise your tiling skills. With luck, you won't have to cut any tiles. And on jobs of this size, there's no need to fit a base batten to support the bottom row.

Tiling small areas

Modern tile adhesive is so effective that for small jobs you don't really need to nail a batten to the wall to support the first row. Even so, you'll find a vertical batten helpful to keep the tiles straight; check it's level with a spirit level and leave the nail heads sticking out so that you can remove them without disturbing the tiles. The secret of putting up tiles is to apply the right amount of adhesive, and to make sure that it's properly grooved. The grooves create suction that help the tiles to stick; they also allow for movement, so that the tiles can be made to lie flat. People used to space tiles with matchsticks, but ready-made X-shaped plastic spacers are cheap to buy and far easier to use. At internal corners between walls, simply trim off one arm of an "X" to form a "T".

> ### Trivia...
> *In 1840 Englishman Richard Prosser patented a technique for producing clay buttons in a press. Ten years later the same process kicked off the Victorian tile craze: decorative tiles appeared in nearly every type of new building, and even on furniture such as washstands and dressing tables.*

If one tile ends up proud of the others, don't try to force it to lie flat – you'll probably crack it. Instead, remove the tile, scrape off the adhesive from both the tile and the wall, lay a fresh bed of adhesive, and try again. After you've laid the first few tiles, you'll quickly get used to applying the adhesive to the right thickness.

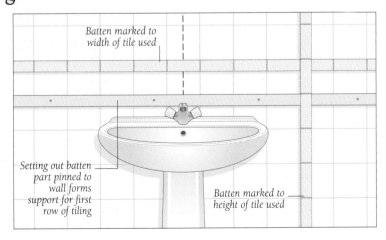

Batten marked to
width of tile used

Setting out batten
part pinned to
wall forms
support for first
row of tiling

Batten marked to
height of tile used

■ **On larger jobs,**
plan where to lay the tiles so that they look centred and don't leave you with odd cuts at edges and corners. The easiest way is to use a batten marked in whole tile widths, allowing for the spacers. Check both horizontally and vertically, then mark where the first tile goes.

TILING A SPLASHBACK ABOVE A BASIN

1 Setting out the tiles

Use a length of wood marked out in whole tile widths – allowing for the gaps – to gauge where to lay the first row of tiles so they're centred.

2 Spreading adhesive

Part-nail a batten vertically to one side to act as a guide. Then use a notched spreader to comb adhesive over the area to a depth of 4–5mm.

3 Laying the first tile

Starting at the vertical guide batten, lay the first tile. Push it with a twisting motion into the adhesive bed and check that it lies flat.

4 Fitting a spacer

Push a tile spacer into the adhesive at the top corner, then continue laying tiles in the same way. Start each new row at the guide batten.

5 Laying border tiles

For a more professional look, remove the guide batten and finish the splashback with oblong border tiles or, as here, contrasting mosaic tiles.

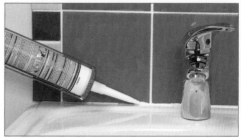

6 Sealing to the basin

Apply grout with a squeegee and wipe off excess with a dry cloth. Rub down the joints, then seal to the basin with bathroom sealant (above).

Cutting ceramic tiles

THE THICKER THE TILES, *the harder they are to cut and shape to fit around awkward corners. So choose your tools wisely: at the very least, you'll avoid lots of costly breakages.*

MAKING STRAIGHT CUTS TO TILES

1 Marking the cut

To mark tiles for cutting, first lay the tile to be cut over the last whole tile, then cover the gap with another tile and mark along its edge.

2 Score and snap

Score down the cutting line with a tile cutter against a metal rule, then lay the tile on a piece of wood or wooden dowel, and snap.

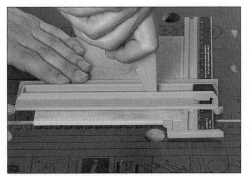

3 All in one

Patent "score-and-snap" tools provide a guide for the tile scorer and a stop for the tile. After scoring, simply press down on the tile.

4 Heavy-duty cutter

Cut thicker tiles in a lever-operated tile cutter. Simply score the tile with the cutting line centred below the levered snapper, and push.

Dealing with awkward shapes

Awkward shapes are trickier than straight cuts and may call for a combination of techniques. Don't make the cuts too complicated or you risk the tile cracking; the grout or sealant will disguise a certain amount of unevenness. Mark curves and gaps with a profile gauge (see below) or a card template; snip the edges of the card to make it follow the line of the curve. Then mark the tile in felt-tip pen.

Create small recesses using the "score-and-nibble" technique, which is also useful for removing very fine slivers if you've measured up wrongly. Cross-hash the waste part with your tile cutter, then snip it off piece by piece. Cut L-shapes and deep recesses with a tile saw, which is accurate but time-consuming. Remove any sharp cut edges using a tile file or carborundum (a hard abrasive) paper.

Cutting tiles to fit around obstacles

With the right equipment, shaping tiles to deal with obstacles is not too tricky.

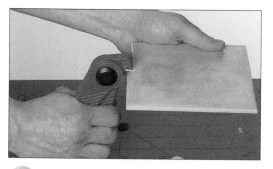

1 Match the shape

To use a profile gauge, first let the sliding feelers mould themselves to the shape of the gap.

2 Mark the tile

Then hold the gauge against the tile and trace the profile in felt-tip pen.

3 Nibble out recesses

If the recesses are small, score the waste with a tile cutter and then use nibblers to snip it off.

4 Cut shapes with a tile saw

If dealing with L-shapes and deep recesses, where the tile might crack, it is safer to use a tile saw.

Laying ceramic floor tiles

CERAMIC FLOOR TILES are laid in much the same way as other types of tile, with the proviso that it is vital to get them level. But again, modern adhesives are a far advance on the old method of laying tiles in mortar.

Setting out the tiles

Clear the room, prepare the floor, and mark a cross in the centre of the room. Lay rows of whole tiles along the arms of the cross (not forgetting to allow for the grout gaps) to see where the cuts fall around fittings and the edges of the room. Wherever you're left with unsightly or narrow cuts, try to get rid of them by adjusting the layout of the tiles. If you have to compromise, do so where it will show the least. When you're happy, re-mark the cross to give you lines to tile by.

If the room isn't a regular shape, set out the tiles to run along the line of the most visually dominant wall as seen from the door. Otherwise, there is a risk that the joints will look askew.

Laying, levelling, and finishing

Starting in a corner, apply the floor tile adhesive with a notched trowel over an area of about a square metre. Spread it to a depth of roughly 5mm unless otherwise recommended and make sure it is well grooved. Then lay out the first few whole tiles, using dowels or spacers to form the grout gaps. Press each tile lightly into place with a slight twist. When the area is filled, check for level with a spirit level and if necessary tap the tiles with a block of wood. If a tile is badly out of line, lift it, replace the adhesive, and re-lay it.

Continue in this way until you've laid all the whole tiles. Leave to dry for a few hours, then – working on boards – fill in the cut tiles. This time spread the adhesive on the backs of the tiles, not the floor, and check for level each time. Leave the floor for 24 hours before grouting gaps and sealing the edges.

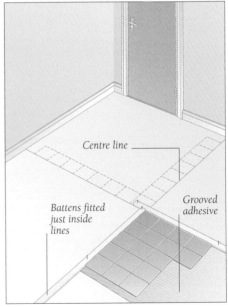

Centre line

Battens fitted just inside lines

Grooved adhesive

■ **Set out guide lines** *and fix two battens at right-angles to form a bay. Start tiling the section furthest from the door.*

FLOOR TILING TIPS

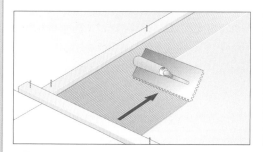

a Spreading adhesive

Cover an area of 1 sq m at a time with adhesive, then draw the notched edge of the trowel through it, holding it at 45° to the floor.

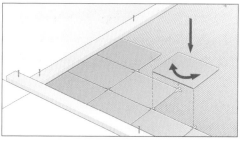

b Laying ceramic tiles

Lay the first tile butting up to both the battens. Don't slide it, but bed it down with a twisting motion. Work outwards from the angle.

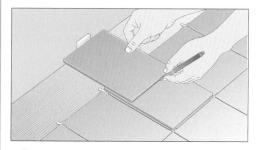

c Cutting tiles

Lay the tile to be cut over the last full tile. Place a spacer between another whole tile and the wall, and mark the cutting line along its edge.

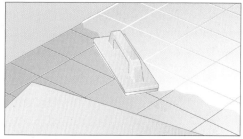

d Grouting joints

Kneeling on boards, work floor-tile grout into the joints using a rubber-based float or a squeegee. Polish with a dry cloth when dry.

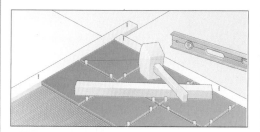

e Laying quarry tiles

Bed quarry tiles into cement-based adhesive and level them by tapping against a wood block. Use 6mm-diameter dowels as spacers.

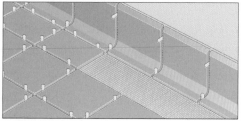

f Fitting skirting tiles

Moulded skirting tiles form a neat edge for quarry tiles, especially where the floor is to be swabbed. Fit them before cutting the edge tiles.

Sealing and grouting

GROUTING THE GAPS *between tiles is the most satisfying part of the whole job, but don't forget to seal around the edges of the surface.*

Every base covered

Leave tiles to dry for 24 hours before grouting. Afterwards, fill any gaps that are likely to move with silicone sealant. The exposed edges of thicker wall tiles can be finished with plastic edging, although this usually has to be bedded down at the same time as the tiles. If there's room, strips of wood moulding, border tiles, or quadrant tiles are all a better option. On floors, any gaps around the edges of the room will hopefully be disguised by skirting. Otherwise, you might consider gluing and pinning wooden quadrant moulding to the existing skirting. Cement-based grout has a tendency to leave smears when you wash it off, in which case a rub with sawdust should cure the problem.

■ **For a smooth edge** *plastic edging strip is bedded into the tile adhesive before laying the final row of tiles. On horizontal edges, some form of border tile is better.*

GROUTING THE TILES

1 Applying

Apply the grout with a squeegee, working it across the surface and into the joints.

2 Washing off

Wash off the excess with a sponge, taking care not to lift grout out of the joints.

3 Smoothing

Smooth the joints to a slightly concave finish using a finishing tool. Leave to dry, then polish.

Whole walls

TILING LARGER AREAS is all about setting out the tiles so that you don't leave unsightly cuts – especially around a window.

Double-check the layout

Whole walls – and even more so whole rooms – need extra-careful setting out to avoid cuts. Windows are often the trickiest places, so plan the tile layout outwards from the main window using the order shown here as a guide. The best place for cuts is behind a door.

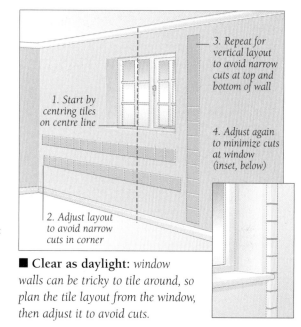

1. Start by centring tiles on centre line

2. Adjust layout to avoid narrow cuts in corner

3. Repeat for vertical layout to avoid narrow cuts at top and bottom of wall

4. Adjust again to minimize cuts at window (inset, below)

■ **Clear as daylight:** *window walls can be tricky to tile around, so plan the tile layout from the window, then adjust it to avoid cuts.*

If you're fixing heavy tiles, work upwards from horizontal and vertical support battens nailed to the wall along the lines of the first rows of whole tiles. After the whole tiles are dry, remove the battens and fill in the gaps with cut tiles. Support any special-purpose tile, such as a soap dish, by taping it temporarily to its neighbours.

A simple summary

✔ Ceramic tiles are a permanent and quite costly feature.

✔ Tiling tools are inexpensive and tile suppliers should stock them.

✔ Make sure the surface is flat, dry, and clean before tiling.

✔ Splashbacks and surrounds are good for practising tiling skills.

✔ Avoiding costly breakages is your reward for careful cutting.

✔ Ceramic floor tiles can create an elegant but informal ambience.

✔ Sealing and grouting makes a satisfying conclusion to the job.

✔ When tiling whole walls, windows present a challenge.

Chapter 9

Staining and Varnishing

As WELL AS BRINGING OUT OUT THE BEAUTY and richness of natural wood, staining and varnishing performs an important protective function – indoors against dirt, outdoors against the elements. But unless the wood is new, your first task will be to strip the existing finish – a time-consuming but ultimately hugely rewarding job.

In this chapter...

✓ Indoor stains and varnishes

✓ Stripping wood

✓ Sanding and sealing floors

✓ Preserving outdoor woodwork

BRING STRIPPED FLOORS TO LIFE WITH STAINED PATTERNS AND VARNISH

Indoor stains and varnishes

STAINS FOR INDOOR WOODWORK *divide into those that accentuate or modify the natural colour of the wood and those that change it completely. Similarly, varnishes are split between the traditional shellac-based type, which needs wax polishing, and modern, maintenance-free polyurethane and melamine-based varnishes.*

Stain without pain

The golden rule is to test the **wood stain** on an offcut – preferably a large one. Softwoods such as pine absorb stain at an uneven rate, which can cause blotchiness. And with hardwoods such as oak, you can end up with a colour that's far from what you imagined.

Surfaces for staining must be clean and dry. If blotchiness looks like being a problem, treat the area with wood conditioner first. Apply the stain in thin coats with a paintbrush or soft cloth, following the grain of the wood. Let the stain dry before re-applying to remove blotches. Remove any excess with a dry cloth. If you are staining drawers, cover them inside and out to prevent warping.

> **DEFINITION**
>
> **Varnish** *forms a protective coating over wood.*
> **Wood stain** *is a dye that colours wood, although some stains also have preservative properties.*

APPLYING WOOD STAIN

1 **Marking out**

Mark the area to be stained with a chalkline. If the design crosses the grain, score along the line to prevent the stain from bleeding.

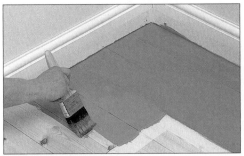

2 **Brushing on**

Use masking tape to protect the surrounding boards. Apply the stain with a paintbrush, following the grain of the wood.

Varnishing tricks

The secret of varnishing is patience – in other words, taking the time to build up many thin coats rather than a single thick one, and sanding between coats to get a really smooth finish. Always follow the instructions on the tin, especially with regard to drying times.

Traditional shellac-based varnishes such as polish and French polish are for furniture only. Apply several coats with a cloth pad or polisher's mop. Then rub down with fine wire wool and wax-polish, or "lift" to a gloss finish by rubbing lightly over the surface with a pad soaked in white spirit (a job requiring no little skill).

Modern polyurethane varnish can be applied with a brush and comes in both matt and gloss finishes. Two-part melamine varnish is similar, but thicker and much harder. With both types, sand between coats for a smooth finish.

Oiling and waxing wood

Oil and wax are easier-to-apply, more natural-looking alternatives to varnish, but they are not as hardwearing.

Wax marks easily, and so is unsuitable for outdoor use or surfaces that may have things put on them.

Furniture oil is ideal for protecting garden furniture and kitchen worktops. The best known types are teak oil and the lighter Danish oil. Apply several coats with a cloth or brush, sanding after each coat to build up a smooth finish. On open grained wood, thin the first coat with 50 per cent white spirit.

APPLYING VARNISH

1 Prepare the surface

Remove grease and dust by wiping down the surface with a rag soaked in white spirit, then apply a thinned first coat of varnish.

2 Sand down

When dry, lightly sand down the surface with glasspaper wrapped around a block. Vacuum away all the dust before continuing.

3 Apply more varnish

Apply one or more full-strength coats of varnish, finishing with the grain. Sand down again between coats for extra smoothness.

Stripping wood

HIDDEN BENEATH LAYER UPON LAYER of old paintwork, there may be some beautiful woodwork just waiting to be rescued – and even if you plan to repaint, there comes a time when old paint just has to go. But if you're varnishing, proceed cautiously: there are plenty of pitfalls to trap the unwary.

The choice is yours

You can strip paint by hand, or remove the offending item and have it professionally dipped in a bath of caustic soda. Stripping by hand is much more laborious, but generally gives better results; dipping tends to make most woods go "flat".

1 **Chemical stripper:** this is available in brush-on liquid, gel form, or as a paste which you apply with a filling knife. It's suitable for all woodwork, and especially for detailed mouldings, but using it can be a slow process. Modern water-based paste and gel strippers are a lot less hazardous (both to use, and to the environment) than the old solvent-based types. Even so, use with care in a well-ventilated room and follow the manufacturer's instructions.

2 **Heat stripping:** this is fast and efficient on flat surfaces, but be careful not to scorch the wood. A heat gun is safer, but slower, than a traditional blowlamp.

3 **Sanding down:** this is hard work, even with power tools, and the paint tends to burn or clog the sander. But it's often the only way to remove the last traces of chemically- or heat-stripped paint without damaging the grain of the wood.

If possible, on old doors and built-in furniture, strip an unobtrusive area to see how easily the paint comes off: wood in Victorian times was sometimes primed with a plaster-based filler, in which case you'll need to get the item dipped. Bear in mind, too, that old doors were never made to be left bare. Once dipped, you may have to strengthen or fill ill-fitting joints and knot holes.

Easy does it

Varnishing accentuates the natural grain of wood, so the last thing you want to do is ruin the grain in heavy-handed attempts to remove the old paint. A variety of scrapers are available for chemical and heat stripping, and the more of them you have to hand the better. Use a stiff-bladed paint scraper for flat surfaces, and a combination shave hook for getting into the crevices of decorative mouldings. Always scrape with the grain of the wood and never force stubborn patches: stop, and apply another coat of stripper. After stripping, give the wood a light sanding with medium abrasive paper or wire wool to remove any remaining particles.

If you use a blowlamp, keep all flammable materials well way from the area and be sure to wear protective clothing. Use a heat-proof shield or pot stand to protect vulnerable areas such as glass window panes or plastics, and catch the drips of burning paint in an old metal tin.

An electric heat stripper takes longer, but is safer and more controllable. Even so, you still need a heat shield to protect window glass from cracking.

■ **Be patient** *with chemical stripper: you may need two or three applications to get through very thick paint.*

Never heat strip old paint that you think might contain lead – it could emit poisonous fumes. Likewise, sanding could release toxic dust. Use a chemical stripper instead.

USING A HEAT STRIPPING GUN

1 **An integral stripping tool**

A gun with an intergral stripping attachment makes short work of flat surfaces. Lay down foil to catch the paint scrapings.

2 **A separate scraper**

Then use a combination shavehook to deal with more intricate mouldings and the awkward corners with adjacent surfaces.

Sanding and sealing floors

STRIPPED AND VARNISHED *floorboards look fantastic and are a lot cheaper than a new carpet if you do the work yourself. Even using hired power tools, however, it is hard work – but the rewards more than justify the effort.*

Sanding down

It almost goes without saying that you should assess the condition of the floorboards before stripping. If they are too badly damaged, you're better off replacing them. And if you're in doubt about the colour, test a small area first. Think about the noise implications, too. Sanded boards can be very noisy for those living below unless entirely covered in rugs. Woodstrip flooring might be a better option in such cases.

To strip the bulk of the floor you need to hire a drum sander. For the edges, hire a smaller orbital edge sander. Make sure you wear full protective gear, including ear defenders, and keep the room well ventilated at all times. Bear in mind that the floor may be out of action for some days.

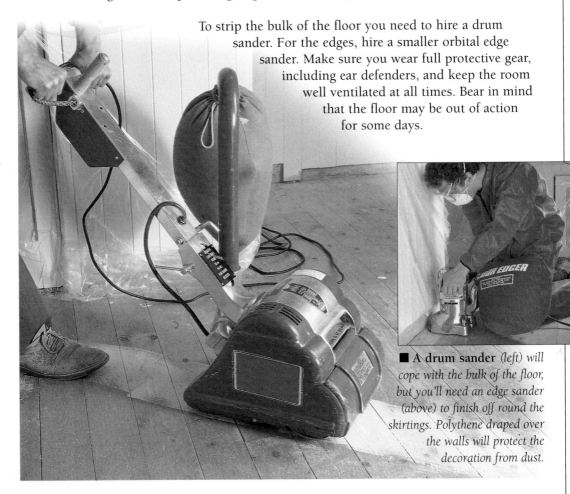

■ **A drum sander** (left) will cope with the bulk of the floor, but you'll need an edge sander (above) to finish off round the skirtings. Polythene draped over the walls will protect the decoration from dust.

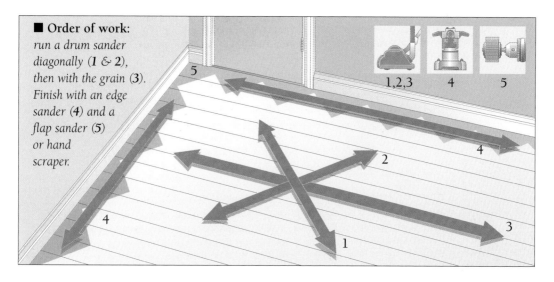

■ Order of work:
run a drum sander diagonally (1 & 2), then with the grain (3). Finish with an edge sander (4) and a flap sander (5) or hand scraper.

Before you start, clear the room and tape up the doors to stop dust spreading. Nail down loose boards, punch down raised nails heads, and fill any cracks. Fill larger gaps with tapered strips of wood glued in with woodworking adhesive.

Start with a coarse abrasive sheet on the drum sander. Slowly run it diagonally across the boards, working back and forth across the room. If necessary, make a second pass in the opposite direction. Then switch to a smoother abrasive and work along the boards. Sand along the skirtings with an edge sander and finish in corners with a small flap sander on an electric drill or a hand scraper.

Never switch on a drum sander while the drum is in contact with the floor or you may damage the boards. Tilt the sander backwards, switch on, and gradually lower it as you move forwards. Likewise, lift the sander off the floor at the end of each run and drape the power lead over your shoulder to avoid accidents.

Sealing up

Seal the boards with at least three coats of polyurethane varnish. There's no need to sand between coats (although the floor will be smoother if you do). Vacuum the room thoroughly before you start and wipe the floor with a rag soaked in white spirit to remove all traces of dust from the wood. Keep the room well ventilated, but close external doors and windows to stop dust blowing in.

It may seem obvious, but remember to work back towards the door when applying the varnish. Use a large paintbrush, keeping a look out for stray bristles. Allow each coat to dry according to the manufacturer's instructions.

Preserving outdoor woodwork

PRESERVING EXISTING TIMBER is a lot simpler and cheaper than replacing rotten wood. The trouble is, it has to be done on a regular basis because otherwise the effects of previous coats will soon wear off.

Pretty tough stuff

While preservative stains can help to brighten the outside of your home, the name of the game here is protection – against the elements, mould growth, and insect attack. Ideally, all outdoor woodwork should be treated with a top-up coat once a year, and you should soak any timber components used for repairs in preservative before you fit them – particularly the cut ends of fence posts and rails. Only very oily woods such as cedar and teak are tough enough to do without preservative, and even these need regular oiling to stop the grain and the joints from opening up.

For new outdoor structures that are to be left in their natural state, always use timber that has been pressure-impregnated with preservative at the factory. You'll find that it lasts much longer than ordinary wood – although you'll still have to soak the cut ends.

Outdoor options

There's a vast array of exterior preservatives on the market, with slightly varying properties, so read manufacturers' leaflets and seek the stockist's advice before you buy.

1. **Creosote:** the traditional outdoor favourite, although once applied it can't be painted over. Oil-based, creosote is highly effective against fungi and insects, but can poison nearby plants. Its potentially harmful vapours soon wear off, however.

2. **Water-based preservatives:** these preservatives don't release any vapours and can be painted over. They provide good protection against termites and fungi, but are vulnerable to insects that don't ingest the wood, and are susceptible to mould.

3. **Solid tablet preservatives:** these are inserted into holes in the wood drilled at regular intervals, and are especially suited to highly vulnerable areas such as wooden lintels, windowsills, and bay window frames.

INTERNET

www.rustins.co.uk

Check out the Rustins site for the full low-down on Britain's largest range of low-emission wood finishes, plus details of prices and coverage.

METHODS OF TREATMENT

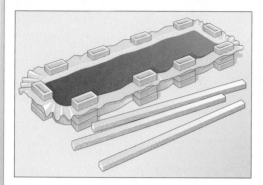

a Home-made preservative bath

Make one for timber components out of a sheet of heavy-duty polythene and building bricks.

b Spray gun

Hire one to spray large areas of outdoor woodwork, but protect nearby plants.

Although preservatives are harmless to humans and animals when dry, they can be dangerous when wet. Keep family pets out of bounds when treating outdoor woodwork and cover water features such as fish ponds. Avoid all contact with your skin.

A simple summary

✔ Surfaces for staining and varnishing need to be free of grease and dust. Then test the stain on a large piece of scrap to see how evenly it absorbs and how the colour turns out.

✔ Always check that doors and floorboards are suitable for stripping, if necessary by testing an unobtrusive area first.

✔ Nearly all varnishes give a better finish if sanded down between coats – but be sure to remove all traces of dust.

✔ Outdoor woodwork needs to be regularly treated with preservative. Otherwise you will leave it vulnerable to attack by mould and insects – as well as at the mercy of the elements.

Chapter 10

Laying Floorcoverings

BALANCE DURABILITY AGAINST DECORATIVE EFFECT when thinking about new flooring and consider the wear and tear that's likely to be inflicted. Does the floor need to be waterproof? Will it be regularly trampled on by muddy boots? And how important is it to have a soft, comfortable surface underfoot? Only you know the answers to these questions – act on them, and your flooring won't let you down.

In this chapter...

✓ Laying sheet vinyl

✓ Foam-backed carpet

✓ Hessian-backed carpet

✓ Woodstrip flooring

✓ Wood block flooring

✓ Vinyl floor tiles

SHEET VINYL IS INEXPENSIVE, EASY TO FIT, AND CONVINCINGLY MIMICS MORE EXPENSIVE COVERINGS

Laying sheet vinyl

FOR SHEER VALUE FOR MONEY, *you can't beat sheet vinyl in rooms that get messy or wet – like the kitchen and bathroom. Modern sheet vinyl not only rivals more expensive materials for looks and durability, but it is incredibly easy to lay and forgiving of mistakes. Unfortunately, the same can't be said of the once-again-fashionable linoleum; laying this is best left to a professional.*

Rooms with straight edges

In most rooms you can simply lay the vinyl in situ. Unroll the sheet and let its weight mould it to the floor. Align the pattern with the most visually dominant wall or run of cabinets, and adjust so that the pattern is balanced all around the room. Roughly trim the vinyl with a utility knife to leave a 50mm overlap all round. Then make release cuts at external and internal corners (see below) so that the vinyl lies flat enough to be trimmed to the walls. There's normally no need to stick the vinyl to the floor, but where you've had to join widths, or there are curling edges, fix them down with double-sided flooring tape, available from your supplier.

Before you actually lay the sheet vinyl, leave it unwrapped and loosely rolled in a warm room for at least 2 days. This will make it more flexible and easier to handle.

TIPS FOR LAYING SHEET VINYL IN SITU

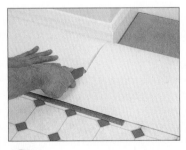

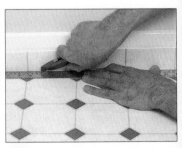

a **At external corners**

Roll back the vinyl over a piece of hardboard. Starting 50mm from the bend, cut back to the edge.

b **At internal corners**

Pull down and cut along the centre of the V-shaped fold, and overlap the resulting flaps.

c **Along skirtings**

Starting at an internal corner, push a straightedge into the angle and trim along it at 45°.

Complicated floor areas

In rooms with lots of obstacles, it's easier to make a paper template and use this to cut the vinyl to fit. Make the template from sheets of heavy paper taped together. Cover the entire floor, leaving a gap of 25mm or so around the edges and around obstacles. Then scribe around the walls and each obstacle using a block and pencil to leave a clear impression on the template.

Remove the template and lay it over the flattened-out vinyl sheet. Using the block to follow the lines you've just scribed on the template, reverse-scribe back onto the vinyl to leave pencil marks showing you where to cut it. This may seem like magic, but believe me, it works! All I would advise is that you cut generously to the waste side – you can always make adjustments by carefully trimming the vinyl once it's in place.

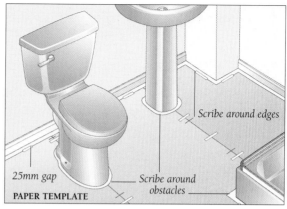

Scribe around edges

25mm gap

Scribe around obstacles

PAPER TEMPLATE

■ **Paper template**: *tape sheets together to a rough fit. Scribe around the obstacles using a block of wood, then scribe back from these lines onto the vinyl.*

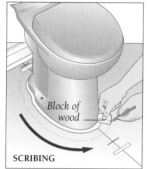

Block of wood

SCRIBING

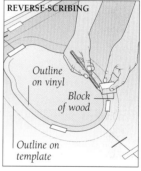

REVERSE-SCRIBING

Outline on vinyl

Block of wood

Outline on template

d **At door architraves**

Make vertical cuts to the floor at each change in profile of the moulding, then trim off the excess.

e **At thresholds**

Trim the edge of the sheet to the middle of the threshold, then screw a threshold strip to the floor.

f **Joining widths**

Overlap the sheets and match the pattern. Cut through both layers, then stick the edges to the floor.

Foam-backed carpet

SIMPLE TO LAY *and highly versatile, foam-backed carpet can be used virtually anywhere in the home. Equally suited to solid or wooden floors, it will even help to hide imperfections in an uneven surface.*

Added backing

Foam-backed carpet, as the name suggests, has its own built-in underlay, although I'd still advise you to fit either paper felt or **spun polyester underlay** beneath it. This added barrier will stop the foam from sticking to the floor, which in turn will

■ **Foam-backed carpet** *is a boon to do-it-yourselfers, as it doesn't need stretching.*

make lifting the carpet far easier should the need arise. It's also a good idea to draw a scale floor plan of the room showing all recesses and doorways before cutting the carpet.

> **DEFINITION**
>
> *As an alternative to paper felt, you could use* **spun polyester underlay** *with foam-backed carpet. Sold in 1.5m wide rolls, spun polyester is particularly good for use underneath carpet that is likely to have heavy furniture placed on top of it.*

Foam-backed carpet is available in 2m, 3m, or 4m widths. Where possible, try to pick the width that gives as few joins as possible – even if this means considerable wastage. Where joins are unavoidable, as in a large L-shaped room, keep them away from heavily used areas, and make sure the pile faces the same way. Foam-backed carpet is graded according to durability. Light domestic is suggested for bedrooms; medium domestic for dining rooms; general domestic for living rooms; and heavy domestic for halls, landings, and stairs.

One of the secrets of successful carpet laying is to fit a new blade to your knife after every 2m or so of cutting. It may seem wasteful, but believe me, it's worth it!

Before fitting, unroll the new carpet outside or in a larger room. Following your scale plan, use a trimming knife to trim it roughly to the shape of the room leaving about 150mm waste all round. Be careful not to let the rolled carpet buckle under its own weight when you move it around or you may damage the foam backing, resulting in unsightly creases in the pile.

Reaching the threshold

Threshold strips are used to join different types of carpet to one another, or to other types of flooring, in doorways. Made of brass, aluminium, or wood, these strips also protect the edge of the carpet for both aesthetic and safety reasons. Use a threshold strip without spikes for foam-backed carpet and cut it to fit the width of the door opening with a junior hacksaw. Fix the strip to the floor with either nails or screws. If you are using nails, protect the strip by placing a wooden batten over it when hammering.

LAYING FOAM-BACKED CARPET

1 Felt underlay

Stick double-sided tape around the edge of the room and staple or tape paper felt to the floor.

2 External corners

Make a straight release cut to the edge of the corner over an offcut of hardboard.

3 Internal corners

Make triangular release cuts at internal corners, as far as it takes for the carpet to lie flat.

4 Trim to the skirting

Score along the edge with the back of the knife, then trim to the skirting; tuck in any fibres.

5 Joining strips

Lay the second strip over the first and cut through both layers against a straightedge.

6 Sticking the joint

Fold back the first strip, lay double-sided tape along the join, and press both strips onto it.

Hessian-backed carpet

WOVEN, HESSIAN-BACKED CARPET should always be laid on a separate underlay. Unlike foam-backed carpet, woven carpet also needs to be stretched during laying to hold it taut by the toothed gripper strips used to secure it around the edges of the room.

Get a gripper

Don't be fooled into purchasing cheap underlay: a thick, good quality rubber or natural felt underlay will prolong the life of a carpet and feel better underfoot.

It's a good idea to lay a paper lining underneath the underlay, to stop dust from rising through the gaps in the floorboards and leaving black lines on the carpet.

Trivia...

It's estimated that around 10 per cent of the weight of an average two-year-old domestic carpet consists of dust mites and their droppings! So if you were thinking of replacing that old carpet, maybe now's the time. There again, perhaps a total change of floorcovering is in order...

Hessian-backed carpet is stretched and fastened onto spiked gripper strips which you nail or glue around the edges of the room with the spikes towards the wall. To do the stretching, you need to hire a special tool called a knee-kicker, plus a carpet fitter's bolster (a bricklayer's or electrician's bolster must not be used because they will damage the carpet). A carpet that is not stretched properly may ruck up and wear unevenly. The advantage of gripper strips is that if this happens, you can simply unhook the carpet and try again.

Start on the wall containing the doorway. Trim and slide the carpet into the grippers along this edge, then spread the rest of the carpet out towards the far wall. Trim the adjacent walls next, using the knee-kicker to push the carpet towards the grippers and then the bolster to secure it on the spikes. The knee-kicker does not require great force – just a firm tap. Finally, check that the carpet hasn't rucked up anywhere in the room and fit it to the far wall.

■ **Use a knee-kicker** *and bolster to push the carpet tightly onto the gripper strips.*

LAYING HESSIAN-BACKED CARPET

1 **Nail down grippers**

Fit gripper strips around the room, leaving a gap two-thirds the thickness of the carpet.

2 **Cut underlay**

Trim the underlay with scissors to butt up to the grippers, and staple or stick it to the floor.

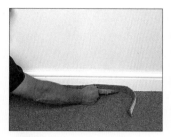

3 **Trim to skirting**

Trim and fit the carpet along the door wall, changing the blade every 2m or so.

4 **Push behind gripper**

After stretching and trimming, use the bolster again to tuck the cut edge behind the gripper.

5 **Threshold strip**

Nail the threshold strip to the floor, then trim along a line running down the middle.

6 **Architraves**

Make vertical cuts down the architrave, trim, then push the edge into the threshold strip.

Joining lengths together

Joining any type of carpet is best avoided if you can. But in an odd-shaped room full of recesses and alcoves, hessian-backed carpet can work out very expensive unless you make use of some of the larger offcuts. Try to position such joins in little used or unobtrusive places.

You can buy special fibreglass-reinforced tape to join lengths together. Position the length of tape under the join and press both pieces of carpet firmly onto it. Although the bond formed by the tape is fairly strong, be careful not to break the join when stretching the carpet. An alternative method of joining is to sew the adjoining lengths together, but this is a job best left to a specialist.

Woodstrip flooring

LAMINATED WOODSTRIP FLOORING *consists of interlocking lacquered panels that are clipped or glued together to "float" on an existing floor. Though not as tough – or as expensive – as solid wood, they have the advantage of being easy to lay and maintain.*

Before you start...

The floor must be level and dry. Cover bumpy floorboards with hardboard and lay plastic sheet over a solid floor. Removing the skirting boards will give you a much neater finish around the walls. The woodstrip will raise the height of your existing floor slightly, so you may need to trim the bottoms of doors to suit. Some woodstrip systems include matching threshold strips to join to other types of floorcovering.

Mind the gap

Begin by covering the existing floor with felt underlay. Lay the flooring panels along the longest or most dominant wall first, leaving a 10mm gap. Use wooden wedges to maintain this gap as you clip or glue the subsequent rows of strips in position. The final row of strips may have to be cut lengthways, in which case don't forget to allow for the 10mm gap. This gap allows the boards to expand with changes in humidity, and is often filled with a cork strip that will be covered up when you replace the skirtings. If it isn't practical to remove the skirting, cover the expansion gap with 15mm quadrant moulding, pinned to the skirting. Paint the moulding to match the skirting or stain it to match the flooring.

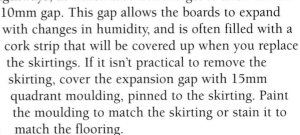

There's no need to cut strips to fit around architraves. Simply cut away the base of the architrave to the same depth as the woodstrip and slide the strip underneath.

■ **Sunset strip:** *laminated woodstrip flooring is both decorative and hard-wearing.*

LAYING THE STRIPS

1 **Leaving room for expansion**

Lay the first strip against the longest wall using wedges to maintain a 10mm gap all round.

2 **Fitting further strips**

Begin the second row with an offcut from the first row and position subsequent lengths.

3 **Protecting tongues**

Hammer the boards together using a grooved block of wood to avoid damaging tongues.

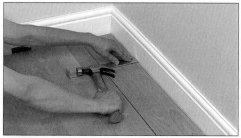

4 **Finishing off**

Use a knocking tool to hammer in the final row of lengths on the opposite side of the room.

Fitting at edges

The last part of the job is the most satisfying – neatly edging your new floor.

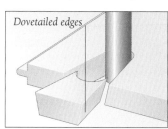

Dovetailed edges

■ **Pipework:** *drill, then cut out a dovetail shape, leaving 2mm clearance around the pipe.*

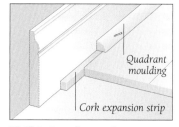

Quadrant moulding

Cork expansion strip

■ **Skirting:** *fit a cork expansion strip, and pin quadrant moulding to the skirting board above it.*

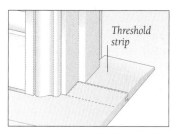

Threshold strip

■ **Architraves:** *cut away the base of architraves to allow the woodstrip to fit beneath them.*

Wood block flooring

ELEGANT, DURABLE, AND LUXURIOUS, *wood block flooring comes in a range of stains and grains. It's ideal for hallways and living areas – including kitchens, if well sealed – but is not recommended for bathrooms.*

Preparing and planning

Wood block systems vary in detail, but the fitting method is basically the same for all interlocking loose blocks. Allowing a 12mm gap for expansion around the edges of the room, you create a "frame" of blocks laid end-to-end on black bitumen flooring adhesive, then fill in the remaining blocks in your chosen pattern. You can also get block "panels" attached to a paper backing, which you lay just like vinyl tiles.

Prepare the room as for woodstrip flooring. Remove all the skirtings and threshold strips if at all possible. Your supplier will advise on quantities, based on your chosen laying pattern (see opposite), and on a suitable underlay. A floor-boarded floor will need levelling with hardboard; solid floors generally need some kind of bitumenized felt underlay. Ask your supplier about adhesive at the same time. Laying the blocks won't require much in the way of special equipment, but with a herringbone pattern, it definitely makes sense to hire a saw table to make the 45° cuts in blocks; sawing by hand is hard work and much less accurate.

LAYING BLOCKS IN A HERRINGBONE PATTERN

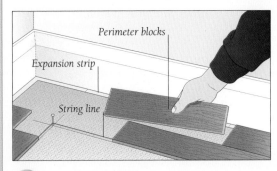

Perimeter blocks

Expansion strip

String line

1 **Set up guidelines**

Mark a 12mm expansion gap around the edge of the room, then set up string lines two blocks' widths in from here and dry-lay the perimeter blocks.

Mitred corner

2 **Lay the perimeter blocks**

Apply adhesive around the perimeter, trim the grooves off the whole blocks, and lay. Then cut and trim the corner blocks to fit and slot them in place.

Laying the blocks

With most patterns, it's customary to glue the blocks around the edge of the room and then fill in the pattern, finishing at a the doorway. The exception to this rule is a basket weave pattern, where you arrange the blocks in "panels" and glue those panels that fall around the edge of the room. Cut away the feet of door frames with a padsaw to accommodate the blocks. Afterwards, replace the skirtings to hide the expansion gaps, or else cover with quadrant moulding. Remember that unsealed systems will have to be sanded and sealed after they are laid.

■ **Three popular laying patterns:** *basketweave, stretcher, and herringbone, which requires more cutting but looks great.*

When laying hardwood flooring, particularly if working on perimeter blocks last, make sure you don't stand on the newly-laid blocks. Kneel on a board to spread your weight evenly.

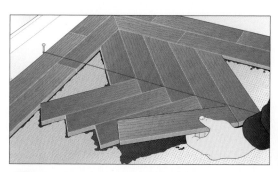

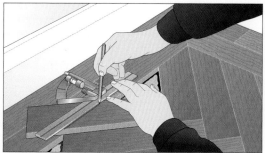

③ **Start the herringbone pattern**

Set up a string guideline for the apex of the outer row of blocks. Dry-lay them first, then mitre the other end to fit at the perimeter.

④ **Fill in the gaps**

Lay the blocks, one herringbone row at a time, over the whole area. Fill the gaps at the edges by marking the blocks in situ using a combination square.

Vinyl floor tiles

RESILIENT VINYL TILES are inexpensive and easy to fit, even in a small room with obstructions. The advice here also applies to cork and carpet tiles.

Dry lay and fit

Make sure the surface to be tiled is clean and level. Whether you're laying glue-down tiles or the self-adhesive type, begin by dry-laying them to centre the pattern and ensure equal-width cuts at the edges. Starting in the quarter of the room furthest from the door, fix the whole tiles in place. Press down from the centre outwards to avoid trapped air. Lay all the whole tiles, then fill in the straight-cut gaps. Tackle any awkward corners last.

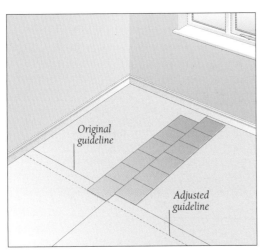

Original guideline

Adjusted guideline

■ **As with ceramic tiles,** *mark a cross in the room and then dry-lay the tiles to see how the cuts fall. Adjust the cross if necessary.*

TILING EDGES

(1) **Mark the profile**

Lay the tile to be cut over last full tile. Use a second tile to mark the profile of the skirting.

(2) **Cut the tile**

Place the tile on a piece of hardboard and cut using a trimming knife and straightedge.

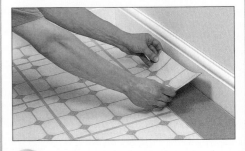

(3) **Fit and smooth down**

Slip the cut tile into place and smooth out to remove any air bubbles.

Corners and curves

To fit a tile against an external corner, use a second tile to mark the profile of one side of the corner, then repeat for the other side. Cut along the lines to form an L-shape. At an internal corner, mark from both walls and cut to form a square.

To tile around plumbing fittings, either scribe the shape onto the cut tile, as when laying sheet vinyl, or cut a cardboard template of the gap and use this to mark the tile; cut slits in the card and press against the outline.

1 Mark first side…

Place the tile over the last full tile on one side of the corner Mark with a second tile.

2 …then the second

Repeat for the other side of the corner, again working from the last full tile.

A simple summary

✔ Sheet vinyl is cheap, relatively simple to lay, and easy to keep clean. It's ideal for kitchens and utility rooms.

✔ Foam-backed carpet is wonderfully versatile, at home virtually anywhere in the house. It is also easier to lay than hessian-backed carpet but not so durable.

✔ Hessian-backed carpet requires more effort to lay than foam-backed but it is more durable.

✔ Laminated woodstrip flooring is easy to lay, hard-wearing, and can be laid on top of existing hard surfaces.

✔ Wood block flooring is ideal for living rooms and halls. It is easy to maintain, but may warp if subjected to excess moisture.

✔ Resilient vinyl floor tiles are inexpensive and highly versatile. They are easy to lay, and are considerably less wasteful than other coverings.

PART THREE

Chapter 11

Doors and Windows

Doors and windows are the most important moving parts of a home and, like all mechanical devices, they need regular maintenance to keep them in good working order.

In this chapter...

✓ Sticking and warping

✓ Casement window repairs

✓ Overhauling sash windows

✓ Patching frames and sills

✓ Hanging a new door

✓ Door furniture and locks

✓ Window furniture and locks

✓ Draughtproofing

Sticking and warping

WHEN A DOOR OR WINDOW STICKS, *it's often the first sign of a potentially more serious problem. So, before you reach for your plane or sander, see if you can trace the root cause.*

Stick with it

Consider planing or sanding as a last resort – after all, once you've done it, there's no going back. Seasonal sticking suggests that the wood is inadequately protected, in which case wait until a spell of dry weather, repaint or revarnish, and then see if the problem goes away. If it doesn't, or if you can rule out swelling due to moisture, check the hinges. Loose hinge screws and poorly fitted hinges are two common reasons for sticking and are easily dealt with. Often, chiselling out or packing the hinge recesses is the easiest way to deal with paint build-up, too. More problematic is sticking due to rotten wood or to loose joints. Fix such faults as soon as possible (they can only get worse), then rehang the door or window and plane to fit.

Doors can stick because the hinge pins have become slack, causing the door to drop and rub against the frame. Rather than buying new hinges, try swapping the old hinges around. Top and bottom hinges wear in opposite directions, so reversing them often does the trick.

CURES FOR STICKING DOORS

a **Loose screws**

Fill old screw holes with glued dowels and trim flush, then drill new pilot holes.

b **Sticking shut**

Chisel out a hinge recess to cure sticking on latch side, but don't remove too much wood.

c **Springing open**

If the door springs open without latching, pack out the recess with a piece of card.

Planing down

Don't attempt to plane down a door or window in situ; remove it and support it securely on a workbench or trestles. Paint build-up is best removed with a Surform or an electric sander; if you need to remove more than 1mm or so, use a block plane.

When planing the bottom of a door, work from the outer edges inwards to stop the visible faces from chipping. And be sure to repaint or reseal afterwards, or the problem will simply recur.

Avoid planing the side edges of a door or window casement if at all possible, otherwise you might find yourself having to reposition the hinges, latch, or other hardware. Adjusting existing hinge positions is a far better move.

■ **Power tools** *make short work of planing the base of a door; work from both edges towards the middle to avoid chipping.*

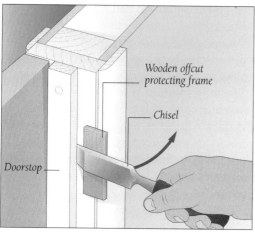

Wooden offcut protecting frame

Chisel

Doorstop

■ **Minor warping** *in a door can often be accommodated simply by prising off the doorstops and repositioning them.*

Cures for warping

Serious warping in a door or window casement is nearly always due to inadequate protection from the elements. If the problem has gone too far, you may have no choice but to remove the affected item, lay it flat in a dry environment, and weight it down with bricks. Given time and dry weather, the door should return to its proper shape within a few days, after which you can repaint or reseal it before rehanging. But check first that the joints haven't opened up or loosened in the meantime. Unless the exposed surfaces of the door have a continuous unbroken seal, the warping may recur.

153

Overhauling sash windows

WHEN A SASH WINDOW *sticks or stops working, it's a sign that the window is in need of a general overhaul. Once you know how sash windows work, the job is easier than it looks – but you will need a helper to lift out the sashes, and you should prepare yourself for some redecorating.*

Removing the sashes

Begin by prising the staff bead away from the frame; running a knife blade down the edge of the bead will help release it from layers of old paint. The inner sash can now be pulled away from the frame. Tie a length of string to each sash cord, then cut the cord between string and sash and lower the sash weight to the bottom of the sash box. Remove the outer sash in the same way, having first released it by prising out the parting bead between the two sashes. Note which weights are for which sash.

Not all sash windows have cords; newer ones use spiral spring balance mechanisms. Check which you have before removing the sashes. Spiral-system sashes rarely need maintenance, but the springs can break. Buy a special tensioning tool to re-balance the springs.

■ **Prise staff beads** *off with a chisel, starting in the middle of each. When refitting, put first the nail 100mm from the corner.*

Replacing sash cords

If a sash cord breaks, causing the sash to go "loose" on one side, replace both cords together. The pockets giving access to the sash box may be screwed, pinned, or just slotted in place, but the chances are they will be covered in layers of old paint that will have to be cut or scraped out first. Pull the weights out through the pocket and sever the old cord. Then tie the old cord end-to-end to the new one with a piece of string, and use the old cord to draw the new cord up the sash box and through the pulley. Attach one end of the new cord to the weight, then nail the other end to the top of the sash.

ANATOMY OF A SASH WINDOW

A traditional sash window with cords and weights is a mechanical marvel: treat it with respect! Make sure you know how the window is constructed before attempting an overhaul. Replacement pulleys, sash cords, and weights are obtainable from hardware stores, as are replacement springs for the newer sprung-balance type.

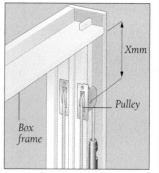

Xmm

Pulley

Box frame

■ **Measure from** *the pulley to the top of the box frame when replacing cords.*

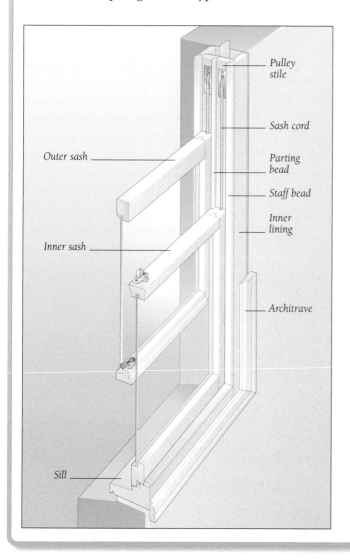

Pulley stile

Sash cord

Outer sash

Parting bead

Staff bead

Inner lining

Inner sash

Architrave

Sill

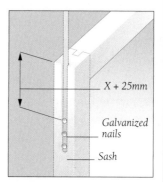

X + 25mm

Galvanized nails

Sash

■ **Add 25mm** *to above distance when nailing new cord to sashes.*

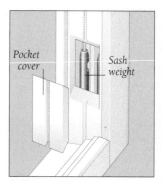

Pocket cover

Sash weight

■ **Pocket covers** *behind the parting bead hide the weights within the box frame.*

Patching frames and sills

EXTERIOR WOODWORK IS FOREVER *at the mercy of rain and that, ultimately, means one thing: rot. Guard against damp penetration by checking door frames and windowsills regularly, and deal with any patches of rotten wood promptly, before they spread.*

Checking for rot

Inspect all exterior woodwork at least once a year for signs of wet rot. Locally flaking or bubbling paintwork is often a sign of moisture retention, but don't rely solely on visual indicators. Test wood with a penknife: if the wood is soft and the knife won't stick in, you've got a repair job on your hands. If detected early enough, you may be able to cure damp patches by inserting wood preservative pellets, then covering them with filler and wood-hardening resin. But be warned: this is a short-term solution, not a preventative measure, and the problem is likely to reappear in the future.

If you encounter rotten wood that is dry, powdery, and covered in a white fungus, call in a specialist immediately. You may have a serious case of the dreaded dry rot — a fungal condition that can spread through the house like wildfire unless given expert (and often drastic) treatment.

Dealing with rot

If you find evidence of rot in your woodwork, be sure to treat it as soon as possible.

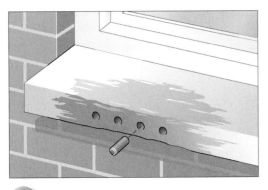

a **Insert preservative pellets**

Damp patches in sills can be treated with wood preservative tablets. Drill holes in the affected area and insert the tablets.

b **Harden soft wood and fill**

Treat soft wood with wood-hardening resin. Make good with heavy-duty filler, sand down when dry, prime, and paint.

Patching frames

Door frames are most likely to suffer lower down, so you should be able to patch rather than replace. Chisel out the affected area and then make a stepped cut into the unaffected wood (see below). Fashion a new piece of wood to fit and coat it in wood preservative. Remove any old frame fixings and drill pilot holes for new ones in a different position. Screw the wood patch in place, countersinking the screw heads and covering them with wood filler. Sand the repair to shape, coat with preservative, and repaint.

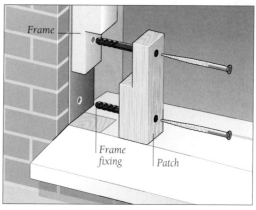

■ **Replace rotten wood** *at the base of a door frame with a patch, secured to the walls with frame fixings, and sealed with non-setting mastic.*

Patching sills

If damp penetration is severe in a windowsill cut back the affected area, drill several holes in the sill, and insert preservative pellets. Then cut a replacement timber patch to fit, and locate this while you mark the position of a drip groove underneath the sill. Chisel out the groove, coat the new patch with preservative, then glue and screw it to the sill. Cover the screw heads with wood filler, sand the patch to shape, and prime and repaint the sill.

If you can't get a clean cut when chiselling out a patch of rotten wood, it's probably because the wood is damp. Try cutting further back into sound timber.

Rotten door sills are seldom worth patching: it's better to saw through the joints with the frame and then dig the old sill out. Take it with you to a builder's merchant to match the profile of the timber.

Before fitting the new door sill, check that there's a layer of damp-proofing; if not, fit a strip of bituminous felt or self-adhesive flashing tape. Then slot the new sill in place and secure to the frame uprights with countersunk screws driven in at an angle.

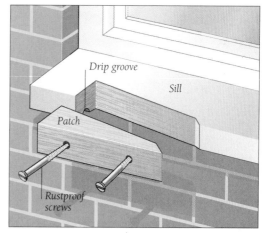

■ **When inserting a patch,** *cut diagonally back into the sound timber to give the repair strength.*

Hanging a new door

NEW DOORS COME IN STANDARD SIZES, *which must be trimmed to fit before hanging. Buy the nearest (larger) size available, and don't forget the hinges and latch that go with it. If the door is a different thickness to the old one, you'll need to prise off the door stops and refit them to suit.*

Measuring up and preparation

Measure the height and width of the opening and then subtract a small amount for clearance before transferring the measurements to the new door; take 3mm off the top and sides, and 6-12mm from the bottom. When trimming to length, take equal amounts from the top and bottom of flush doors, but only trim the bottom edge of a panelled door. Trim small amounts with a block plane or power planer, working from the corners towards the middle to avoid chipping the edges. If you need to remove more than 5mm, use a circular saw and finish with a plane.

Test-fit the door in the opening before you proceed by standing it on wooden wedges. Doors are heavy, so you may need help.

When you are happy with the fit, remove the door to fit the hinges and other hardware. If you're starting from scratch, fit the upper hinge 175mm from the top of the door; and the lower hinge 250mm from the bottom. On a fire door, fit a third hinge 100mm below the top one.

Fit upper hinge 175mm from top of door

Latch side identified by key symbol on top edge

Latch block

Fit lower hinge 250mm from bottom of door

Plane a 3° bevel on closing edge of door

■ **A flush door** *must be hung the correct way round so that the latch will be bedded in solid timber.*

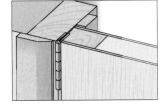

■ **The door latch** *(left) should be set approximately 950mm from the bottom of the door; a butt hinge (right) needs to be centred between the door and frame.*

FITTING DOOR HINGES

1 Marking out

Lay the hinge on the door edge and mark around the leaf with a pencil or knife.

2 Mark depth

Mark the depth of the hinge recess on the face of the door using a marking gauge.

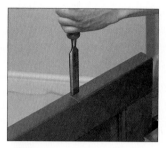

3 Score lines

Cut around the marked lines to the same depth as the recess using a chisel (bevel to waste).

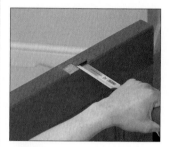

4 Chisel out

Chop out the waste, working from the line on the face, with the bevelled edge upwards.

5 Test and clean

Test-fit the hinge, then shave along the recess until you get a perfect fit.

6 Fit hinge

Mark and drill pilot holes for the hinge, then screw the leaf in position.

Fitting to the frame

Once you have fitted the hinges, wedge the door in the doorway at the right level and carefully mark the hinge positions on the frame. Make good or extend the old hinge recesses as appropriate. Mark and chisel out new recesses just as you did for the door. Test fit the door with one screw to check you've measured correctly and that your hinge recesses are deep enough. If it sticks, try fractionally increasing the depth of the hinge recesses and test fit it again. When you're satisfied with the fit and the door opens and closes freely, fit the remaining hinge screws, replace the stops (if necessary), and add locks and handles as required. If it's an exterior door, make sure that you prime and paint or seal the door immediately, before it has time to warp.

Door furniture and locks

YOU'VE HUNG YOUR NEW DOOR, it opens and closes perfectly, and it's been given a coat of paint. Now all that remains is to secure it against prying fingers or the outside world.

Door furniture

A door handle and closer set is the minimum requirement for an internal door, and is very easy to fit (see right). Rooms where you may need some privacy, such as a bathroom, can be fitted with simple surface-mounted bolts, and you may want to fit door closers to keep the warmth in. Doors leading to garages should always be fitted with locks. Door furniture for external doors is also sold in sets, which may include knocker, handle, and fingerplate. You may also want to consider a letterbox, security chain, and peephole viewer.

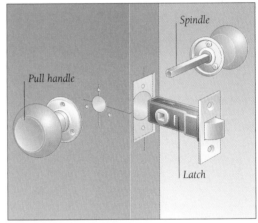

■ **Door handle/latch sets** *come in all shapes and sizes. If privacy is required in a room, fit bolts rather than locks.*

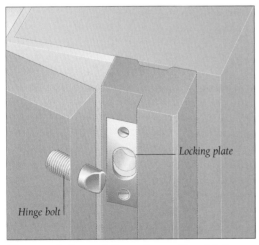

■ **Hinge bolts and frame bars** *offer added protection against hinges and locks being forced, or the frame itself being smashed.*

Locks and security

A door is only as strong as what's around it. Fitting hinge bolts (see left) will prevent the hinges from being forced – simply drill circular recesses in the door and frame. Buy screw-on metal bars to reinforce the frame itself. The minimum requirement for exterior doors is a deadlocking rim latch, but you'd be well advised to fit a mortise deadlock as well. This is fitted in the edge of the door, which must be at least 44mm thick. Narrow-stile versions are available for glazed doors. Prepare the mortise by drilling a series of overlapping holes to the depth of the recess, then clean up the sides with a chisel – the lock should be a snug fit.

FITTING A RIM LATCH

1 **Position lock**

Mark the position of the lock and holes on the door, using a template if provided.

2 **Drill cylinder hole**

Drill the cylinder hole from one side then, when the bit breaks through, from the other.

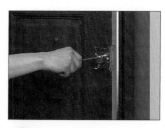

3 **Fit backplate**

Position the backplate on the door and fix in position using woodscrews.

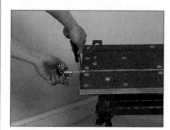

4 **Trim connecting bar**

Fit the cylinder in the hole and mark the bar for length. Trim with a junior hacksaw.

5 **Position keep**

Fit the lock and mark where it strikes the frame. Position the keep accordingly.

6 **Recess keep**

Chisel out the recess for the keep in the door frame, test-fit, then screw the keep in place.

Fit a rim lock one-third of the way down the door and a mortise lock one-third of the way up for maximum strength.

Test-fit the lock with the bolt extended so that you can pull it out again. Having fitted the lock, cut a recess in the door frame for the keep (the metal plate or box that receives the latch). Take care not to weaken the frame timber when you do this.

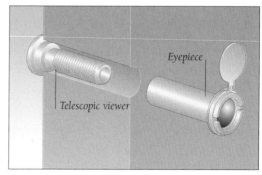

Eyepiece

Telescopic viewer

■ **A peephole viewer** *gives a wide-angle view to the outside. Fit the threaded section from outside, then screw on the eyepiece.*

Window furniture and locks

HALF OF ALL DOMESTIC BREAK-INS *are made via a window. If you don't want to be included in that statistic, fit window locks.*

Fitting window furniture

Window furniture, in the form of stays and handles, will keep your windows open and closed but not secure. Always fit locks, too. Some window locks – such as stay locks, spindle clamps, and locking cockspur stops – can be used with existing furniture, but if in any doubt I advise you to buy new. Choose lockable handles and stays with clamps. Fitch fasteners and Brighton fasteners are good for sash windows. For added security, make sure surface-mounted locks can't be dismantled. Use tamper-proof screws, or choose locks with casings that cover their fixings.

■ **Key safety issue:** *never leave keys in locks. Remove after use and keep close at hand, but out of sight.*

Choosing and fitting window locks

The shape and construction of a window largely determines which locks to fit, but you should also consider ease and frequency of use before buying. Mortise rack bolts are unobtrusive, and ideal for wooden casement windows. The bolt is recessed into the edge of the casement and operated by a splined key through the face of the casement. Sash windows can be secured in a number of ways, the most popular being dual screws, which are fitted through both sashes, and sash locks, which are mounted on the inner sash to permit partial opening.

INTERNET

www.yale.co.uk

Find out what's available for securing the windows in your home from this site. You'll find advice on dedicated locks for casement, sash, wooden, metal, and PVC windows.

As with doors, window locks are only as good as their mountings and keeps, so make sure the woodwork is in good condition before fitting.

It may seem obvious, but don't leave the keys to window locks in or around the locks where they could be reached from the outside by breaking a pane of glass. Always keep the keys out of sight, but make sure they can be easily found in case you need to open a window in an emergency.

LOCKING CASEMENT WINDOWS...

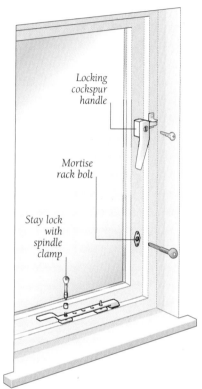

Locking
cockspur
handle

Mortise
rack bolt

Stay lock
with
spindle
clamp

The type of casement lock required will depend on what make of window you have and where it is situated. For frequently opened windows, use an automatic lock (see right). You will need a key to open the window, but it will lock on its own when closed.

AUTOMATIC LOCK

...AND SASH WINDOWS

For maximum security it's advisable to fit sash locks in pairs. Older sash windows are usually wooden, so dual screws and sash stops are good options. The surface-mounted sash push-bolt (see right) is also popular. It doesn't require a key to lock it, but can't be opened without one.

SASH PUSH-BOLT

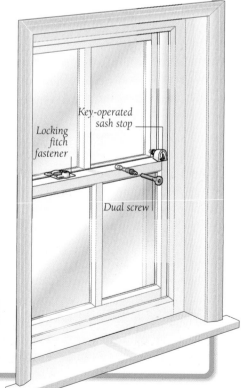

Key-operated
sash stop

Locking
fitch
fastener

Dual screw

Draughtproofing

IF YOU WANT TO KEEP THE HEAT IN you've got to keep the cold out. Sealing doors and windows to prevent draughts could help cut your heating bills by up to 10 per cent, so what are you waiting for?

Search and seal

Use the flickering flame of a candle to locate the source of draughts and make good any cracks or gaps in door and window surrounds. Seal any gaps around frames with flexible waterproof sealant and repaint where necessary. Clean door frames and window sashes and fit draughtproofing strips. Doors should also be fitted with threshold draught excluders. Purpose-built draughtproofing is also available for letterboxes, cat flaps, and keyholes.

Windows must remain easy to open after draughtproofing. Providing adequate ventilation around the home is very important, as it reduces the risk of damp and condensation.

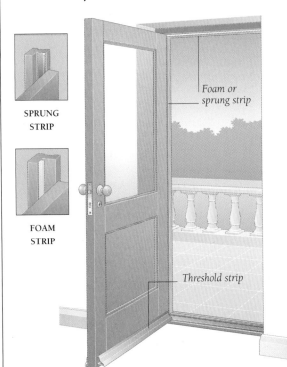

SPRUNG STRIP

FOAM STRIP

Foam or sprung strip

Threshold strip

Draughtproofing doors

There are two types of draughtproofing for door frames: compression strips and sealing strips. If the door closes against a doorstop you will need a self-adhesive foam compression strip; if it moves across the frame, fit a brush or sprung sealing strip. A wide variety of threshold strips is available, including brush strips, compressible strips, and two-part interlocking seals (see below). The choice depends on how your door opens and the size of the gap to be sealed.

■ **A wide variety** *of door draughtproofing is available, including foam or rubber compressible strips, brush strips, and two-part interlocking seals.*

BRUSH STRIP   **COMPRESSIBLE**

TWO-PART

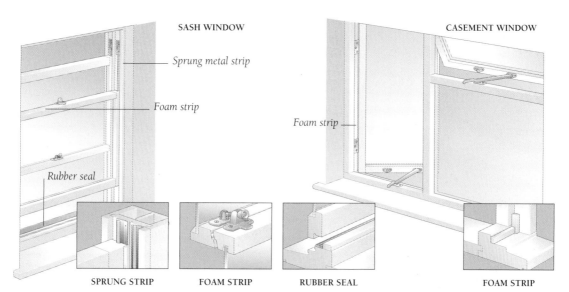

SASH WINDOW

Sprung metal strip

Foam strip

Rubber seal

CASEMENT WINDOW

Foam strip

SPRUNG STRIP   FOAM STRIP   RUBBER SEAL   FOAM STRIP

Draughtproofing strips for windows

Compressible strips are made of foam or rubber and are self-adhesive. Sprung metal strips are nailed to the runner grooves of sash windows, then "sprung" with a special tensioning tool. Brush strips are pinned to the staff bead of sash windows.

■ **You can draughtproof** *your windows in several different ways. The diagram above illustrates what you can use and where to use it.*

A simple summary

✔ Don't rush into sanding down a sticking door or window: there may be an easier means of repair.

✔ Carry out repairs sooner rather than later: they'll only get worse.

✔ Overhauling sash windows isn't as difficult as it looks.

✔ Keep an eye out for rot. Dry rot requires specialist attention.

✔ Doors are sold in standard sizes and need to be trimmed to fit.

✔ It's well worth fitting a mortise lock as well as a deadlocking rim latch to an exterior door.

✔ Install locks on all your upstairs and downstairs windows.

✔ Draughtproofing can save up to 10 per cent on heating bills.

Chapter 12

Floors and Staircases

CREAKS IN WOODEN FLOORS AND STAIRS don't only make things go bump in the night; they also cause premature wear in whatever is laid over the top and, in extreme cases, lead to accidents. Get to grips with any repairs before you lay a new floorcovering, or go the whole way and give the floor a brand-new level surface.

In this chapter...

✓ Fixing staircase faults

✓ Repairing stair banisters

✓ Wood floor repairs

✓ Levelling a wood floor

✓ Levelling a solid floor

A CREAKING STAIRCASE MAY BE DAUNTING...BUT IT CAN BE FIXED

Repairing stair banisters

IT SHOULD COME AS NO SURPRISE to learn that the most often used safety feature in homes with stairs is the banister. Handrails, balusters (spindles), and even the supporting newel posts can all become loose over the years, necessitating urgent repairs.

Checking for faults and making repairs

The most common banister fault is a loose baluster. Although some movement in balusters is to be expected, you should attend to breakages and balusters that fall out without delay. In staircases with closed (solid) strings (the sloping timber supporting the treads), the balusters are housed in grooves in the string and the underside of the handrail, where they are separated by pinned wooden spacers. On stepped or cut-stringed staircases, the feet of the balusters are housed in the treads behind mouldings.

Broken balusters can sometimes be repaired without being taken out. Prise the split sections apart and apply woodworking adhesive, then press together and clamp tightly. Likewise, you may be able to secure a loose baluster by driving screws at an angle into its housing.

More worrying are loose handrails and newel posts. A handrail can be secured at the newel post end by reinforcing the existing joint with a 75mm No.10 screw, counterbored and driven in at an angle. Afterwards, cover the screw with a plug of matching wood glued in place. Where the end of a handrail is built into a wall, secure it with a metal angle bracket; or, for a proper repair, hack out the plaster around the rail, wedge it tight where it is cut into the brickwork, then make good the damage.

■ **On closed-string staircases,** *the balusters sit in the handrail and are held in place by spacers (top inset). The string is grooved and also uses spacers (middle inset). Cut-string balusters are notched into the tread and are held in place with mouldings (bottom inset).*

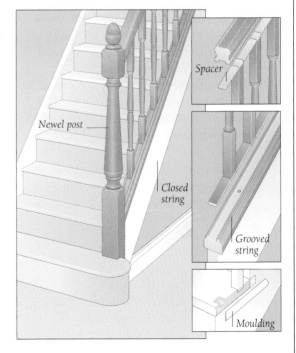

Newel post

Spacer

Closed string

Grooved string

Moulding

REPLACING CLOSED-STRING BALUSTERS

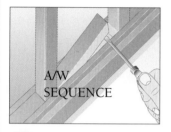
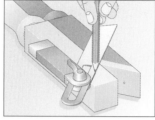

1 **Take out spacer**

Prise out bottom spacer in front of the baluster and the top spacer behind it.

2 **Cut angles**

Use a sliding bevel to transfer joint angle to new spindle, and replace in banister.

3 **Replace and finish**

Nail spacers back in place, at top and bottom, with one panel pin in the centre of each.

REPLACING CUT-STRING BALUSTERS

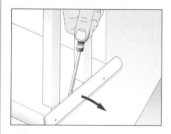

1 **Remove moulding**

Prise off the planted moulding that holds the baluster in the tread.

2 **Hammer free**

The baluster will be nailed to the handrail, so tap free against an offcut of wood.

3 **Pin back**

Cut new baluster and replace. Pin moulding back in place and nail to the handrail.

Loose newel posts are the most serious problem, as they are structural timbers that support the banister. If you can gain access from underneath, coach-bolting the newel post to the adjacent floor joist is the most satisfactory repair. Otherwise, screw the post to the string with long No.10 countersunk woodscrews. If the cap of a newel post becomes loose or gets knocked off, drill the base to accept a length of dowel, then glue back in place.

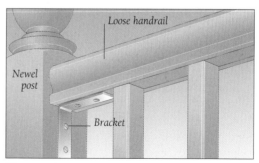

■ **Loose handrails** *can be fixed by securing to a newel post or wall with a metal bracket.*

Wood floor repairs

RAISED OR DAMAGED FLOORBOARDS *are a safety hazard, as well as annoying, so don't delay in fixing them. Use the same techniques to gain access to pipes and cables beneath the floor.*

Creaking and damaged boards

Floorboards are prone to swelling and splitting over time. This can cause the nails to work loose and the boards to creak, and can lead to excessive carpet wear. If you're lucky, loose boards can be secured with additional nails or screws, but badly damaged sections may have to be removed and replaced. To do this, you'll have to cut across a board in situ, which is best done with a circular saw. Set the saw to the exact board thickness to avoid pipes notched into the joists. The cut should fall exactly halfway over a joist, which you can gauge by checking where other joints between boards are; double-check by inserting a piece of card into the gaps. If the board is tongued-and grooved, you'll have to saw down one edge as well. Afterwards, it should be possible to lever up the cut end, insert a batten underneath, and spring the damaged section free of its other fixings.

Before making repairs to isolated floorboards, check the flooring as a whole. If the entire floor appears to have bowed or warped, it may be due to a joist problem. This must be looked at by a professional.

LIFTING SQUARE-EDGED BOARDS

1 **Cut at a joist**

Use a circular saw, set to the thickness of the boards, to release the damaged section.

2 **Lift the end**

Use a claw hammer and a bolster together to lever the cut end free of the joist.

3 **Spring the board**

Slip a batten under the board and stand on the raised end to spring the other fixings.

REPLACING TONGUE-AND-GROOVE BOARDS

(1) Remove the tongue

Sever the tongue from the board by cutting down one edge with a circular saw.

(2) Lever out

Lever up the edge of the board with a bolster chisel over an offcut of hardboard.

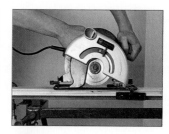

(3) Cut to size

Cut off the lower (thinner) side of the groove on new board. Fit it tongue first and nail down.

Patching boards and filling gaps

Gaps between boards are best filled with slivers of wood, cut lengthways to a wedge-shaped profile with a circular saw. Glue the slivers, tap into the gaps with a mallet, then plane flush with the surrounding boards. As a final precaution, double-check that all nail heads are driven below the surface of the boards.

If you can't find an exact replacement for the existing boards, buy timber that's wider and thicker. Trim it to length and width, then chisel notches in the ends to accommodate the joists so that the patch sits flush with the other boards.

Other types of wood floor

Use a similar technique to cut out damaged sections from a plywood or chipboard floor, noting where the joints between the boards fall. Floors of this type rarely cause any trouble unless they get wet and swell, in which case the chances are that the adjacent boards will also be affected. If possible, remove the skirtings first, then lift entire sections and replace them; cutting out small sections is likely to weaken the integrity of the floor and may lead to creaking.

■ **Nail into joists** *at an angle (left) with cut floor brads parallel to the grain. If for some reason you can't nail directly into a joist, attach a batten to the side of it (right) and screw into this.*

Levelling a wood floor

LEVELLING AN EXISTING BOARDED FLOOR with hardboard or plywood is a lot easier than replacing the floor itself, and will feel better underfoot as well as prolonging the life of the floorcovering. If you're laying sheet floorcoverings or wood block flooring, it's an essential first step.

Preparing the floor

Don't expect too much of the new layer: secure loose boards, replace damaged sections of board, and make sure all fixings are driven just below the surface.

Hardboard provides an ideal surface for most floorcoverings, but if you're planning to lay ceramic tiles, nail down 12mm exterior-grade plywood instead. For sheet floorcoverings, carpets, and soft floor tiles, lay hardboard up to the skirting, leaving a 3mm gap. For hard floorcoverings it is advisable to first remove the skirtings and cut away the bottom of architraves, then replace skirtings over the completed flooring. Remove doors that open into the room for trimming, or hire a door saw.

Boarding the floor will make underfloor ventilation more critical. Check that outside floor vents and airbricks are intact and free from blockages so that air circulates freely in the floor cavity.

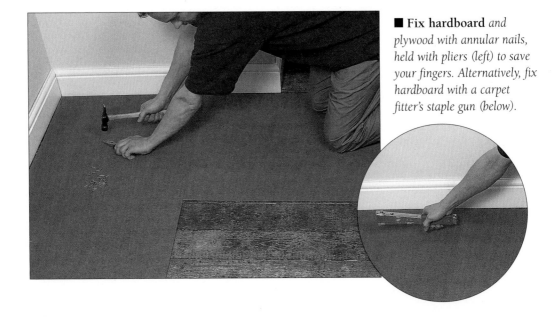

■ **Fix hardboard** *and plywood with annular nails, held with pliers (left) to save your fingers. Alternatively, fix hardboard with a carpet fitter's staple gun (below).*

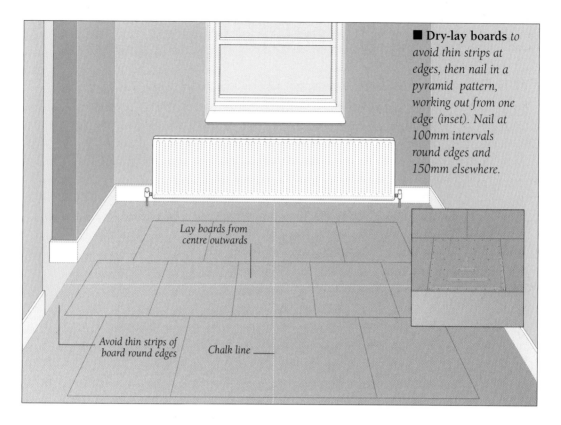

■ **Dry-lay boards** *to avoid thin strips at edges, then nail in a pyramid pattern, working out from one edge (inset). Nail at 100mm intervals round edges and 150mm elsewhere.*

Lay boards from centre outwards

Avoid thin strips of board round edges

Chalk line

Fitting the sheets

Buy tempered hardboard, or condition it yourself by spraying with warm water and then standing it in the room prior to fitting for 48 hours. Get 1200 x 600mm flooring panels, which are easier to handle than full sheets. Mark centre lines across the floor and dry-lay sheets outwards from here, staggering the joints between rows. If you're left with narrow strips of less than a floorboard's width around the edges of the room, adjust the layout accordingly. Hardboard should be laid rough side up if you plan to lay tiles, to provide a key for the adhesive, otherwise smooth side up.

Don't forget to provide access panels for essential underfloor services. The panel should match the existing one underneath. Screw it in place so that both panels can be lifted together in an emergency.

Once you are happy with the layout, fix down the whole sheets, working from one edge outwards in all directions to prevent the board from bowing up. Then cut pieces to fit the gaps around the edges. Check the level of the floor at regular intervals, and if necessary pack underneath the sheets with card or board to get them flat.

Levelling a solid floor

GIVE A ROUGH CONCRETE FLOOR *a smooth, level surface before tiling using self-levelling compound – a remarkable latex-based powder that finds its own level when mixed with water and dries to a tough finish.*

Using self-levelling compound

The existing floor should be free of dust and dirt, and must be completely dry. Ideally, plumbing fixtures or fitted units should be unscrewed and propped clear so that the

compound can be laid beneath them. If not, make sure you protect them with tape. Before you start, run over the floor with a spirit level and check for high and low spots. Mark these, so that you can pick a "route" for pouring the compound that starts at the lowest point and ends at the door. Fit battens across doorways to contain the liquid. Spread the liquid compound over the floor with a plasterer's float, working quickly so that the first batch doesn't harden before you've finished pouring. It may take two applications to get it absolutely level.

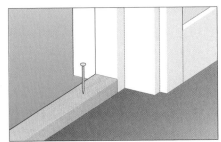

■ **Fit battens** *across doorways to contain the compound. You can remove them when it has fully hardened.*

Levelling a floor

Using self-levelling compound makes levelling a solid floor a surprisingly simple job.

1 **PVA preparation**

You don't need to remove ceramic tiles before using a self-levelling compound. Prepare the surface with a coat of PVA.

2 **Making good**

Fill any cracks and gaps in the floor surface with mortar. Allow to dry thoroughly before using self-levelling compound.

3 Pour out compound

Pour the self-levelling compound onto the floor, starting in the corner furthest away from the door. Don't attempt to cover too large an area at once.

4 Spread out

Spread the compound with a float. When you're finished, check the level and fill any low patches with a thin mix of compound.

If you think your floor might be damp, tape polythene over the suspect area and leave for a couple of days. A mist under the polythene means that damp is penetrating the damp-proof membrane laid under the existing concrete screed. Have the fault repaired before you level the floor.

A simple summary

✔ Creaking floorboards and stairs don't always signal damage, but check to be on the safe side.

✔ Ensuring that stair banisters are secure is absolutely essential for home safety.

✔ Damaged floorboards and stairs are dangerous; fix them before an accident occurs.

✔ Provide a smooth base on timber floors for floorcoverings by laying hardboard; for heavier floorcoverings such as ceramic tiles, use plywood to support the extra weight.

✔ Self-levelling compound makes the job of levelling solid floors straightforward. Simply pour it over the floor surface.

Chapter 13

Shelves and Storage

STORAGE SPACE IS SOMETHING few homes have enough of – and even when they do, it's seldom long before it runs out. Making the most of empty wall space is often the answer, using shelves for the things you want to display and built-in cabinets or cupboards for items that you'd rather hide away.

In this chapter...

✓ Open-track shelving

✓ Built-in shelving

✓ Changing cabinet doors

✓ Fitting kitchen cabinets

✓ Building in cupboards

✓ Building in a wardrobe

ALCOVE UNITS AND RECESSED SHELVING CAN CREATE A LUXURIOUS AMBIENCE

Fitting kitchen cabinets

BECAUSE KITCHEN CABINETS *are modular in size, it's relatively easy to substitute new for old. The important thing is to work in the right order: after you've removed the old units, take the opportunity to inspect the plumbing and electrics, and make any necessary alterations. Also, make good any damage to the walls behind the units or you'll forever be plagued with dust or pests.*

Installing the cabinets

Position the base cabinets first (see below), but don't fix them. Mark vertical lines on the wall to set the intervals of the wall cabinets above them and draw a horizontal line not less than 450mm above the work surface to mark where the cabinets will sit. Remove the base units and fit temporary support battens along this line. Starting at a corner or end unit, lift the first wall cabinet into position and mark the wall fixing holes; if the cabinet isn't level, pack under the support batten with bits of card. Fit all the wall cabinets in the same way and, if necessary, join them together with cabinet connectors. Then fix the base units to the wall, double-checking that they're level. Finally, fit the drawers and hang the doors.

Before removing old units, turn off the electricity and water and disconnect the cables and pipework. Remove wall cabinet doors to reduce the weight. Get help to support the doors while releasing the fixings.

FITTING A BASE CABINET

1 Assembling the carcass

Fit the hardware to each panel and join them together. Then fit the back panel and the adjustable feet.

2 Levelling with feet

Position the corner unit and adjust the screw feet until the top aligns with your guidelines.

3 Fixing to the wall

Mark through the fixing holes and remove the unit. Install wall fixings to secure the cabinet.

Fitting a worktop

Fitting lengths of straight worktop is relatively easy, but an inset hob presents more problems. Support the back edge of the worktop on a wall-mounted batten. To make the cut-out, first drill a starter hole for your jigsaw blade at each corner. Screw a guide batten to the waste along one side, cut this side out, then repeat for the opposite side. Now repeat the process for the other two sides, shifting the worktop along to support the waste. Join lengths of worktop using concealed connectors drilled and cut into the underside to pull the lengths together.

INTERNET

www.villagers-
collection.co.uk/
villagers_kitchens.htm

This site includes a wide range of kitchen units, planning advice, and even kitchen appliances.

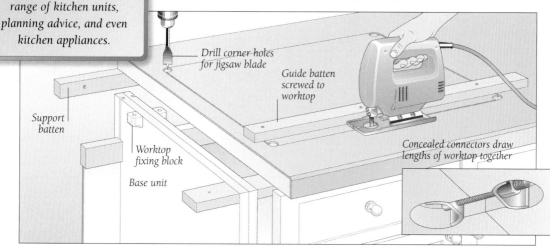

Drill corner holes
for jigsaw blade

Guide batten
screwed to
worktop

Support
batten

Worktop
fixing block

Base unit

Concealed connectors draw
lengths of worktop together

■ **To make a cut-out** *in a worktop, start by drilling a starter hole in the corners. By fixing a guide batten parallel to the edge to be cut, you ensure that your jigsaw cuts dead straight.*

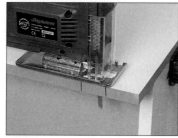

4 **Fitting around pipes**

If pipes obstruct the unit, mark the side panel to fit, leaving 3mm clearance all round.

5 **Notching a side panel**

Cut in from the edge and cut out the notch with a jigsaw. Cut to the exact shape in an exposed panel.

6 **Fitting a plinth**

Shape the plinth to fit round the skirting. Screw plinth clips on the centre line to align with the feet.

Building in cupboards

LIKE SHELVES, A CUPBOARD *can be built into a recess to make the most of an otherwise "dead" area. Add shelves above and finish with decorative wooden mouldings for a traditional "dresser" look.*

Designing the cupboard

If the recess is deep enough and is reasonably square, you can opt for the simplest form of built-in cupboard: alcove shelving with added doors. Install the shelves first, then add a supporting framework for the doors and countertop. But if the walls of the recess are uneven, badly out of square, or simply not deep enough to provide usable storage space, add side panels as well and pack behind them with plywood to create a squared-up carcass. Cover the gaps between the side panels and the wall with strips of wooden moulding, pinned and glued.

Make up doors from the same material as the top and shelves and hang in the frame using ordinary brass butt hinges. Fit magnetic catches to the central frame member to act as stops. Finally, cut the top to overhang the doors and fix it to the top of the door frame using plastic knock-down (KD) joint blocks.

Don't forget that installing a built-in cupboard may cover a much-needed electrical socket, or make it difficult to use. If necessary, relocate the socket or refit it higher up in the cupboard.

MAKING A SIMPLE CUPBOARD FRAME

1 Attach battens

Fit plinth battens flush with the skirting to support the base of the new cupboard.

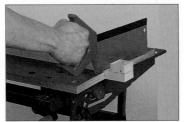

2 Build frame

Build the cupboard frame from 50 x 50mm timber. Use halving joints to put the frame together.

3 Fit cupboard base

Cut the base to fit over the plinth battens and finish at the front edge. Fit any further shelves above it.

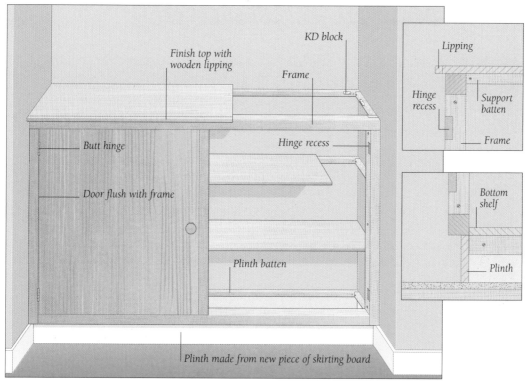

Finish top with wooden lipping

KD block

Frame

Lipping

Hinge recess

Support batten

Frame

Butt hinge

Hinge recess

Door flush with frame

Bottom shelf

Plinth batten

Plinth

Plinth made from new piece of skirting board

■ **The simplest form of built-in cupboard** *consists of a halving-jointed timber frame over alcove shelves on batten supports. Finish the edge of the countertop with a strip of pinned-and-glued wooden lipping (top inset), and use a plinth of matching skirting board to finish the base (lower inset).*

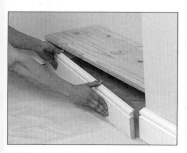

4 **Fit new skirting**

Cut a new piece of skirting board to length and screw and glue to the ends of the plinth battens.

5 **Install frame**

Position frame on top of skirting and screw it to the wall, checking that it is square and plumb.

6 **Cupboard doors**

Make up doors to fit the frame, then mark and cut hinge recesses in the frame uprights.

Building in a wardrobe

CREATE MORE BEDROOM STORAGE with a ready-made sliding door kit. All you need is a clear wall with around 600mm in front of it.

Fitting considerations

Sliding door kits come in standard sizes and a range of finishes, including mirrored. Aluminium height reducers and clip-on fascias are supplied to take up any gaps between the doors and ceiling. The only important fitting consideration is that the top track is screwed to a joist (or to several joists, if they run at right angles). Fit out the space behind the doors with poles or ready-made cabinets as desired.

FITTING SLIDING DOORS

1 **Cut tracks to fit**

Once you have carefully measured from wall to wall, cut the tracks to length.

2 **Fit top track**

Having secured height reducers to the joists, fit the fascia panel and secure the top track.

3 **Secure bottom track**

Use a plumbline to locate the bottom track and screw it to the floor through the carpet.

4 **Fix fascia**

A secondary fascia may be needed to hide the top track. This simply clips in place.

5 **Insert door**

Lift the sliding door into the roller mechanism located in the top track.

6 **Fit slider**

Fit the sliding wheel into the bottom track and test that the door closes smoothly.

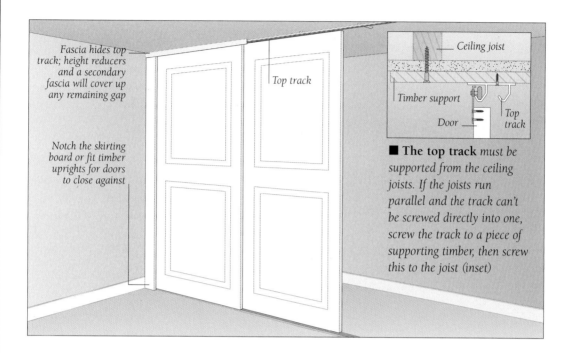

Fascia hides top track; height reducers and a secondary fascia will cover up any remaining gap

Notch the skirting board or fit timber uprights for doors to close against

Top track

Ceiling joist

Timber support

Door

Top track

■ **The top track** must be supported from the ceiling joists. If the joists run parallel and the track can't be screwed directly into one, screw the track to a piece of supporting timber, then screw this to the joist (inset)

A simple summary

✔ Track shelf systems are easy to fit, and the spaces between the shelves are easily adjusted to keep pace with the family's changing storage needs.

✔ Fit shelves and built-in cupboards in alcoves and recesses, where they will intrude least on existing living space.

✔ Changing cabinet doors is an effective and affordable way to brighten a tired kitchen.

✔ When installing kitchen cabinets, use the base units as a guide for positioning the wall units, but fit the wall units first.

✔ Transform a room and make the most out of a recess or alcove by building in a cupboard.

✔ Extra bedroom storage is easily created with a ready-made sliding door kit. Always attach the tracks for the sliding doors to a joist.

Chapter 14

Walls and Ceilings

STRUCTURAL WORK ON WALLS AND CEILINGS is best left to a builder – if only because of the mess involved and the potential hidden pitfalls. But don't despair: building a new partition is well within the scope of the do-it-yourselfer, as is adding decorative moulding and cornices.

In this chapter...

✓ Panelling and boxing in

✓ Making openings in walls

✓ Building a partition wall

✓ Decorative plasterwork

✓ Repairing moulding

✓ Fitting coving and cornices

✓ Tracing damp faults

PLASTER CEILING COVING AND WOODEN ARCHITRAVE PUTS THE FINISHING TOUCHES TO A PERIOD-STYLE ROOM

Panelling and boxing in

IF YOUR WALLS ARE IN POOR CONDITION *or covered with pipes and wires, but are free from damp, consider panelling them with tongue-and-groove boards, wallboard, or sheets of grooved MDF. And you can use the same techniques to box in pipes by fitting the panelling over a timber framework.*

Preparing for strip panelling

Tongue-and-groove strip panelling is normally nailed vertically against supporting rows of horizontal battens, screwed to the wall at roughly 500mm intervals – but there's no reason why you can't reverse this, or even nail boards diagonally. The key to an invisible fixing is to nail each strip through its tongue before slotting the next strip in place (called secret nailing). You can buy special mouldings to finish internal and external corners and to finish the top of half-height panelling. In theory, you should remove all skirtings, architraves, and other mouldings before you start and then replace them once the panelling is in place. In practice, this isn't always possible, and you may find yourself having to fit additional mouldings around doorways to hide the gaps.

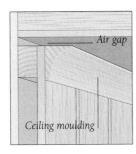

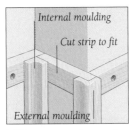

■ **Leave an air gap** *for ventilation on full-height panelling (top). Finish internal and external corners with special mouldings (above).*

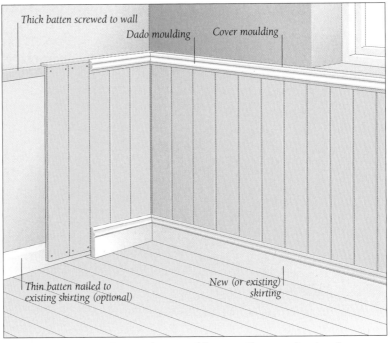

■ **Fix vertical panelling** *to horizontal battens. If you are leaving the existing skirting in place, it can act as one of the fixings.*

FIXING TONGUE-AND-GROOVE PANELLING

① Fit support battens

Screw the support battens to the wall. Use a spirit level to check they're level and flat.

② Scribe cut strips

Measure up for any cut strips. If necessary, scribe the strips and trim to fit the wall.

③ Secret nailing

Face-nail the groove edge of the first strip, and secret nail through the tongue at an angle.

④ Subsequent strips

Use an offcut to knock subsequent strips together, then secret nail the tongues.

⑤ Dealing with corners

Fit an internal corner moulding, then measure the gap and cut a strip lengthways to fit.

⑥ External corners

Do the same at external corners, then pin the decorative top moulding in place.

Wallboards and solid panelling

Wood-fibre wallboard can be used to resurface a wall that is reasonably sound and flat. It is glued, rather than supported on a batten framework, but is not as robust as timber panelling. Cut the boards to size with a sharp knife and smooth the cut edges with abrasive paper, then stick to the wall on bands of the manufacturer's recommended adhesive and check that they lie flat. Leave gaps at the top and bottom to allow air to circulate behind the boards and cover with wooden moulding. Solid panelling – chipboard, plywood, or MDF – needs a supporting framework of 50 x 25mm timber and is a better choice than strip panelling for boxing-in. Screw the panelling to the frame and fill or, if you need access, use dome-head screws.

Making openings in walls

AS YOUR NEEDS CHANGE, you may want to add or remove a wall, or create a new door opening. If the wall is loadbearing (see below), then it's time to get professional help. But non-structural walls are easily created or rearranged using plasterboard over a framework of timber studs.

Removing a partition wall

Non-structural partition walls are usually timber framed, but in older houses, they may just as easily be brick or concrete block. Similarly, in a timber-framed house, a stud wall may be loadbearing. The illustration on the right should help you check – but if you are in any doubt at all, get expert advice.

Removing any type of wall creates clouds of dust. Clear the room as far as possible, seal off, and wear the appropriate protective gear.

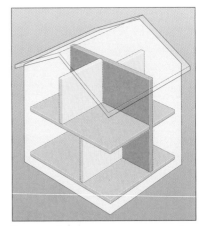

■ **A wall that rises continuously** *through a house is probably loadbearing and shouldn't be interfered with.*

First, remove any skirtings and mouldings. Then with the electricity disconnected, remove any light switches and wiring. Reconnect the outlets and tie or tape them safely out of the way until you're ready to relocate them. On a masonry wall, loosen the brick or blockwork with a club hammer and bolster and try to remove it with the plaster intact to keep down the dust. On a frame wall, prise away the plasterboard with a claw hammer or wrecking bar, then dismantle the framework – horizontal timbers (noggins) first, followed by the vertical studs, and then the head and sole plates. Make good any holes in the wall and ceiling with fresh strips of plasterboard.

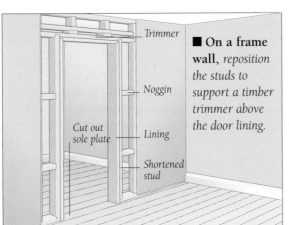

Trimmer

■ **On a frame wall,** *reposition the studs to support a timber trimmer above the door lining.*

Noggin

Cut out sole plate

Lining

Shortened stud

Opening up a doorway

You can save yourself a lot of work here by buying a prefabricated door

CREATING A DOORWAY IN A FRAME WALL

1 Brace door lining

Nail a batten diagonally across the prefabricated door lining to brace it square.

2 Mark position

Cut away the plasterboard and mark the height of the lining on the exposed studs.

3 Construct top frame

Cut through the intervening studs and reposition them with a horizontal trimmer above.

4 Rebuild side frames

Strengthen the frame either side of the door with noggins, nailed through the studs.

5 Wedge and fix frame

Position the lining and wedge it in place. Check it is true, then nail to the frame.

6 Fix plasterboard

Resurface the frame with plasterboard. Ensure the joints are centred over the trimmer.

lining and an internal door to match. On a stud wall, cut back the plasterboard around the site of the opening with a trimming knife, mark the position of the doorway, then dismantle the studwork. Shorten the studs to support a 100 x 50mm timber trimmer above the doorway and rebuild the frame with supporting noggins. Finally, wedge the door lining in the opening, check that it is square, then fix to the frame and replaster.

On a masonry wall, mark the position of the prefabricated doorway. Then use a club hammer and bolster to chop a slot in the brick or blockwork immediately above the doorway to accommodate a 100 x 50mm timber trimmer extending 150mm to each side. Bed the trimmer on mortar and leave to dry. Then cut away the rest of the opening and screw the door frame in position using frame fixings at 400mm intervals.

Building a partition wall

A NON-LOADBEARING STUD PARTITION *wall is the quickest way to create two rooms out of one. Build the framework from 100 x 50mm timber screwed to the floor and ceiling joists, then simply clad with plasterboard.*

Positioning the wall

The position of the wall is governed by the sole plates (see opposite), which on a timber floor must be screwed through the floorboards and into the joists. If the wall is to run parallel with the joists, locate the nearest joist and sit the sole plates directly over the top. Follow the same principle for the header plate. If the ceiling joists run parallel and "miss" the plate, fit timber noggins between the joists from above to provide a secure fixing.

Building the timber frame

Aside from the sole and header plates, the rest of the frame can be nailed together using 75mm round head wire nails. As when creating a new doorway, save yourself time by using a prefabricated lining for the door opening, with short studs to either side supporting a trimmer above. Elsewhere, space the studs at 400mm intervals, skew-nailing them to the sole and wall plates. Then brace the spaces in between the studs with noggins, staggered so that you can nail through the studs into the ends.

CONSTRUCTING THE FRAMEWORK

1 **Fit header plate**
Get help to support the header plate while you screw it to the joists – or along one joist.

2 **Fit the sole plate**
Hang a plumbline from the header plate to make sure that the sole plate goes directly beneath it.

3 **Secure end studs**
If necessary, cut out sections of skirting, then screw the ends studs to the adjacent wall.

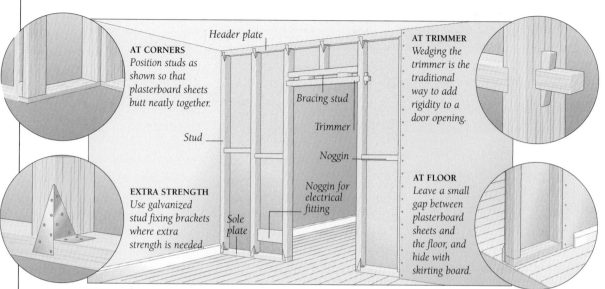

AT CORNERS
Position studs as shown so that plasterboard sheets butt neatly together.

Bracing stud

Trimmer

Stud

Noggin

EXTRA STRENGTH
Use galvanized stud fixing brackets where extra strength is needed.

Noggin for electrical fitting

Sole plate

AT TRIMMER
Wedging the trimmer is the traditional way to add rigidity to a door opening.

AT FLOOR
Leave a small gap between plasterboard sheets and the floor, and hide with skirting board.

■ **Key design features** *of a stud wall; use stud brackets and wedge trimmer for extra strength.*

Cladding the frame

Nail plasterboard to one side of the frame, arranging for the joints to coincide with the frame members where possible. If desired, make the wall sound less "hollow" and improve the soundproofing by packing in between the frame with insulation roll. Then clad the other side of the wall, and fill the joints and nail holes in the plasterboard in the usual way (see p. 62).

4 **Fit intervening studs**

Skew-nail the ends of the studs to the header and sole plates, taking care to keep them vertical.

5 **Frame the opening**

At an opening, sit a horizontal trimmer across two shortened studs, then add bracing studs above.

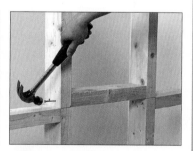

6 **Fit noggins**

Fit bracing noggins between the studs, staggered so that you can nail into the ends.

Decorative plasterwork

PLASTER MOULDINGS *add the finishing touch to a period-style room, and can be repaired, too.*

Fitting a ceiling rose

Fit a ceiling rose with a pendant light fitting or as a stand-alone feature. A small rose can simply be glued in place using plaster moulding adhesive, but a very heavy rose will be provided with lugs or holes for screwing to the ceiling joists. Before applying the adhesive, strip off any lining paper and make sure the surface is dust-free. Support the rose from below, using a timber prop topped by an offcut of hardboard or plywood, while the adhesive dries.

■ **A ceiling rose** *provides a visual centrepiece in a period-style room, especially when complemented by a chandelier-style pendant light fitting.*

FITTING PANEL MOULDINGS

Use a plaster panel moulding kit to add decorative interest to a flat wall or ceiling. Simply glue the strips in place with moulding adhesive, working in from the corners Do a dry run first, and mark the positions of the corner pieces in pencil.

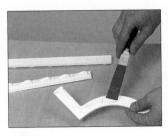

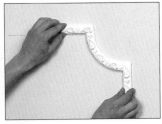

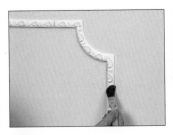

① **Apply adhesive**	② **Start at a corner**	③ **Finish the joints**
Spread adhesive over the back of the moulding with a flexible filling knife.	*Position the first corner moulding against your pencilled guideline.*	*Press fine-surface filler into the joints with your finger, then smooth with a damp brush.*

Repairing plaster mouldings

Decorative plaster ceiling cornices can simply be glued in place like other mouldings, although you'll need to support the heavier type with nails while the adhesive sets. But if your house is old, and a section of moulding is damaged, you have a choice: remove the existing moulding and replace the lot; or make up a sheet plastic template to match the profile of the existing moulding and use this to shape a plastered repair.

A repair is only feasible if the damaged section is less than about 300–400mm long. Stiffen the plastic with hardboard and screw on a handle. Transfer the profile of the moulding to the template using a profile gauge and cut it to shape with a coping saw or jigsaw. Nail a batten to the wall below the damaged area and fit guide battens to the template (see below) so that it can be held in the correct position on the wall.

Fill the damaged section with repair plaster or plaster of Paris, using pieces of zinc gauze or plasterboard scrim tape for support where necessary; the batten underneath the moulding will hold the plaster in place. Then, while the plaster is still wet, draw the template across it to shape it to the correct profile. If it starts to drag, dampen the repair with water and try again.

Do any final shaping and finishing when the plaster has dried. The ideal tool for shaping is a portable power drill equipped with a small abrasive wheel. Smooth any blemishes in the plaster with fine surface filler before painting.

REPAIRING A PLASTER CORNICE

1 **Make a template**

Use a profile gauge to copy the cornice onto a sheet of plastic, and make up a wooden frame.

2 **Apply repair plaster**

Nail a batten to the wall below the cornice, then fill the damage with repair plaster.

3 **Shape the profile**

Run the template along the batten so that it moulds the repair to the cornice shape.

Repairing moulding

MOULDINGS FOR SKIRTING BOARDS, ARCHITRAVES, and *other wooden decorative features are available in countless sizes and profiles from specialist timber suppliers. Replacements are simply nailed to the wall with lost-head nails, but repairing original mouldings may require more ingenuity.*

Repair or replace?

If large sections of mouldings are missing, remove the rest and opt for wholesale replacement. Prise off the old moulding with a bolster, using an offcut to protect the wall. For a repair, your best bet is to try to match the profile of the original moulding using individual lengths of narrow strip moulding, then fill the gaps between them.

To avoid damaging the surrounding decorations when removing mouldings, cut around the joint between the moulding and the wall with a trimming knife before prising it away.

Fitting new mouldings

● **Architrave mouldings:** these form a decorative frame around doors and hide the joint between the door lining and the wall. Nail or screw them in place.

MITRING A DOOR ARCHITRAVE

1 **Mitre the upright**

Mark the inside of the mitre on the architrave, 2mm from the inside corner of the door lining.

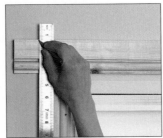

2 **Mitre the top**

Mitre and fit the uprights, then use them to mark the outside mitres on the top section.

3 **Final fixing in place**

Mitre the ends of the horizontal length, fix it in place, then pin through the mitre as shown.

REPAIRING SKIRTING BOARDS

a Removing skirting

Use a bolster chisel and timber offcut to prise skirting board away from the wall.

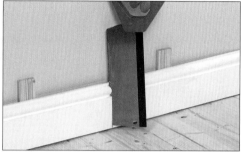

b Cutting out a section

Wedge the prised-away board clear of the wall and cut into it at 45° at both ends.

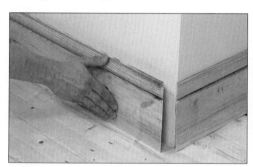

c Mitring external corners

At external corners, mark the inside of the mitre at the corner of the wall.

d Scribing internal corners

Use an offcut of skirting to mark the profile on the back of the new length.

- **Dado and picture rails:** these can add interest to plain walls and will visually lower a high-ceilinged room by dividing it into horizontal bands. Nail or screw in place.

- **Skirting board:** this protects the foot of a wall and can be used to disguise the expansion gaps around the edges of floorcoverings. If there is a pipe or other obstruction in the way, create a box skirting – screw battens to the wall above and below, then nail the skirting board to these.

Other parts of the house, for example staircases and panelled walls, tend to be finished with one or other of the above, often in conjunction with narrower strips.

Fitting coving and cornices

CORNICE IS THE GENERAL TERM *for a variety of special-purpose mouldings used to cover the joints where walls and ceiling meet. The best-known type of cornice is coving – a plain concave moulding that comes in a variety of materials including plaster, foamed plastic, and timber.*

A choice of styles

Aside from coving, cornices come in a vast range of styles and materials, and in sizes from 32mm square to 400 x 100mm. You should be aware that the terms moulding, coving, and cornice are often used interchangeably in builders' merchants. Avoid possible confusion by asking to see suppliers' catalogues and pointing to the items you want. The more ornate types of cornices are generally made of paper-covered fibrous plaster or foamed plastic, and include replicas of ancient Greek, Roman, Georgian, and Victorian designs. Like other mouldings, they are glued in place using special moulding adhesive, although the heavier types need reinforcing with nails or even screws. Some types of cornice are designed to be nailed over battens screwed along the joint between the ceiling and wall. This is useful if the ceiling line is very uneven, since it allows you to set the battens (and hence the mouldings) level and then fill the gaps above.

Some coving and cornice kits come with matching pieces for internal and external corners, which gets around the need to mitre adjacent pieces.

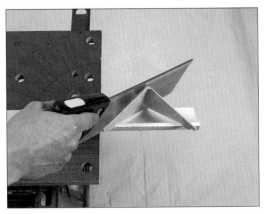

■ **Some makes of coving** *come with a template that hooks over the moulding to act as a cutting guide in two planes. Use the different sides of the template for internal mitres (above left) and external mitres (above right). Clamp the coving securely and cut the mitres with a tenon saw.*

FITTING PLAIN CEILING COVING

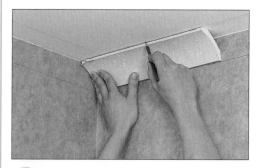

① Mark guidelines

If the room is wallpapered, use an offcut of coving to pencil lines around the wall and ceiling showing where the coving will go.

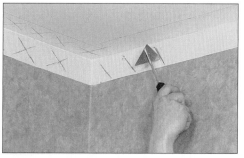

② Key the surface

Cut along the lines with a trimming knife, then strip away the paper in between. Afterwards, score key lines in the wall plaster.

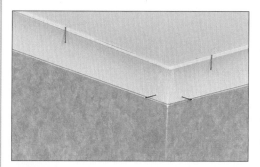

③ Glue and pin in place

Spread adhesive all over the back of the coving and press in place. Hold the edges of the coving with masonry pins while the adhesive dries.

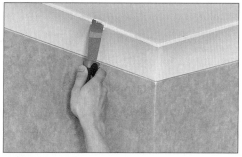

④ Fill the joints

Fill any gaps in between, above, and below the coving with more adhesive, and sponge smooth before it hardens. Remove pins after 24 hours.

Fixing cornices

Follow the manufacturer's instructions on how to fix their particular make of cornice. At the very least, both the wall and ceiling should be dry, dust-free, and stripped of old wallpaper. If the ceiling line is very uneven, you may want to do a dry run first to see where the low points are – or even draw a horizontal line around the room and fix the coving to this to ensure that lengths line up. As a rule, start in a corner and work from either side of this to end in the most unobtrusive part of the room. Afterwards, fill any gaps with interior filler.

Tracing damp faults

DAMP RUINS DECORATIONS *and can lead to rot in structural timbers.*
The trick is not to make temporary repairs, but to locate the source of the trouble
and put it right – even if this means calling in expert help.

Beware the penetrator

Penetrating damp affects all houses, but is most common in
older houses with solid brick walls, which become porous with
age. Houses with cavity or timber-framed walls are less likely
to suffer, although they are by no means immune. The
giveaway is that the damp gets worse after a period of heavy
rain. Common causes include:

- Damaged pointing and broken bricks on a masonry wall.
- Defective flashings on roofs, parapets, and bay windows.

> ### DEFINITION
>
> With **penetrating damp**,
> *water seeps into a house from*
> *outside, through cracks in*
> *walls, and around windows*
> *and doors.* **Rising damp**
> *soaks up from the ground into*
> *solid floors and the lower*
> *parts of masonry walls.*

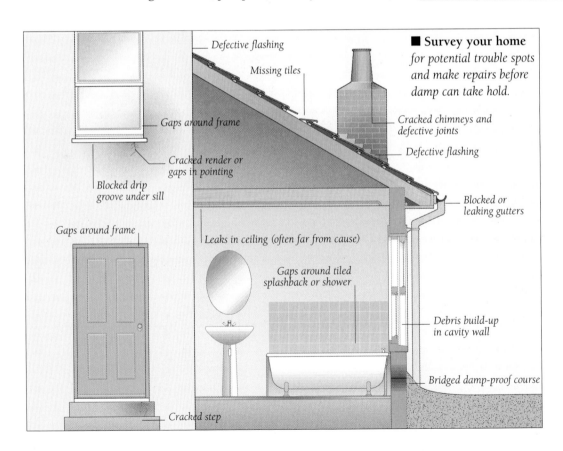

Defective flashing

Missing tiles

Gaps around frame

Cracked render or
gaps in pointing

Blocked drip
groove under sill

Gaps around frame

Leaks in ceiling (often far from cause)

Gaps around tiled
splashback or shower

Cracked step

■ **Survey your home**
for potential trouble spots
and make repairs before
damp can take hold.

Cracked chimneys and
defective joints

Defective flashing

Blocked or
leaking gutters

Debris build-up
in cavity wall

Bridged damp-proof course

- Gaps between door or window frames and the surrounding wall.
- Defective downpipes or guttering.
- Defective or blocked drip grooves on the underside of window sills, causing water run-off onto the wall below.

Note that if water gets into a ceiling cavity, it will find the weakest spot to leak through – which may be some distance from the point of entry.

The damp also rises

To prevent *rising damp*, houses in the UK built after 1880 should have their walls protected by some form of damp-proof course (DPC) built into the brickwork about 150mm above ground level. Similarly, solid concrete floors should have a bituminous or polythene damp-proof membrane (DPM). If there is no DPC, or the DPC is "bridged" (for example, by an adjoining wall or a build-up of soil), ground water will rise up into the masonry and leave damp patches on the plaster to a height of around 1 metre. If a DPM is accidentally breached, the floor will become damp. Repairing, replacing, or fitting a DPC or DPM is best left to a firm of specialists, who should be prepared to guarantee their work against future problems recurring.

A simple summary

✓ Tongue-and-groove strip or wallboard panelling is great for hiding walls in poor condition – but they mustn't be damp.

✓ Thinking of knocking a hole through a wall? Check whether the wall is loadbearing first; if it is, leave the job to a builder.

✓ A timber-framed stud partition wall is the easiest way to split one room into two. Make the job even easier by fitting a prefabricated door lining.

✓ Much decorative plasterwork can simply be glued in place.

✓ Match old wooden decorative mouldings by combining several different types of strip moulding.

✓ If your existing ceiling cornice is badly damaged, you're better off replacing it.

✓ Don't just treat the symptoms of structural damp, pin down the root cause – even if this means calling in a specialist firm.

Chapter 15

Heating and ventilation

T HERE IS NOTHING QUITE AS COMFORTING as a warm, cosy home. But rooms can soon become stuffy and overbearing without proper ventilation. Keeping the cold out while allowing fresh air in is the name of the game when it comes to heating – and if you can allow yourself the luxury of an open fire, then so much the better.

In this chapter...

✓ Insulating your home

✓ Ventilation and condensation

✓ Fires, stoves, and gas fires

✓ Renovating a fireplace

✓ Replacing a fire surround

RECLAIMING AN OLD FIREPLACE CAN TAKE TIME, BUT IT IS CERTAINLY REWARDING

Insulating your home

INSULATION SAVES ENERGY, which should save you money – not to mention the planet. There are plenty of insulation products on the market, all with fitting instructions, but it pays to know the facts before you buy.

Getting your priorities right

Recent buildings should be insulated to a high standard, but you can make major improvements to older ones, even if they're insulated already. Insulation materials are rated by their U-value – the rate at which they lose heat per square metre. So a material with a high U-value will be as effective as a greater thickness of a lower U-value material, which is useful where space is restricted, such as between the joists of a loft floor. In theory, it's more efficient to insulate the outside of a building; inside the house, insulation reduces the temperature on the cold side, which can lead to condensation problems unless the area is properly ventilated. However, exterior insulation is seldom practical unless you plan to fit cladding or weatherboards.

The heat loss is greatest from those areas that are hottest relative to their surroundings. That makes hot water pipes and storage cylinders the most obvious candidates for insulation – and if you're elderly or on a low income, you'll almost certainly get a grant from the council.

PAYBACK TIMES

Be warned: it may take some time to recoup your investment. The table below shows roughly how long.

Hot water cylinder/pipes	1 year
Loft floor	1–2 years
Radiator foil	1–2 years
Draughtproofing	2–3 years
Flat roof	2–4 years
Floor	3–5 years
Wall cavity	5 years
Window	5+ years
Solid wall	10+ years

Methods of insulation

Use tubular foam insulation for pipes and a British-Standards-approved jacket for the hot water cylinder. Glass fibre blanket roll is still the most popular choice for insulating loft floors, but it must be handled with care – wear overalls, a mask, and gloves. For insulating between roof rafters and in between ground-floor joists, you'll probably find it more convenient to cut slabs of expanded polystyrene to a tight fit. Rest floor insulation on battens, pin or staple a polythene sheet over rafter insulation, then, ideally, nail sheets of thermal board over the rafters. Exterior insulation and its associated damp-proofing is best left to the professionals.

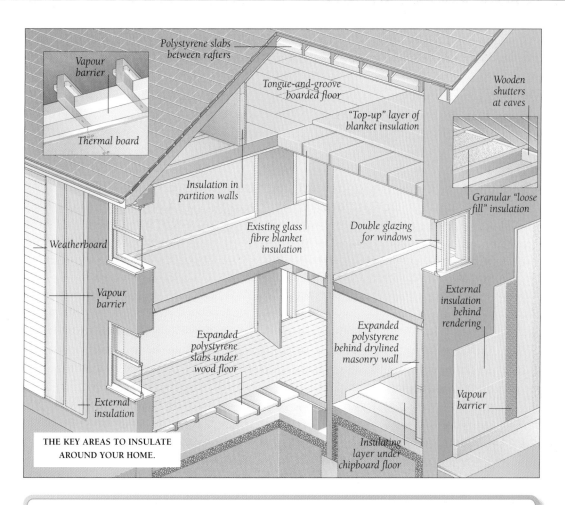

Vapour barrier

Thermal board

Polystyrene slabs between rafters

Tongue-and-groove boarded floor

"Top-up" layer of blanket insulation

Wooden shutters at eaves

Insulation in partition walls

Weatherboard

Existing glass fibre blanket insulation

Double glazing for windows

Granular "loose fill" insulation

Vapour barrier

External insulation behind rendering

Expanded polystyrene slabs under wood floor

Expanded polystyrene behind drylined masonry wall

External insulation

Vapour barrier

Insulating layer under chipboard floor

THE KEY AREAS TO INSULATE AROUND YOUR HOME.

INSULATING PIPES

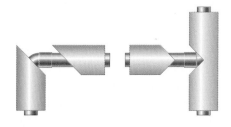

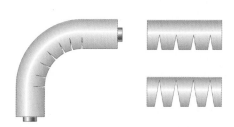

1 **Insulating joined pipes**

Mitre the ends of foam pipe insulation to cover a 90° bend. Cut matching V-shapes for a T-joint. Tape or cement all joints and tape the edges.

2 **Insulating bent pipes**

Make V-shaped cuts in the slit side of foam pipe insulation to fit around bends. Gauge the spacing of the cuts to suit the bend radius.

Ventilation and condensation

WARM, WELL-INSULATED ROOMS are all well and good, but without adequate ventilation you could find yourself with condensation problems. If not tackled quickly, these can lead to damp and mould growth.

Damp-busting

When air is warm, it absorbs moisture until it reaches saturation point, or comes into contact with a colder surface. At this point, the moisture is released, causing condensation. A flow-through of air will deal with the first cause of condensation, so open windows regularly to "clear the air". Dealing with the second rests on providing adequate heating and insulation. The most vulnerable areas are those in which there is a dramatic temperature difference between the outside and inside.

Ventilation is critically important in rooms housing conventionally flued boilers or gas fires, both of which need a constant flow of fresh air in order to burn. Make sure that installed vents in doors and windows are functioning, and open the room door if you turn on the extractor fan.

■ **The illustration shows the places** *most at risk from condensation. An insulated roof space is particularly vulnerable due to the temperature difference, so make sure it is well ventilated.*

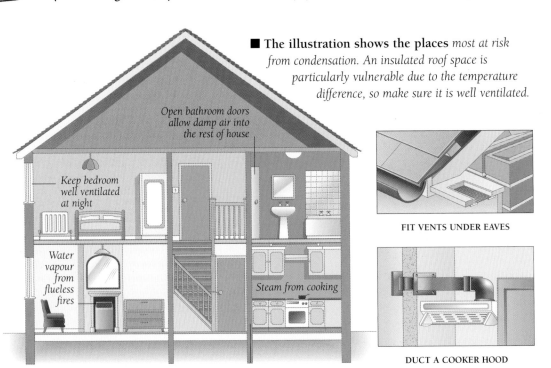

Open bathroom doors allow damp air into the rest of house

Keep bedroom well ventilated at night

Water vapour from flueless fires

Steam from cooking

FIT VENTS UNDER EAVES

DUCT A COOKER HOOD

Preventing condensation

A combination of warm surfaces and frequent air changes should provide the answer.

■ **Expanded polystyrene tiles** *on the ceiling help stop damp from meeting a cold wall.*

■ **Insulating lining** *keeps walls warm. Paste the wall first, then hang the lining.*

■ **Extractor fans** *remove damp air from rooms. The fan output should match the type of room: 215 cubic metres per hour for a kitchen; and 55 cubic metres per hour for a bathroom.*

■ **A de-humidifier** *extracts water from the air. It collects the water in a reservoir or the water can be fed out via a pipe through the wall.*

■ **Anti-condensation paint** *is ideal for use in bathrooms and kitchens. It contains insulating particles and is applied directly to the walls.*

■ **Polythene vapour barrier** *will prevent water vapour from penetrating ceilings and saturating the insulation. Staple to joists through pieces of card.*

Fires, stoves, and gas fires

EVEN IF YOU DON'T PLAN TO INSTALL A FIRE, *it still makes sense to have a basic understanding of how fires and flues work.*

The importance of flues

All domestic fires and boilers have two basic requirements: air to keep them alight and a means of expelling smoke and fumes. A chimney is the traditional way to satisfy both needs. The flue carries smoke out of the house, while at the same time creating an updraught that draws fresh air to the fire. If you plan to install a new fire in an old fireplace, never assume that the flue will be in full working order and free from blockages. Failure to have the flue cleaned regularly will also adversely affect the draw, causing fumes to spill back into the room. And make sure that there is adequate ventilation, if necessary by installing door and window vents.

■ **Open fires** *are not especially efficient or easy to clean, but there's no more welcoming sight on a cold winter's night.*

Although gas and oil fires will work perfectly well with a conventional flue, most modern types are designed to work in conjunction with a balanced flue that expels fumes through a duct in an outside wall, while at the same time drawing in fresh air. This gives you more freedom with positioning.

Never have a gas appliance fitted and serviced by anyone other than a CORGI registered engineer (Confederation for the Registration of Gas Installers). It is illegal for anyone else to receive payment for work carried out on gas systems and appliances.

Assessing the options

As you examine the alternatives in the heating department there are a number of considerations that that should not be ignored.

● **A wood-burning stove** is one of the most economical and effective ways of heating a room. It warms both through convection and radiation, and loses less heat through the chimney than a conventional open fire.

● **Gas and oil fires** may need additional ventilation if they use a chimney flue. Old asbestos or steel external flues are vulnerable to back-draughts and are best replaced with a modern balanced type. Employ a carbon monoxide gas detector if you suspect that fumes are blowing back into the room.

● **Open fires** look great but aren't very efficient: more than half of the heat generated is lost up the chimney.

■ **A gas or oil fire** *can be fitted with a balanced flue on any outside wall.*

■ **A wood-burning stove** *can't be used with an old steel chimney flue lining; have the lining removed.*

■ **An open fire** *simply requires the chimney flue to be free from blockages and leaks.*

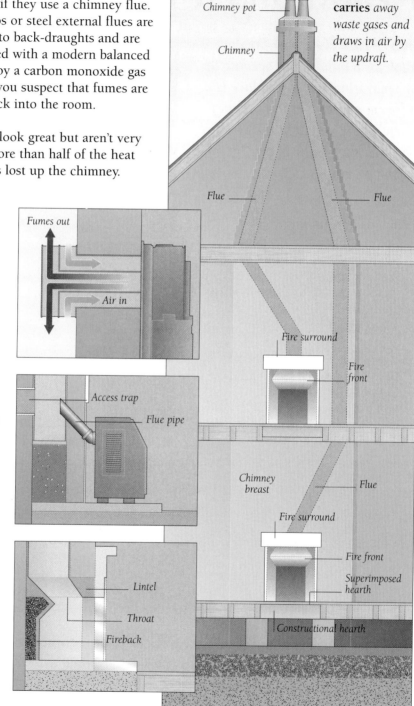

■ **The flue carries** *away waste gases and draws in air by the updraft.*

Chimney pot

Chimney

Flue — Flue

Fumes out

Air in

Access trap

Flue pipe

Fire surround

Fire front

Chimney breast — Flue

Fire surround

Fire front

Superimposed hearth

Constructional hearth

Lintel

Throat

Fireback

Replacing a fire surround

A NEW FIRE SURROUND adds the finishing touch to a restored fireplace. Alternatively, you may simply want to change the existing surround to fit in with a new decorative scheme.

Out with the old

Old cast-iron fire surrounds can be very heavy, so enlist help before attempting to remove one. The surround will be screwed to the wall through fixing lugs buried in the plaster. Expose the lugs by chopping away the plaster right around the surround, then lever the surround away from the wall with a crowbar. Timber and plaster surrounds may also be fixed with additional concealed battens, but can be removed in the same way.

Brick and stone surrounds can simply be demolished; chop through any metal wall ties securing the surround to the masonry behind. If the removal process causes a lot of damage to the chimney breast, you may need to render the wall with repair mortar before proceeding. Also check that the hearth and fireback are in good condition, and make any necessary repairs.

Hire an angle grinder to cut around the edge of a recessed fire surround. This will make the surround easier to remove from the wall and should cause minimal damage to the surrounding plasterwork.

Fitting a new surround

A surround kit provides the easiest route to restoring the outside of your fireplace.

1 **Lay the new hearth**

Some surround kits come with a hearthslab. Bed this on mortar on the concrete sub-hearth.

2 **Fit the inset**

Fit asbestos-substitute rope between the tiled inset and the fireback, and screw to the wall.

3 **Fit the surround**

Assemble the surround on the floor and lift into position. Screw it to the wall, then make good.

In with the new

Modern timber surrounds tend to be sold in kit form. You simply glue and screw the parts together, then fix to the wall on support battens. Brick and stone surrounds are also sold as kits, often with the parts numbered to aid construction, and are easily customized to fit a particular space. A traditional cast-iron surround is simply screwed to the wall through its fixing lugs.

After fitting, fill any gaps between the surround, the fireplace, and the surrounding masonry with fire cement, which is heat-resistant to prevent cracking, then repair the plasterwork and wallcoverings.

■ **Fireplaces with tiled insets** *often have a brass trim to cover the gap between the inset and the fireback.*

A simple summary

✔ Insulating your house properly will save you money in the long run. Insulating your loft floor will pay you back in 1–2 years. Lagging your hot water cylinder and pipes should pay you back within a year.

✔ When attempting to keep the heat in and the cold out, don't forget that your home also needs to be adequately ventilated. Open fires and fires or boilers with a conventional flue need a steady flow of fresh air.

✔ Make sure that you have the flue professionally swept and inspected before you reinstate or fit a new fire in an old fireplace.

✔ Many older fireplaces used asbestos in their construction. Always wear a mask and gloves when opening one up.

✔ Replacing a fire surround can transform a room and will add the finishing touch to a fireplace you have just restored.

PART
FOUR

Chapter 16

Fences and Gates

FENCES, GATES, AND DECKING all have to take the worst that the weather – and the family – can throw at them. No wonder they develop faults! In this chapter, I'll show you how to put up a fence that will last the course, and how to make repairs to existing timber structures.

In this chapter...

✓ Erecting a fence

✓ Repairing fences and gates

✓ Repairing decks

Erecting a fence

PUTTING UP A FENCE is the quickest and least expensive way to mark a boundary. Fences come in all shapes and sizes, but all of them are erected in broadly the same way.

The basic choices

If security and privacy are your main concerns, the choice is between a woven panel or some form of close-boarded fence. But for simply marking a boundary, remember that open fencing will be more stable in high winds and won't need as much maintenance.

Preparing the site

Begin by clearing all obstacles, including rubble, old fence posts, tree roots, any plants, and paving. Level off the ground, then run a string line to mark the line of the fence and place pegs where the posts are to go. There are no hard and fast rules on spacing: on a panel fence, the width of the panels will determine how many posts you need; otherwise space them at a minimum of 2 metre intervals.

If the site is sloping, the height of the fence will have to be staggered to match. This is relatively easy to arrange for open fencing, but for a panel or close-boarded fence, you may prefer to level the site in terraces so that the

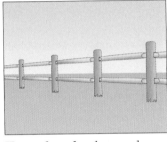

■ **Ranch style:** *cheap and easy to erect and maintain. Rails can be nailed or jointed to posts.*

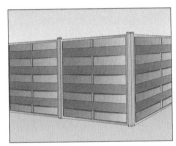

■ **Woven panel:** *good for privacy in sheltered areas. Panels are often available prefabricated.*

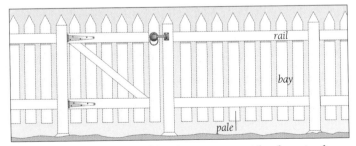

■ **Picket fence:** *easy to build and attractive, a picket fence is often the first choice for the front of a property. Pales can be pointed or curved and are generally spaced 25–50mm apart.*

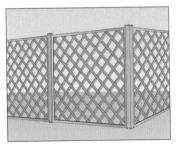

■ **Lattice fence:** *can be built from scratch or from panels. More stable in high winds.*

boards are all the same height within a bay. If the fence has to run across a slope, cut back the ground a minimum of 300mm beyond the higher side.

Setting the posts

Set the posts in the ground, reinforced with hardcore (rubble used as a foundation) and concrete, or in spiked metal sockets (see below). A hired post-hole borer will make digging the post holes easier. Brace the posts with timber battens nailed to wooden pegs in the ground and leave for 24 hours until the concrete has set. Main posts are the corner and gateposts; between are line posts. The space between two posts is called a bay.

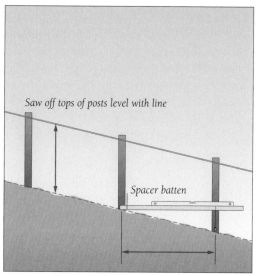

Saw off tops of posts level with line

Spacer batten

■ **On a sloping site**, *use a spirit level and straightedge to ensure the posts are parallel to one another, and use a string line to mark their heights.*

SETTING POSTS IN METAL SPIKES

Setting fence posts in hardcore and concrete is economical, but it is also hard work unless the ground is exceptionally soft, in which case you have no choice. Otherwise use spiked sockets as shown here. Matching bolt-down sockets are available for continuing the fence across a stretch of concrete.

1 **Driving in**

Set the spike vertical with a spirit level, then insert the drift and hammer into the ground.

2 **Locating the post**

Soak the cut end of the post in preservative, position in the socket, and recheck it's plumb.

3 **Fit post**

In this system, the posts push-fit into the sockets, which also hold the gravel board brackets.

Putting up the fence

It's usually easier to build a fence one bay at a time, starting with the first two posts, then the rails or panel brackets, and then the panel itself. But if you're setting the posts in concrete, set them all at the same time using a string line and spacer batten as a guide and double-check that the post spacings match the length of the panels or rails. Screw a post adjoining a wall to the wall itself, using expandable wall anchors.

Most types of fence panel are held on brackets screwed to the insides of the posts. If you have to cut a woven fence panel down to size, simply prise off the end-fixing battens and saw through the panelling, then replace the battens. When the fence is complete, nail fence caps to the posts to finish them.

On a home-made fence, secure the rails in mortises in the posts. Mark the positions of the rail ends, then drill out the mortises with an equivalent sized drill bit and tidy up the edges with a chisel. Secure the joints with a single galvanized nail.

Avoid making cuts in fence timber where at all possible, as this increases its vulnerability to rot. Where you do have to saw components to length or chisel mortises in fence posts, soak the cut areas in preservative before assembly.

Trivia...

In 1874 Joseph Glidden patented barbed wire, and almost overnight the character of the American Great Plains was transformed. As the open range became fenced in, the cattle drive became a thing of the past – an event later lamented in Cole Porter's song "Don't Fence Me In".

ERECTING A PREFABRICATED PANEL FENCE

1 **Set the first post**

Drive in a metal socket for the first post using the tool supplied or an offcut. Check it goes in straight.

2 **Secure post**

On this system, the post is secured by tightening the clamp bolts on the socket itself.

3 **Set second post**

Space the second post to the exact length of a panel and check that it, too, is straight.

MAKING AND FITTING A GATE

Many fence systems include ready-made gates, but for a home-made picket or close-boarded fence, it's easy to make your own using offcuts of rail and pale timber. Make up a square frame to the size of the opening, using pinned mortise and tenon joints to hold the timber together. Nail on the pales or boards, then prop the gate in the opening and adjust the frame until it fits. Remove the gate, being careful not to disturb the set of the frame, and cut a piece of timber to fit as a diagonal brace across it. Screw or nail the brace in position, then hang the gate.

1 **Test-fit gate**

Prop the gate in the opening to adjust the fit. Mark the hinge positions at the same time.

2 **Add a brace**

Mark the timber for the brace directly against the gate, saw to shape, and fix in place.

3 **Recheck the fit**

Double-check the fit of the gate in the opening before cutting in and fitting the hinges.

4 **Mark bracket positions**

Prop the panel between the posts and mark the bracket positions with a pencil.

5 **Fit panel brackets**

On this system, the brackets come with self-tapping screws that allow you to screw them straight in.

6 **Fit panel**

Prop the panel back in place, double-check that it is level, then screw it to the brackets.

Repairing fences and gates

FENCES AND GATES ARE MORE EXPOSED *to the elements than most outdoor structures. Damaged rails or boards, loose or rotten posts, and gates that sag are all-too-familiar headaches for fence-owners.*

Stopping the rot

The buried part of timber fence posts, the joints between posts and rails, and the gravel boards fitted along the base of close-boarded fences are all especially vulnerable to rot and insect attack. Below are some typical problems and the best course of action:

● **Rotten fence posts:** these should be replaced if at all possible, but if this looks likely to disrupt the structure of the fence, you can fit a concrete spur instead.

● **Rotten boards and panels:** not worth patching; your time will be better spent scouring local timber merchants for a replacement, or making up a new board from impregnated timber.

● **Rotten rails:** these are more of a problem. Avoid having to make a wholesale replacement by fitting galvanized brackets, which can be used to strengthen a section of rail or the mortise joint at the post. Special brackets are available for repairing the triangular arris rails often found on close-boarded fences. Gravel boards are designed to rot before the rest of the fence, so be sure to replace them before the rot spreads.

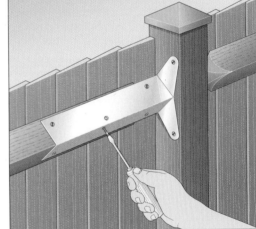

■ **Mending a damaged arris rail:** *special galvanized brackets are available for mending damaged sections of arris rail. Secure with galvanized screws.*

Wooden post caps are there for a reason – to stop the tops of fence posts from rotting. So be sure to replace a cap that's rotten or has been knocked off; it's a lot easier than replacing the post.

Leaning posts and loose rails

If a post is leaning, but otherwise sound, dig a hole around the base about 200mm wide and deep. Use a spirit level to ensure the post is upright, then secure it with three

REPAIRING A ROTTEN POST

  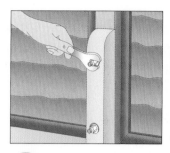

1 Dig hole for spur

You can hire a post-hole borer or simply use a spade to bore or dig the hole for the spur.

2 Position spur

Drop the spur into position and mark fixing holes through to the post.

3 Bolt to post

Fasten the spur to the post with galvanized bolts, washers, and nuts.

bracing battens nailed to the top of the post and to stakes driven in the ground. Pack the hole with about one-third hardcore and two-thirds repair concrete.

To secure a loose rail, make up some small wooden wedges and soak them in preservative. When they are completely dry, glue the wedges and drive them into the mortise and tenon joint with the post until the rail holds firm.

Repairing timber gates

Curing a dropped gate is often simply a matter of replacing the hinges, but if the gate itself is sagging, you should be able to brace it (see right). Check that the gate is square by measuring the diagonals (which should be equal). Wedge or reglue any loose joints at the same time.

If one of the gateposts is loose, cut a matching bracing post from impregnated timber. Dig a hole 600 x 600mm and fill it two-thirds with hardcore and one third with repair concrete. Embed the matching bracing post against the existing post in this hole. Fasten the bracing post to the loose post with carriage bolts.

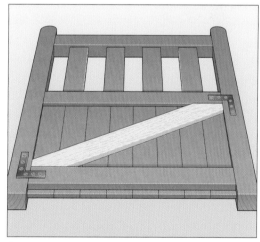

■ **Bracing a dropped gate:** *square up the gate and fit a diagonal brace running upwards from the hinge side. Reinforce the joints further with L-shaped brackets.*

Repairing decks

DECKS, LIKE OTHER OUTDOOR STRUCTURES, *will last for years if properly maintained. But if the deck has been neglected, you may find yourself having to patch rotten boards or structural members.*

Deck maintenance schedule

1 Clean the deck once a month. Clear out the gaps between boards with an old knife to prevent wet dirt from becoming lodged there, then hose down.

2 Smooth roughened timber with medium-grade glasspaper; use a power sander for large areas. Spot-seal the sanded areas with primer or preservative woodstain, then refinish the whole area.

3 Replace a damaged board by cutting out the damaged section of a long board over joists – to span at least three joists – or by replacing the entire length of a short board. Treat the new board before fixing, and use rust-proof screws (two per joist).

4 Refasten loose boards by removing the old fixings, clamping the board to the joist, and fitting new rustproof screws.

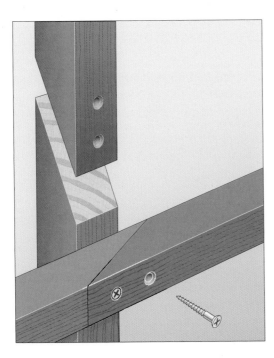

5 Treat rotten timber using preservative pellets and liquid wood hardener (see p. 158). Patch non-structural timbers using diagonal scarf joints (see left), and replace rotten structural timbers. If replacing a joist or beam, temporarily support the structure with props, spreading the load with stout (100 x 50mm) wood.

6 Brace flexing posts with Y- or X-shaped angle braces bolted to the posts and to each other to form a rigid framework.

■ **Repair non-structural timber** *using a scarf joint, angling the joint so that the exposed face slopes downwards to prevent rainwater from running into it. Secure the joint with waterproof adhesive and rust-proof screws or bolts.*

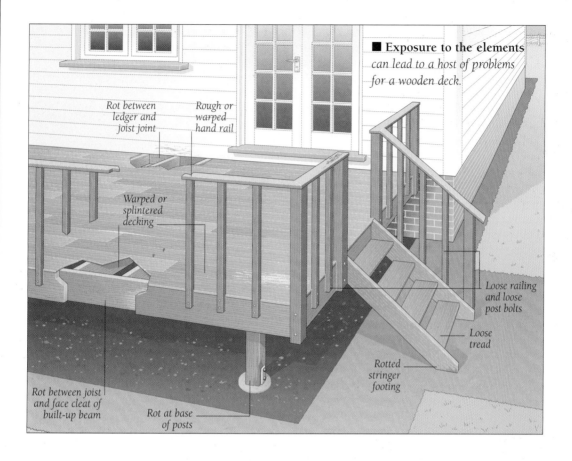

Rot between
ledger and
joist joint

Rough or
warped
hand rail

■ Exposure to the elements
*can lead to a host of problems
for a wooden deck.*

Warped or
splintered
decking

Loose railing
and loose
post bolts

Loose
tread

Rotted
stringer
footing

Rot between joist
and face cleat of
built-up beam

Rot at base
of posts

A simple summary

✔ Fences are the quickest and cheapest way to establish a boundary. Basically, your choice is between a home-made fence or a system sold complete with prefabricated panels.

✔ Use a post-hole borer or spiked metal sockets to take the hard work out of setting fence posts.

✔ You can buy metal reinforcing brackets and concrete support spurs for making repairs to an existing fence without disturbing the structure.

✔ Clean and inspect a deck once a month and treat any rotten timber with preservative pellets at the first sign of trouble.

Chapter 17

Paths and Patios

WHEN IT COMES TO CREATING THE RIGHT IMPRESSION, few outdoor improvements have as much impact as a paved path or driveway. And at the back of the house, you can use the same techniques to extend your living space by bringing the "inside out" with a paved patio or sundeck. In all cases, careful planning is the key to avoiding wastage and future drainage problems.

In this chapter...

✓ Repairs to paved areas

✓ Planning a patio

✓ Laying paving

✓ Laying concrete

✓ Building a deck

A PAVED AREA: PERFECT FOR A SMALL GARDEN

Repairs to paved areas

CONCRETED AREAS AND PAVING SLABS *suffer a lot of wear and tear. If you don't want to go to the trouble of resurfacing them, then it will pay you to catch repairs early.*

Replacing a broken slab

Replace a broken slab as quickly as possible to avoid accidents. Lever out the old one using a wrecking bar held against a lump of wood. If the old slab was bedded in mortar, dig out out the old mortar bedding, level the site, and bed the new slab on dabs of repair mortar. If the old slab is bedded in sand, throw in a few more handfuls of sand and level it out before slotting in the replacement.

If you can't find a replacement slab or paver, "borrow" one from a less obtrusive area, taking care not to damage it as you lift it. Fit a new paver in its place, or simply patch with concrete.

REPAIRING SURFACE DAMAGE

Use ready-mixed repair mortar to patch concrete, adding a little PVA adhesive to the mixing water to help the mortar adhere. Likewise, coat the crack or hole with neat PVA before you fill it. Even this won't help the patch to stick unless the mortar has sufficient bulk, so enlarge very narrow cracks or shallow holes first.

1 **Prepare the crack**

Use a club hammer and cold chisel to open out a narrow crack for filling. If you can undercut the edges of the crack, so much the better.

2 **Level the repair**

Open out holes to help the repair adhere, coat with PVA adhesive, then patch with mortar. Use a batten to level it with its surroundings.

REPAIRING ASPHALT

Holes in asphalt are often the result of slippage or subsidence in the underlying surface. You can usually stabilize this to prevent future damage by clearing out the hole and filling it with repair concrete, before resurfacing the hole with a mixture of cold asphalt and stone chippings.

1 **Stabilize the hole**

Brush out the loose asphalt and excavate the hole back to a stable surface. Coat with PVA adhesive, then part-fill with repair concrete.

2 **Refill with asphalt**

Mix the cold asphalt in a bucket with the stone chippings and pour into the hole. Tamp down firmly with the end of a wooden beam.

Stains and algae

Tackle oil and petrol stains at once – a long-standing oil stain will be that much harder to remove and may dissolve an asphalt surface. Cover the spill with sand or sawdust and remove as much of the residue as you can. Then apply a degreasing agent with a stiff brush and flush with water.

Get rid of slippery green algae quickly for safety's sake. Algae often takes hold on hard surfaces that are permanently in the shade. Pour a solution of fungicidal concrete cleaner and water over the affected area and brush well in.

■ **To mend a cracked edge,** *prop or peg a timber batten against the damaged area to act as a former. Clear out any loose debris, coat the damaged area with PVA adhesive, then patch with repair concrete in the usual way.*

Planning a patio

CAREFUL PLANNING *is the key to creating a paved area. Think carefully about what the area will be used for, how you're going to deal with obstructions, and how the paving will be drained of surface water.*

Choosing a hard surface

Appearance, cost, and durability are all important factors when choosing a hard surface. Concrete is inexpensive, versatile, and strong enough to take the weight of vehicles (if laid to a depth of 100mm or more), but loses out in the looks department. Asphalt and gravel are a cheap alternative for driveways, but need regular maintenance. Next up the scale are engineering bricks, shaped pavers, and concrete or reconstituted stone paving slabs, all of which can simply be bedded on sand if the ground is reasonably stable – if not, cover the site with hardcore to a depth of 50mm and bed the slabs or pavers on strips of mortar. At the luxury end of the market are natural stone slabs, to which the same considerations apply. Most suppliers also offer a range of matched edging pieces.

THREE TECHNIQUES FOR SETTING OUT

Set out an area to be paved with string and wooden pegs, and use them as a guide when excavating.

a **Pegs and string**

Mark out a paved area or concrete slab with wooden pegs and string lines. Hold a spirit level and straightedge between pegs to check for high spots.

b **Sprinkle with sand**

If the lines get in your way when you come to lift turf or excavate the topsoil, sprinkle sand along them to act as a guide, then remove the lines.

c **Use a beam compass**

To set out a curve, drive a large nail through a length of batten to match the curve's radius, then use this device to score the line of the curve in the ground.

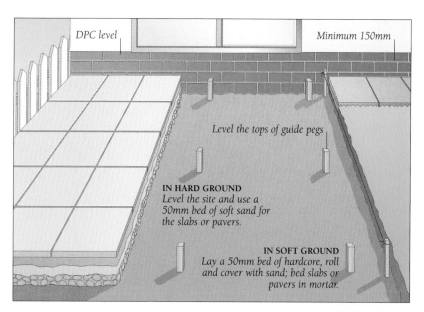

■ A paved area *will probably need excavating to keep it clear of the house's damp-proof course (DPC). Use wooden pegs, levelled with a spirit level and wooden straightedge, to gauge the depth of the excavation and to provide a slight slope.*

DPC level

Minimum 150mm

Level the tops of guide pegs

IN HARD GROUND
Level the site and use a 50mm bed of soft sand for the slabs or pavers.

IN SOFT GROUND
Lay a 50mm bed of hardcore, roll and cover with sand; bed slabs or pavers in mortar.

Planning considerations

Unless the site is small and square, draw a scale plan on 5mm graph paper (make each square represent 250mm) to help you estimate quantities.

1 If the paved area is against a house wall, make sure it is at least 150mm below the level of the damp-proof course (i.e., the door frame). This may mean excavating. The paving should slope away from the house to promote water run-off – a fall of about 20mm per metre is sufficient.

2 Manhole covers will need to have their frames built up to the height of the paving. If the cover is very old, replace it with a modern flush-fitting type. These have recessed covers that can be paved or concreted over.

3 Terrace a steeply sloping site with "steps" of concrete. Excavate and cast the steps one at a time, starting at the top of the slope, and allow 2–3 days for drying before moving on to the next one.

4 Minimize cutting, both by your choice of paving material and by the way you deal with obstacles. Leave trees and borders unpaved, if possible allowing sufficient space for you to pave around them with whole slabs or pavers.

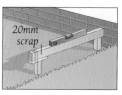

20mm scrap

■ Add a slope *by fixing a scrap of wood to your straightedge.*

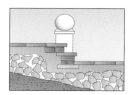

■ Level a sloping *site by terracing it with steps of concrete.*

■ Minimize cutting *when planning spaces around obstructions.*

237

Laying paving

LAYING PAVERS OR PAVING SLABS *on a bed of sand isn't difficult, but you can make the job a lot less hard work by hiring a plate vibrator to compact the sand bed and a block splitter for cutting tiles.*

It takes two

Providing the site is level – and you don't lose your way with the pattern – it's hard to go wrong laying paving on a sand bed. Even so, the job is a whole lot easier if you have a helper. Your chief consideration is how to deal with the edges. One option, especially if the pavers are small, is to fit concrete edging blocks on a bed of mortar. Otherwise, fit battens around the edges of the paved area supported on wooden pegs and use these as a guide to levelling the sand bed. Pour the sand, rake it out, and compact it with the plate vibrator. Then use a heavy timber beam to level the sand against the edging blocks or boards and you're ready to lay the pavers. Level the pavers a square metre at a time, adding sand if one sits too low, or tapping with a block of wood if the paver stands proud of those around it.

BASKETWEAVE

SQUARE HERRINGBONE

INTERLOCKING

Pavers should sit a minimum 150mm below house damp-proof course

Large slabs can be edged with bricks or edging slabs, or else left unedged

Bed of sand

Hardcore foundation

■ **Firm foundations** *are essential for stable paving. Block pavers (inset) must be contained by an edging bedded in mortar.*

PAVING A DRIVEWAY

1 Level the sand bed

Line the edges of the site with boards and use these as a guide to levelling the bed of soft sand.

2 Lay the whole pavers

Lay the whole pavers according to your chosen pattern. Kneel on a board to spread your weight.

3 Alternate the pattern

Alternate patterns in "panels" if you wish. Use a batten as a guide, working from the edges.

4 Deal with obstacles

Obstacles such as manhole covers need to have their frames reset level with the new surface.

5 Cut pavers to fit

A hired block splitter will make short work of any pavers that need to be cut to fit.

6 Compact and fill

After laying the pavers, brush sand into the joints and compact them with a plate vibrator.

Laying concrete

A CONCRETE SLAB *is a quick, effective way to provide a hard base, and you can use the same techniques for other areas, too. For a path or patio, make the slab 75mm thick; on a driveway or foundation, increase this to 100mm.*

Preparing the site

Mark out the site with pegs and string. Make a foundation slab 100mm larger all round than whatever is to sit on top. Excavate the site to the proposed depth, allowing an extra 100mm for a layer of hardcore, and level out. Lay down the hardcore, compact it with a plate vibrator or garden roller, then line the hole with timber boards to match the slab thickness. Hold the boards in place by nailing them to wooden pegs.

Use a strong concrete mix of 1 part cement to 2½ parts sand to 4 parts gravel. This way, 1 cubic metre of concrete needs six 50kg bags of cement, ⅓ cubic metre of sand, and ½ cubic metre of aggregate.

CONCRETE PATHS

On a straight path, excavate and level the site, and mark it out with wooden pegs. Check with a spirit level that the tops of the pegs are all the same height, then erect timber formwork boards between them. The width of the boards should match the combined depth of the concrete and hardcore (normally 175mm). After you've poured the concrete, the boards can be used to level it.

If the path curves (inset), drive in extra pegs to mark the line. Then part-saw through the formwork boards at 25mm intervals so that they bend easily, and fasten them to the pegs.

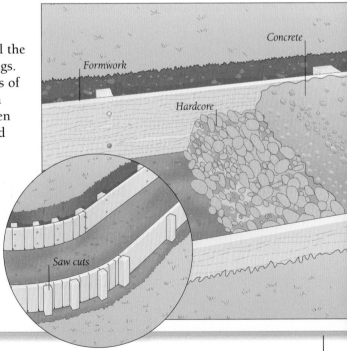

Concrete

Formwork

Hardcore

Saw cuts

Pouring the concrete

If you're concreting a large area, position 10mm thick softwood boards across the site at 3 metre intervals. These will be removed later to form expansion gaps that will stop the concrete from cracking or buckling. If the slab is against a house wall, position a strip of 10mm thick fibreboard along the junction to form an expansion gap here, too.

Mix the concrete with just enough water to bind the dry ingredients. If you are working on a large area, it's almost certainly worth hiring an electric mixer. Tip the mix into the excavated area, taking care not to disturb the formwork. Spread and level the wet concrete with a shovel or rake, ensuring that all corners and gaps are completely filled. Then use a timber beam to compact the concrete, and chop it off level with the top of the formwork boards. Cover the slab with weighted-down sheets of polythene and leave to cure for 3–7 days before removing the formwork. Dig out any expansion strips and fill the gaps with sand or repair mortar. In very hot conditions, dampen the slab daily to prevent cracking. Afterwards, backfill around the slab with topsoil.

Finishing the surface

Finish the surface as the concrete dries. In dry conditions you may not have long before it becomes unworkable.

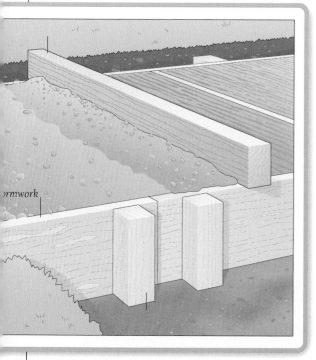

ormwork

a **Fine-textured finish**

Spray the surface with water from a garden spray and smooth with a wooden float or spade.

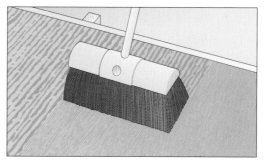

b **Rough finish**

To provide a grippier surface, lightly sweep over the levelled concrete with a stiff broom.

Building a deck

TIMBER DECKING provides a natural transition from an indoor living space to an outdoor recreation area.

Building a deck

First decide whether to rest the deck on the ground, on loose-laid joists, or on a framework of posts criss-crossed by timber joists. Decking more than 450mm above the ground should have a handrail, and you may need to provide steps for access. When selecting timber, choose western redwood or cedar, or softwood that's been pressure-impregnated with preservative. Plot the position of the deck and its support posts (a rectangular deck will need at least six posts). Then dig holes, set the posts, and fill the holes with concrete. Construct the framework by nailing pairs of cross-joists to either side of the corner posts; nail the edges of the joists level with the tops of the posts to ensure that the deck platform will be flat. To stop weeds growing, spread a 20mm-deep layer of chipped bark or pea shingle over the site. Then nail the supporting joists across the cross-joists and attach the planks with screws or nails. Leave a 5–10mm gap between each plank to allow for drainage.

To prevent the decking boards from cupping and bowing, lay them with the bark side uppermost. Look at the end grain: the bark side is on the outside of the curved annual ring lines

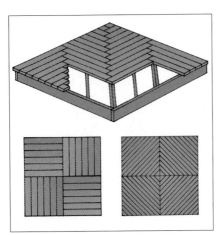

■ **Simple solution:** *prefabricated decking squares are available in a variety of patterns from large DIY stores.*

An easier way

You can also buy prefabricated timber decking panels with wooden slats in ready-made timber frames. Like individual boards, these can be laid over joists resting directly on the ground, or on a framework supported by posts.

The panels tend to look better laid with the slats pointing in alternate directions. Secure the panels to the joists using rust-proof fixings.

INTERNET

www.tda.org.uk

A site packed full of information, design ideas, and product suggestions for constructing timber decking, steps, and handrails. Well worth a visit.

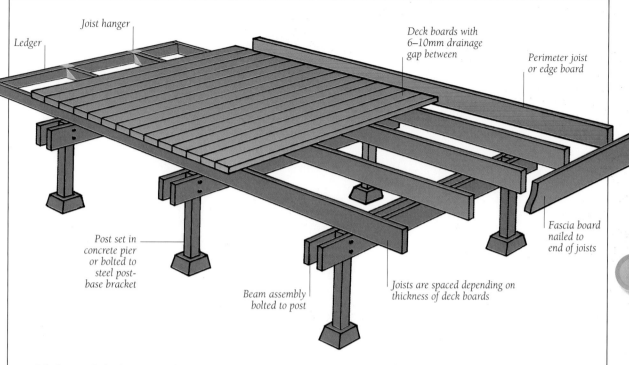

Ledger

Joist hanger

Deck boards with 6–10mm drainage gap between

Perimeter joist or edge board

Post set in concrete pier or bolted to steel post-base bracket

Beam assembly bolted to post

Joists are spaced depending on thickness of deck boards

Fascia board nailed to end of joists

■ **Elevated decking** *must be supported by stout posts on firm footings. Extra rigidity will be achieved by securing one edge to the house wall with masonry anchors. A range of hardware makes assembly straightforward without the need for woodworking joints. Follow the manufacturer's recommendations for joist span.*

A simple summary

✔ Repair a damaged paved or concreted area as soon as possible, to prevent accidents.

✔ Careful planning of a paved area avoids problems during building and saves on materials.

✔ Pavers and slabs can normally be laid on a bed of soft sand and finished with edging blocks.

✔ Concrete is a quick and very economical way to create a hard-standing area. Lay over a bed of hardcore to prevent future problems with subsidence.

✔ A timber deck is a great alternative to a patio, especially if the ground is sloping or uneven. Regularly maintained, it should last for years.

Chapter 18

Walls and Roofs

REGULAR INSPECTIONS OF THE OUTSIDE of your home will show up any minor faults before they turn into major disasters, and as long as you have a head for heights, there's plenty you can do yourself. But take my advice and stop short of a main roof: working safely at a height calls for special equipment and is best left to a professional.

In this chapter...

✔ Gaining access outside

✔ Repairing masonry

✔ Cladding and weatherboards

✔ Repairs to flat roofs

REPAIRS TO LOW ROOFS ARE WITHIN EASY REACH

Gaining access outside

A LADDER IS FINE for making quick inspections, but if you need to carry out any kind of substantial repairs to the outside of the house, you're better off hiring an access tower.

Safely does it

Scaffold towers, complete with clip-on ladders, are easily hired, usually on a free delivery/collection basis. Designs vary in detail, but most have tubular sections that simply slot together, with bolt-on crossbraces between them. Working platforms and toe boards generally consist of short lengths of scaffold board with brackets for attaching to the framework. A tower over 2m high also needs fitting with outriggers to keep it stable. Bear in mind that erecting a tower is a two-person job. Afterwards, lash the tower to any structurally secure part of the house, such as a window mullion or wall bracket – but not a rainwater pipe.

■ **A ladder stay** *is a worthwhile investment if there's nothing to lean a ladder against, or if you have doubts about the soundness of the structure.*

a Putting up an extension ladder

Pull out the extension to the required height, hook it over the rungs, then tilt the ladder towards you as you carry to the wall.

b Positioning the ladder for safety

Pull the ladder out from the wall a minimum of one quarter its total length. Make sure the ladder sits on a firm footing and cannot slip.

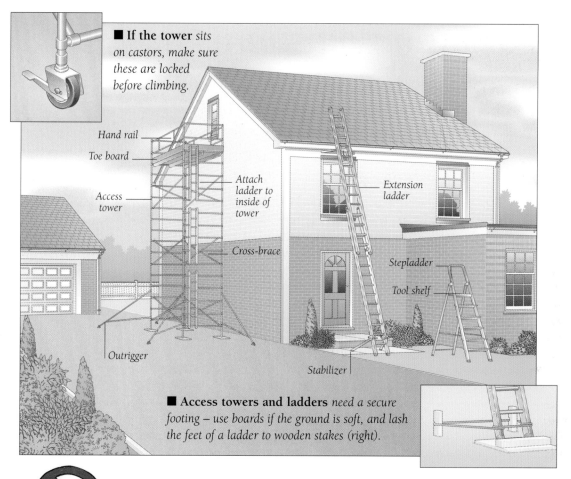

■ **If the tower** *sits on castors, make sure these are locked before climbing.*

Hand rail

Toe board

Access tower

Attach ladder to inside of tower

Cross-brace

Outrigger

Extension ladder

Stepladder

Tool shelf

Stabilizer

■ **Access towers and ladders** *need a secure footing – use boards if the ground is soft, and lash the feet of a ladder to wooden stakes (right).*

My advice about working on a pitched roof is: don't. Even if you have a head for heights, the risks involved in working in such an unfamiliar environment just aren't worth taking. And in any case, hiring the right access equipment will probably cost you more than paying for a yearly inspection by an expert.

Working on flat roofs

Most flat roofs aren't designed to be walked on, so protect the existing surface with a walkway of planks or boards. Even if you can gain access from a window, you'll probably need a ladder as well for passing up materials and passing down debris. In this case, make sure the ladder extends at least five rungs above the line of the roof so that it doesn't accidentally get kicked away – and you can see where to climb onto it.

If you need to use a flat roof as a base for a ladder to reach higher up, sit the ladder on a sturdy piece of board with a batten screwed to it to stop the feet from slipping.

Repairing masonry

MASONRY WALLS *are by no means immune to the effects of weathering, especially pointing and large, flat areas of cement* **render**. *The trick is to make repairs before damp takes hold.*

FLUSH

Repair, then repoint

Old age and excessive exposure can both cause *pointing* to deteriorate, placing brick walls at risk from damp. If the whole house needs repointing, leave the job to a builder. It's often just a localized area that's at fault. Crumbling bricks, loose flashings, and leaking rainwater pipes are some of the most likely culprits. Chimney stacks are also vulnerable. If your house has a flat roof bordered by parapet walls, check the condition of the coping stones used to top the walls: damage here can allow water to seep into the brickwork below.

ROUNDED

DEFINITION

Masonry *includes stonework and brickwork.* **Render** *is a waterproof layer applied in the same way as plaster.* **Pointing** *is the weatherproof joint between bricks.*

Clear out old mortar joints with a cold chisel. Dampen the area before rolling in repair mortar with a pointing trowel. Flush pointing is rubbed smooth with sacking as the mortar dries. Rounded pointing is shaped with an old metal bucket handle or similar tool while still wet. Finish weatherstruck pointing with a trowel held against a timber batten.

WEATHERSTRUCK

Repointing a wall

Repointing protects your home from the elements, and smartens up your house.

1 **Chop out old mortar**

Use a club hammer and cold chisel to clear out the crumbling mortar. Brush clean and dampen.

2 **Apply new mortar**

Use your trowel to roll the repair mortar into a sausage shape, then force it into the joints.

3 **Finish the joints**

Create a weatherstruck joint with the trowel held at an angle, then trim the mortar against a batten.

PATCHING DAMAGED CEMENT RENDER

1 Cut back the damage

Use a club hammer and bolster to hack back the damaged render to a sound edge. Undercut the edges if you can, to help the repair mortar grip.

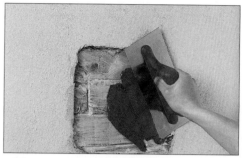

2 Prepare the patch

Chop out damaged pointing and brush off any loose dust, then coat the damaged area with PVA adhesive to provide a key for the repair.

3 Apply repair mortar

Mix up some repair mortar with added PVA adhesive and apply to the patch in thin layers, cross-hatching the surface.

4 Finish surface

Lever the final coat with a batten and then, while it is still wet, texture it with a sponge or throw stone chipping into it.

Damaged render

Cracks in a rendered surface can allow moisture to penetrate between the render and the underlying masonry. If you leave it untreated, the render will eventually "blow" – that is, part company with the wall. You can tell if this has occurred, because a blown area will sound hollow when tapped. You can repair cracks and small blown patches yourself, by hacking back the render to a solid edge – where it is still firmly stuck to the brickwork – and applying repair mortar. But if the damage is extensive, it will only be a matter of time before the entire wall has to be taken back to the masonry and professionally re-rendered.

Cladding and weatherboards

EXTERIOR CLADDING, *whether in the form of tiles, shingles, or timber or plastic boards, is your home's front line of defence against the elements. A little tender loving care on a regular basis will ensure that it stays that way.*

Types of cladding

- **Tiles**: whether clay, natural or synthetic slate, or concrete – are more resistant to fire than timber cladding and require less maintenance. With clay tiles, ornamental and coloured versions are often mixed together to create unique patterns.

- **Wood shingles**: these vary in durability according to what timber they're made of. The best type are made from Western red cedar, which needs virtually no maintenance.

- **Timber weatherboards**: these are fixed so that the lower edge of one board overlaps the top edge of the board below, or else are tongue-and-groove.

- **Synthetic cladding**: generally made from uPVC plastic or glass fibre and resembles painted weatherboards. It is virtually maintenance-free, requiring only the occasional wash-down. However, both timber and plastic cladding need to be fixed with room for the boards to expand and contract, otherwise there is a danger that timber boards will distort and plastic boards will crack.

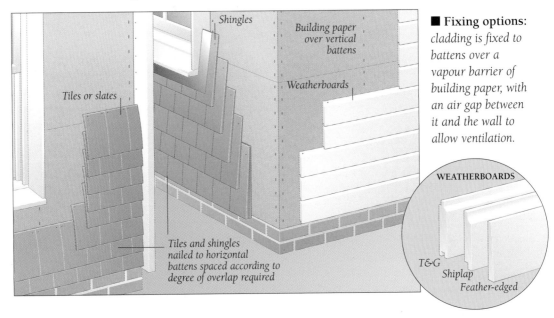

Shingles

Building paper over vertical battens

Tiles or slates

Weatherboards

Tiles and shingles nailed to horizontal battens spaced according to degree of overlap required

■ **Fixing options:** *cladding is fixed to battens over a vapour barrier of building paper, with an air gap between it and the wall to allow ventilation.*

WEATHERBOARDS

T&G
Shiplap
Feather-edged

REPAIRING DAMAGED SHINGLES

As on roofs, shingles are fixed to overlap each other so that the joints are completely weatherproof. When replacing a shingle, hold it in position and mark the cutting line so that the bottom edge will align with its neighbours.

1 **Cut through the fixings**

Split the damaged shingle with a chisel and cut through the nails with a hacksaw blade.

2 **Nail on the replacement**

Slide the new shingle under the ones above and nail it in position in line with adjacent fixings.

REPAIRING DAMAGED WEATHERBOARDS

Replace a damaged section of timber weatherboard with a piece of timber of the same profile. Nail the new section to the underlying battens, whose positions are revealed by the rows of existing nails.

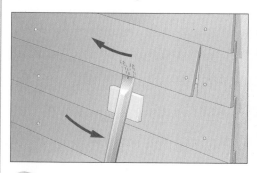

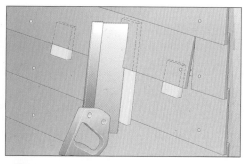

1 **Lever up the board**

Using a crowbar over a protective offcut of timber, prise away the damaged board to loosen its fixings.

2 **Cut and fill**

Wedge the board proud of the surrounding cladding and cut away the damage. Cut and fit a matching piece, and nail to the battens.

Repairs to flat roofs

THERE ARE AS MANY TYPES OF FLAT ROOF *as there are pitched roof, but the ones that cause the most problems are those covered in layers of bitumen felt, often finished with stone chippings. Although you can patch leaks in the felt yourself, it's a strictly short-term solution. A felted roof has a lifespan of around 20–25 years, and when it starts to leak, it's usually time to replace it.*

Dealing with blisters and cracks

Once a felt roof starts to blister, it's only a matter of time before the felt cracks and allows water to seep in through the boards underneath. Inside the house, the leak may appear some distance from the blister, as water will run along the joists until it finds a weak point. The only way to be sure of the extent of the damage is to sweep away the stone chippings and then examine the felt closely. At the same time, check the flashings and rainwater system around the edge of the roof, both of which are more likely sources of trouble.

Blisters are repaired by slitting along them and then applying a patch bedded in "cold" bitumen compound. The materials are generally sold together in kit form. Make sure you treat all suspect areas in one go, then, when the patches are dry, apply a final coat of the compound and redistribute the stone chippings.

PATCHING BLISTERING ROOFING FELT

1 **Slit blister**

Slit along the blister, peel back the edges, and coat with bituminous repair compound.

2 **Nail back flaps**

Nail down the flaps with galvanized clout nails, then apply more repair compound.

3 **Cover with patch**

Bed a patch of new felt over the wet compound, nail the edges, then coat with more compound.

Repairing flashings

Flashings, the waterproof joints between roofs, house walls, and chimney stacks, are a common source of leaks. Metal flashings that are perished should be replaced, but more often the problem is with the mortar joints around them: rake the joints out and repoint, then seal any remaining gaps with bitumen mastic. Felt flashings can often be repaired in the same way as roof felt, but again, check that the mortar joints around them are sound. Mortar flashings are useless: remove them, coat the area with bituminous primer, then apply two or three overlapping strips of self-adhesive flashing.

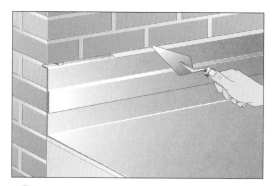

a **Repoint the mortar joints**

The mortar joints are the most vulnerable areas around metal flashing. As long as the metal itself isn't perished, repoint as you would for brickwork.

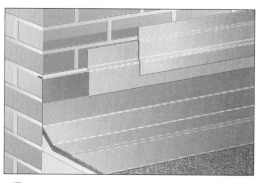

b **Using flashing tape**

Replace mortar flashing with self-adhesive flashing tape. Coat the area with special primer and allow to dry. Apply in overlapping strips and roll flat.

A simple summary

✔ Use a ladder for inspections and minor repairs only. For major repairs, always hire a scaffold tower to give you safe access.

✔ Before repointing mortar joints or patching areas of cracked render, look for any structural faults that may have caused them to deteriorate prematurely.

✔ The big risk with wall cladding is that damp will penetrate behind the boards. Repair any damage as soon as you spot it.

✔ Repairs made to flat felted roofs can only ever be regarded as a stopgap. When felt starts to blister, it's a sign that the roof needs re-covering.

Chapter 19

Gutters and Drainage

FAULTY GUTTERS AND DOWNPIPES are the most common causes of structural damp in homes, usually because they have suffered years of neglect. Inspecting your rainwater system once a year may sound like a chore, but believe me, it's a small price to pay compared with the cost of replacing ruined decorations and rotten structural timber. In this chapter, we'll also look at what to do if the rainwater has nowhere to go and your garden isn't draining properly.

In this chapter...

✓ *Fixing gutters and downpipes*

✓ *Garden drainage*

CLEAN OUT RAINWATER GUTTERS ANNUALLY TO AVOID BLOCKAGES OR SAGGING

Fixing gutters and downpipes

GUTTERS AND DOWNPIPES *need regularly inspecting for debris that could cause blockages or cause the guttering to sag. You'd be amazed how much dirt, crumbling mortar, leaves, and twigs can accumulate in the space of a year.*

Guarding against blockages

Clean out gutters on a regular basis, having first blocked the outlet with a rag to stop debris entering and blocking the downpipe. Afterwards, pour water into the gutter and check for leaking joints and sagging sections. If fallen leaves are a particular problem, it may be worth nailing plastic mesh over the guttering. Wire mesh balls are available to protect the downpipe outlet.

Never place a ladder directly against a rainwater system.

Either lean the ladder against the house wall below the roof line or – better – fit a ladder stay and extend the ladder beyond the roof line so that you have something to hold on to as you work. If you have to replace a section of guttering, hire a scaffold tower rather than risk overbalancing.

CORRECTING SAGS IN GUTTERING

a **Re-align the brackets**

If a large section is sagging, or the bracket fixings are loose, remove the guttering and refit the brackets using a taut string line as a guide.

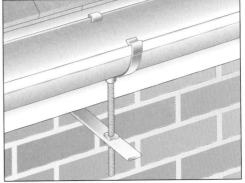

b **Fit a support bracket**

If the problem is confined to a single joint or bracket, you may be able to correct the sag by fitting an adjustable support bracket.

Making repairs

If a gutter or downpipe is leaking, first establish the cause. The weak spots on any rainwater system are the joints between sections. With a cast-iron system, the putty sealing the joint may have perished, or a connecting bolt could be rusted through. If the guttering is plastic, it may be that a seal has perished or dislodged. Plastic guttering can crack, and metal guttering will corrode if not maintained. All downpipes are vulnerable to cracking during a frost if partially blocked.

Make emergency repairs by binding the joint or damaged section with waterproof tape or self-adhesive flashing tape. But bear in mind that these are only stopgap measures.

REPAIRING LEAKING CAST-IRON GUTTERS

a **Seal leaking joints**

You may be able to cure a leaking joint by forcing mastic into it. If not, dismantle the sections and replace the seal, or bed on mastic.

b **Patch holes with epoxy resin**

Patch cracks and rust holes in the gutter with a two-part epoxy resin repair kit, having cut a reinforcing patch to cover the damage.

Repair or replace?

Rainwater systems come in all shapes, sizes, and materials, so if you need to replace a damaged part, your biggest headache is likely to be finding one to match. Take a section of the original guttering with you to your supplier – especially if you need to replace a perished rubber joint seal, which are notoriously prone to leaking unless they are an exact fit. If the worst comes to the worst, remake the joint using a bed of waterproof mastic in place of the old seal. If you have a cast-iron or aluminium system, your top priority is to keep it in good condition and to treat signs of corrosion as soon as they appear. Metal guttering lasts for years if properly maintained.

While you're about it, check the soundness of the gutter's fixing brackets and the fascia board to which it's attached. If there's any sign of rot around the fixings, patch in a new section of board or remove the stretch of gutter and replace the board entirely. Metal downpipes are prone to rot at the back (check with a mirror). The only cure for this is to replace the downpipe or to patch in a plastic section.

Don't bother to repair asbestos-cement guttering, which is still to be found on some older properties. Dismantle the entire system and replace it with a plastic or seamless metal type. Contact your local authority about where to dispose of the old guttering safely.

Replacing gutter and downpipe sections

If you can't find the parts, or a section of the system is damaged, you'll find it easier to replace an entire run. Ask your supplier about conversion pieces for joining the new system to an existing one; the same applies to sections of downpipes. Plastic guttering is easy to remove, but for cast-iron, you'll need a helper. The joints between sections are normally bolted together with putty seals, but you may have to saw through the bolts with a hacksaw. Set the brackets for the new guttering in place using a taut string line. The run should fall towards the downpipe by about 25mm for every 15m of its length.

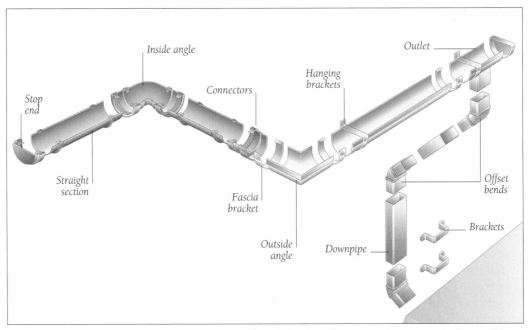

Inside angle

Outlet

Hanging brackets

Connectors

Stop end

Straight section

Fascia bracket

Outside angle

Downpipe

Offset bends

Brackets

■ **A typical rainwater system.** *If you're opting for wholesale replacement, draw a rough sketch of the run and use this diagram to note what parts you need.*

Garden drainage

STOPPING RAINWATER *from damaging your home is only half the battle. It's just as important to ensure that the water drains away properly – that is to say, neither so slowly that it causes the ground to become waterlogged, nor so fast that it leaches nutrients from the soil.*

Improving the soil

Garden drainage is first and foremost an issue of soil type. In clay soils, for example, rainwater tends to collect on the surface rather than drain down into the subsoil. Excessively sandy soils, by contrast, tend to drain too rapidly, depriving plant roots of much-needed moisture and causing the topsoil to dry out. The remedy is to dig in one or more additives over a period of time – anything up to a year – so that you gradually "improve" the soil and change its drainage properties.

■ **Dig in soil improvers** *to a depth of around 300mm and thoroughly mix them with the existing soil. Don't expect instant results: soil improvement can only ever be a gradual process.*

If you're unsure how well your soil drains, try this simple test. Dig a hole about 200mm square by 300mm deep and fill it with water. If the hole drains within 10 to 20 minutes, you've got sandy soil that drains quickly; if it takes more than 8 hours to drain, you have a drainage problem.

Consult a local garden centre to find out what soil improvers are popular in your area, bearing in mind what you plan to plant. Generally speaking, very heavy clay soils benefit from being mixed with well rotted compost or manure to aerate them and break up the particles. But plants such as lavender or succulents thrive in much faster-draining, sandier soils, in which case the soil might also benefit from being dug through with fine sand.

Creating a land drainage system

If your garden is seriously and more or less permanently waterlogged, a land drainage system could be the answer. Here, rainwater is channelled down a network of perforated plastic pipes to a rubble-filled pit called a soakaway (see opposite), where it is dispersed underground. You can use a land drain to tackle just a few square metres of boggy ground, or extend the system over the entire garden. The pipes are laid on a bed of 10mm pea shingle, usually about 750mm below the soil surface. Arrange for a central "spine" pipe to run through the most badly affected area, with branch pipes extending herringbone-fashion on either side at 1.5–2m intervals.

Begin by marking out the pipe runs on the surface using pegs and string. Remove and reserve any turf, then excavate the trenches. The ideal depth is 750mm, but stop before this depth if you reach clay. The trenches should slope very gently – about 25mm per metre – towards the soakaway. Line the base of each trench with pea shingle to a depth of about 50mm and compact it with a heavy piece of timber. Then cut the spine pipes to length with a hacksaw, allowing for open joints wherever they meet a branch pipe. Assemble the branch pipes and lay all the pipes in their trenches. Leave 10mm gaps at the joints, then cover the joints with squares of heavy-duty polythene sheet. Cover the pipes with gravel to a depth of about 50mm, taking care not to disturb their position, then replace the subsoil and topsoil.

Before excavating the trenches, check with your local authority and utility providers that the system won't collide with any pipes or cables already laid beneath the garden.

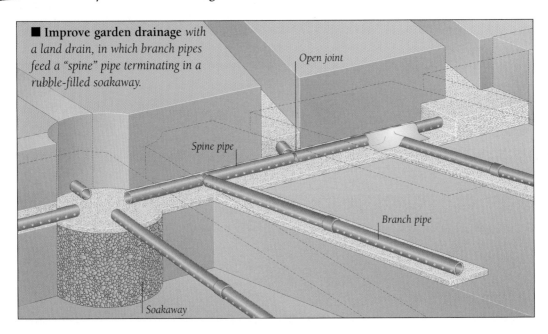

■ **Improve garden drainage** *with a land drain, in which branch pipes feed a "spine" pipe terminating in a rubble-filled soakaway.*

Open joint

Spine pipe

Branch pipe

Soakaway

Building a soakaway

A soakaway is simply a deep pit filled with layers of rubble, pea shingle, heavy-duty polythene sheet, and earth. The rubble gently disperses the water from the land drain below ground, while the polythene stops surface water flooding into the pit from above.

Site the soakaway at one end of the spine pipe, at least 5m away from the house. Make the hole between 1m and 1.5m square, depending on the size of the garden, and excavate it to a depth of roughly 1m below where the spine pipe enters. Fill the hole with loose rubble or hardcore to just below the pipe inlet, then lay a length of spine pipe to extend into the soakaway by about 300mm. Cover the hardcore and pipe with pea shingle, compact it, and lay the polythene over the top. Replace the subsoil, topsoil, and any turf, and the drainage system is complete.

■ **The spine pipes of a** *land drainage system end in the soakaway – a pit filled with hardcore and pea shingle, and covered with subsoil, topsoil and turf.*

A simple summary

✔ Inspect your rainwater system once a year (preferably autumn). Clear out any debris that could cause a blockage and repair any obvious faults.

✔ If you experience difficulty getting parts, or if runs are sagging in more than one place, it may be easier to dismantle the entire system and replace it.

✔ Poor garden drainage often points to a soil problem, especially if the soil contains a high proportion of clay. Dig in soil improvers over a period of time to improve the soil's drainage properties.

✔ Laying a land drain system may be the only cure for a persistently waterlogged garden.

PART FIVE

Chapter 20

Know your Plumbing

TIME SPENT GETTING TO KNOW YOUR HOME'S plumbing system won't be wasted, especially if you learn how and where to turn off the water in an emergency. Faultfinding, too, becomes easier once you know the order in which to approach things. But, as with electrics, if there is something you don't understand, seek professional advice.

In this chapter...

✓ Where the water comes from

✓ Where the water goes

✓ How water gets heated

✓ Where to turn the water off

✓ Hot water troubleshooter

Where the water comes from

UNDERSTANDING HOW WATER *is supplied and distributed around the home is the first – and most important – step towards becoming a confident home plumber.*

The mains point

All the water entering your home comes through a single underground pipe, called the mains, which is controlled by an outside stopcock. The pipe should then run in a straight line, through the foundations, to a main stopcock inside your home, and from there to the cold tap in your kitchen. So far, so good. But from this point on, you will find variations in the way water is supplied to the rest of your home.

In the UK, water is usually distributed by one of two methods: directly from the mains or indirectly via a storage tank. Work out which type of system you have from the diagrams below. The actual layout may vary, but the principles are the same.

If you are unsure whether a tap is fed by the mains or from a storage tank, turn it on and place your thumb over the spout. If the water squirts out around your thumb, even when you apply maximum pressure, then the tap is mains-fed.

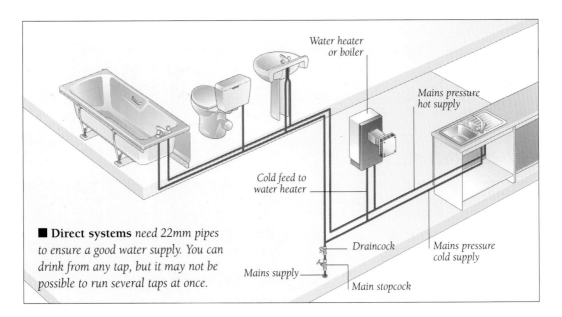

Water heater
or boiler

Mains pressure
hot supply

Cold feed to
water heater

■ **Direct systems** *need 22mm pipes to ensure a good water supply. You can drink from any tap, but it may not be possible to run several taps at once.*

Draincock

Mains pressure
cold supply

Mains supply

Main stopcock

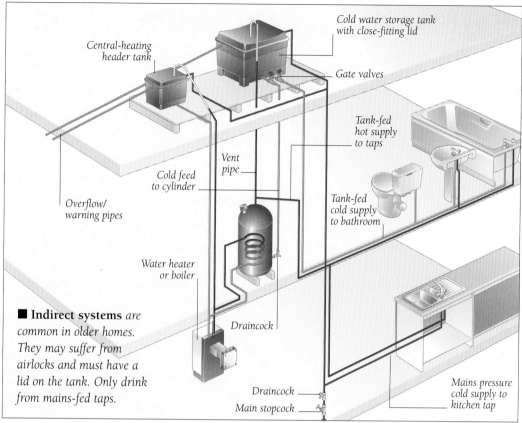

Central-heating header tank

Cold water storage tank with close-fitting lid

Gate valves

Tank-fed hot supply to taps

Vent pipe

Cold feed to cylinder

Tank-fed cold supply to bathroom

Overflow/ warning pipes

Water heater or boiler

Draincock

Draincock

Main stopcock

Mains pressure cold supply to kitchen tap

■ **Indirect systems** *are common in older homes. They may suffer from airlocks and must have a lid on the tank. Only drink from mains-fed taps.*

Direct system

All the cold outlets are supplied directly from branches of the mains pipe. Hot water is supplied via a cylinder or boiler that heats the water as it is fed through. Direct systems are simpler, but the pressure can cause pipes to hammer and lead to premature wear in fittings.

Indirect system

An indirect system uses a cold water storage tank (normally in the loft) to distribute cold water throughout the house. Water is piped into the tank at mains pressure through a float valve that closes when the water level reaches its upper limit. Water leaves the tank at gravity pressure to supply non-drinking cold water outlets and the hot water cylinder. Cold water enters the base of the cylinder, is heated, and rises out of a vented pipe at the top to supply hot taps. The kitchen sink cold tap and any garden taps are fed directly from the mains.

STOPCOCK   GATEVALVE

SERVICE VALVE

■ **Stopcocks** *have a crutch head, washers, and a flow direction arrow. Gatevalves have a wheel head, no washers, and water can flow either way. Service valves have a quarter-turn mechanism.*

Where the water goes

GETTING WATER OUT OF A HOME *is often trickier than getting it in.*
Most drainage systems rely on gravity to move the waste water, and it doesn't
take much to block the flow in a near-horizontal drain or waste pipe.

Tracing drain runs

All drain runs start at a trap, also known as a U-bend, which holds a small amount of water to stop smells from the drains entering the home. This is a brilliantly simple idea, but it does leave the first part of the run prone to blockages.

From the U-bend, the effluent travels via a sloping *waste* pipe or *soil* pipe to a vertical stack or a second U-bend known as a gully. In homes over 40 years old, the upstairs waste pipes often feed to an outside hopper that discharges via its own waste stack into an open gully. Downstairs waste pipes discharge directly into the open gully, and effluent from the toilet is discharged via a separate outside soil stack direct to the drains.

In newer homes, both waste and soil pipes are connected to a single stack, which is often built-in rather than fixed to an outside wall. This stack is vented to stop vacuums from forming and emptying the traps. It should also have access panels known as "rodding eyes" wherever pipes join it, to allow for blockage clearance. If it isn't practical for waste pipes to join the stack, they may be run to an enclosed gully known as a back inlet. Likewise, a downstairs toilet may be connected directly to the drains via a soil pipe and U-bend.

Main drainage

Irrespective of the age of a property, all stacks and gullies discharge into the main drains. In the UK, these are defined

DEFINITION

Plumbers make a distinction between **waste**, *the outflow from a sink, basin, bath, or shower, and* **soil**, *the effluent from a toilet. Historically, the two systems were kept separate until they entered the drains. These days, they are combined at the drainage stack earlier in the run.*

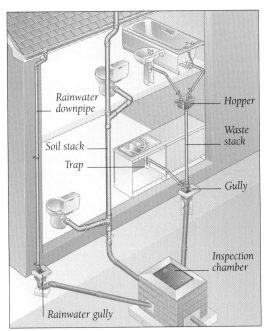

Rainwater downpipe

Soil stack

Trap

Hopper

Waste stack

Gully

Inspection chamber

Rainwater gully

■ **Older two-pipe systems** *with separate waste and soil stacks tend to be easy to unblock, but are vulnerable to frost.*

as the network of pipes feeding the public sewer, and are the homeowner's responsibility. But in some older homes, where the drains are shared between two or more properties, the local authority may have "adopted" the drains as a sewer. This is good news, as it means your drains will be cleared and maintained for free!

Non-mains drainage

In rural areas the drains discharge into a cesspit or septic tank, rather than a sewer. This is like having your own sewage treatment works, and you should receive a discount on your water bills. You can also claim a discount if your rainwater discharges via a soakaway, rather than into the main drains.

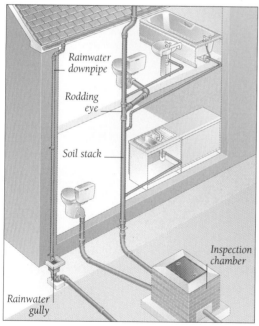

■ Modern single stack *systems often have a separate back inlet gully to handle waste from a kitchen and utility room.*

MAINS DRAINAGE

Underground, the drainpipes from stacks, gullies, and rainwater downpipes run in straight lines to an inspection chamber. From here, there is normally a single pipe connecting the drains with the public sewer in the road.

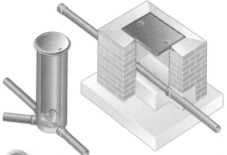

ⓐ **Inspection chambers**

Installed wherever underground soil or waste pipes join the main house drain (and also where a drain changes direction) to provide access for clearing blockages. Older types (above right) are brick-built, with concrete channels called benching. New types (above left) are moulded in plastic.

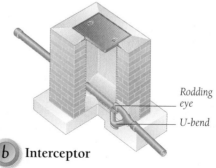

ⓑ **Interceptor**

Older houses have a second interceptor chamber where the house drain joins the public sewer, which has a built-in U-bend to provide a further barrier against smells and a rodding eye to aid unblocking.

How water gets heated

WATER CAN BE HEATED IN BULK *by a boiler or an electric immersion heater, or in smaller quantities by some form of instantaneous heater, such as an electric handwash unit or an electric shower.*

Instantaneous water heater

Also known as multipoint heaters or instantaneous boilers, instantaneous water heaters are common in small apartments. Cold water enters the heater under mains pressure. When a hot tap is turned on, the boiler senses the flow of water and fires its gas or oil burner, which raises the temperature of the water as it passes through a heat exchanger. The flow of hot water is determined by the power of the burner, which means that in winter the flow rate is reduced. More sophisticated boilers partially overcome this problem by having a built-in reservoir that stores a little hot water ready for use.

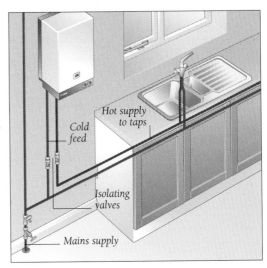

Hot supply
to taps

Cold
feed

Isolating
valves

Mains supply

INSTANTANEOUS WATER HEATER

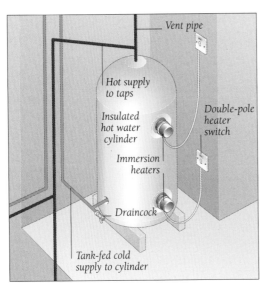

Vent pipe

Hot supply
to taps

Insulated
hot water
cylinder

Double-pole
heater
switch

Immersion
heaters

Draincock

Tank-fed cold
supply to cylinder

IMMERSION HEATER

Immersion heaters

One of the most common methods of heating water, an immersion heater is often incorporated in an indirect central heating system (see opposite) as a back-up if the boiler breaks down. The simplest method of controlling an immersion heater is with a times witch. A night storage cylinder is more efficient, in that it uses two immersion heaters. The lower of the two uses cheap off-peak electricity to heat the contents of the cylinder during the night, while the upper one provides a fast top-up facility during the day. Immersion heaters are particularly vulnerable to limescale, but you can now buy scale-resistant types for use in hard water areas.

Indirect central heating

The most common way of heating water is via an indirect cylinder connected to a "wet" (that is, with radiators) central heating system. In the cylinder is a coil that transfers heat from the water heated by the boiler to the water that flows from the taps. Keeping the boiler water self-contained stops the radiators from rusting and prevents a build-up of limescale. Top-up water for the boiler comes from a separate feed and expansion tank. Water for the cylinder comes from the cold storage tank.

In modern, fully pumped systems, motorized valves, thermostats and a programmer make it possible to control both the flow and temperature of the boiler water and radiators separately. In older systems, the boiler water circulates through the hot water system by convection only, and the only means of controlling its temperature is the boiler's own thermostat. Fitting a pump to the hot water part of the system will increase the flow rate by up to 100 times.

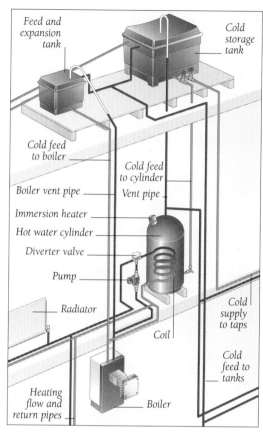

Feed and expansion tank

Cold storage tank

Cold feed to boiler

Cold feed to cylinder

Boiler vent pipe

Vent pipe

Immersion heater

Hot water cylinder

Diverter valve

Pump

Radiator

Coil

Cold supply to taps

Cold feed to tanks

Heating flow and return pipes

Boiler

INDIRECT CENTRAL HEATING

Unvented cylinders

The water in an unvented cylinder is heated like any other type of cylinder. The difference is that an unvented cylinder takes its water supply directly from the mains, rather than from a storage tank. As a result, the pressure at taps and shower heads tends to be greater and can be balanced against the pressure of the mains supply. And because there is no need for a storage tank, the system is ideal for homes with no loft space. Unvented systems incorporate a number of safety devices to prevent overheating or excessive pressure. All work carried out on this type of system should be left to a qualified professional.

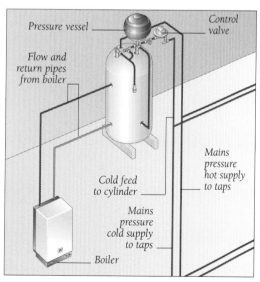

Pressure vessel

Control valve

Flow and return pipes from boiler

Mains pressure hot supply to taps

Cold feed to cylinder

Mains pressure cold supply to taps

Boiler

UNVENTED CYLINDERS

Where to turn the water off

KNOWING HOW to turn the water off and drain down the system will take the panic out of plumbing emergencies and save a fortune in call-out charges. But don't wait until the worst happens: try it now, so that you can be sure that all stopcocks and other valves are in good working order.

Going with the flow

Check the diagrams on pp. 264–65 and work out how they relate to your home. Your ultimate line of defence against leaks is the main stopcock, where the water enters the house. If you can turn this off, then any leak – even in the heating system – will eventually stop. If you can't find the main stopcock, check with a neighbour; if they have the same type of house, the stopcock is likely to be in the same place. If you have a direct system, this is all the emergency information you need. But if you have an indirect system, with tanks in the roof space, it will be better if you can isolate parts of the system locally. Draining down the tanks themselves often causes airlocks.

1. In an ideal world, all taps, float valves and other fittings would have a stopcock or service valve on their pipes, allowing them to be isolated for maintenance. It's worth a look, but don't be surprised if you have to search further down the line.

2. Screwdriver-operated service valves are most likely to be found on newer taps and toilet float valves – look for a chrome fitting on the pipe with a slot in the side. When the slot is at right-angles to the pipe, the water is off; when it's in line with the pipe, the water is on. But be warned: service valves often weep when they are turned. Washing machine supplies should have special lever-operated valves where the supply hoses meet the pipes.

3. If you have to search further back down the line, look for gatevalves on the main feed pipes leaving the cold water storage tank, or in the airing cupboard, where the hot water cylinder is. Closing the main cold feed gatevalve will isolate all non-mains cold outlets. Closing the cold feed to the hot water cylinder will isolate all the hot taps, by stopping water from entering the cylinder. Don't look for a valve on the pipe leading out of the cylinder: this pipe must be kept open to vent the system.

Unfortunately, old gatevalves are notoriously prone to seizing. On no account try to force a seized valve, or you may have a flood on your hands. Either isolate the supply further back down the line, or use a pipe-freezing kit.

Draining heating systems

Before you drain a heating or hot water system, turn off the boiler and pump by turning off the electricity supply to the heating controls. Central heating systems are drained at the lowest point via a draincock. This is often found on the boiler, on nearby pipework, or poking through the outside wall just above ground level. On open-vented systems, turn off the mains water supply to the feed and expansion tank, or tie up the float valve arm with string. On sealed systems, water won't re-enter the system until you turn on the filling valve. To aid draining, open the bleed valves on some upstairs radiators.

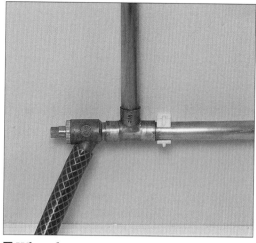

■ **When draining** *your central heating, find the draincock (usually at the lowest point of the system), connect a hose and turn with a spanner to open.*

USING A PIPE FREEZING KIT

If you can't turn off the water, use a pipe freezing kit to create an ice plug in the pipe. Chemical spray kits give you only about 10–15 minutes to work, so use this time to install a service valve or stopcock that will allow the rest of the job to be done at a more leisurely pace. Alternatively, hire an electric freezing kit from a hire shop. For the pipe to freeze, the water in it must be (a) cold and (b) not flowing. If you can't stop the flow by any other means, hammer the pipe flat and freeze it about ½ metre further back. When the ice plug forms, cut the pipe downstream and fit a valve.

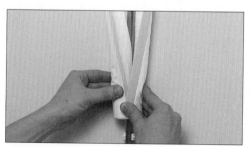

① **Wrap the pipe**

Having stopped the flow through the pipe, wrap the foam muffler around the pipe where you want to freeze it.

② **Spray the muffler**

Spray the muffler and wait for the chemicals to start working. Give a second squirt and listen for a gentle cracking as the ice plug forms.

Hot water troubleshooter

WHEN THE HOT TAPS run cold or dry up altogether, try not to panic. You can sort many problems out without professional help, and even if you can't, you will save money if you can point the plumber or heating engineer in the right direction. Below are three common problems and how deal with them:

1) Water flows, but is cold or lukewarm

Assuming that any room thermostats and water heating controls are correctly set, this points to a fault in the heater.

● **For a boiler or instantaneous heater:** consult the maintenance handbook and check that the pilot light is on. If it has gone out, there may be a reset button to press before you can relight it. This should be accessible without removing the casing. Afterwards, check that the heating controls are set to "hot water constant" and look for signs of life in the heater. If the pilot light keeps going out, either the pilot light unit itself is faulty, or the system is overheating. If the hot water system is pumped, the overheating is probably due to a seized pump. If the boiler or heater also supplies radiators, and these remain hot, a motorized control valve may have seized shut. In all cases, call in a heating engineer. If the pilot light is working, but the controls appear to have no effect on the heater, replace the fuse in the electrical supply and try again. If nothing happens this time, the fault is in the controls themselves – call an engineer.

● **For an electric immersion heater:** check the relevant fuse or circuit breaker at the consumer unit. There will also be a replaceable fuse if the heater is supplied from a fused connection unit. If neither of these make any difference, the heater itself is faulty and should be replaced.

2) Water doesn't flow at all

This suggests that the cold supply to the system has been cut off. Irrespective of whether your system is direct or indirect (see pp. 264–65), check if emergency work is being carried out in the road.

● **On an indirect system:** check for a blockage or airlock, both of which only afflict tank-fed supplies. If the storage tank is empty, waggle the float arm up and down. If only a dribble of water appears, the float valve is blocked and needs overhauling or replacing (see pp. 282–83). If the tank is full, there is probably an airlock somewhere between the cold feed to the cylinder and the hot taps. If you have separate hot and cold taps, you may be able to clear the blockage by connecting a hose between the affected hot tap (if they're all running dry, choose the most convenient one) and the kitchen cold tap or an outside tap (both of which will be at mains pressure). Open the hot tap fully, partly open the cold tap to shoot mains-pressure water back through the hot pipes, then close both taps in reverse order. Try the hot tap to see if the airlock has cleared; if it hasn't, repeat the entire process.

3) Water scalding hot; gurgling noises in pipes

Water that is too hot is dangerous and can cause pipes and taps to scale up in hard water areas. Switch off the boiler, heater, or immersion heater immediately.

● **With an indirect system:** check that the thermostat on the outside of the hot water cylinder is set to 60°C; if there isn't one, check the boiler's own thermostat.

● **With an instantaneous heater:** the temperature of the water output will be preset. If the water overheats, you have no choice but to call an engineer.

● **With an electric immersion heater:** there will be a thermostat inside the heater casing. Turn off the electricity, unscrew the casing and check that the setting is at 60°C. If it is, the thermostat is probably faulty. Unscrew the electrical connections, make a note of which wire goes where, then unscrew the thermostat and take it to a plumber's merchant to obtain a matching replacement.

A simple summary

✓ Water supplies can be direct, which means all outlets are fed from the mains, or indirect, in which all outlets except the kitchen cold tap and any outside taps are fed from a storage tank.

✓ Older drainage systems treat the waste water from sinks, baths, and basins separately from the soil discharged from toilets. In newer systems they're combined.

✓ Water is heated instantaneously, or indirectly via a hot water storage cylinder.

✓ Practise turning the water off so that you don't get caught out in an emergency.

✓ Most hot water faults can be traced by a process of pure logic, and many can be put right without professional help.

Chapter 21

Home Plumbing Jobs

ONCE YOU'RE FAMILIAR with how your system works, there are plenty of plumbing jobs you can tackle yourself – from simple repairs to taps and float valves, to the more substantial alterations needed to accommodate a new sink, basin, bath, or shower.

In this chapter...

✓ Clearing blockages

✓ Mending leaks in pipes

✓ Curing leaks in taps

✓ Repairing valves and toilets

✓ Replacing taps

✓ Making alterations

✓ Plumbing in new fittings

✓ Shower alterations

PROTECT PLATED FITTINGS FROM SERRATED JAWS WITH A CLOTH

Clearing blockages

MOST BLOCKAGES *inside the home are soon cleared using chemicals, a plunger or a wire snake. You'll probably want to call in a specialist to clear a main drain – but don't be fazed by their jargon and high-tech equipment: most blockages are easily cleared using good, old-fashioned drain rods.*

Taking the plunge

If you can't reach a blockage because it's too far down, let the water in the pipe do the work for you. Water can't be compressed, so any force that you apply at one end of a water-filled pipe will be transferred to the other. Use a plunger to exert this force and you won't just push on the blockage, but pull on it as well. Buy an all-purpose plunger for the sink, bath, and shower, and a larger double-headed plunger for toilets and drain gullies. Sink blockages tend to be fat or soap, which respond better to chemical cleaners that clean the entire length of the waste pipe. Take care when using such compounds and always follow the instructions.

Avoid blockages by disposing of cooking fat in the bin, not the sink; likewise with left over rice and pasta.

BLOCKAGE CURES

a Clearing with cloths

If you don't have any tools to hand, use a couple of cloths to clear a blockage. Place one cloth over the sink overflow, then scrunch up the other, and pump up and down on the plug-hole.

b Using a plunger

Fill the sink with water and block the overflow with a cloth. Smear soap around the plunger to help form an airtight seal, then pump up and down vigorously over the plug-hole.

Clearing the trap

If a blockage doesn't respond to plunging, dismantle the trap over a bucket and use a wire snake or a vacuum cleaner with a water suction facility to reach further down the pipe. There may be an alternative access point in the vertical drain stack, although if the pipe is cast iron, the screws are likely to be rusted or painted over. It's very rare for soil pipe blockages to occur beyond the toilet trap.

Outside, open gullies are a common source of blockages. To clear, simply lift the grid and scoop out the debris. If the main drain is blocked (usually revealed by gurgling or back-flow in the waste and soil pipes), call in a drain-clearance firm. Be sure to get a firm price quoted over the phone, inclusive of call-out charges, and don't pay a penny more.

WASTE PIPE WISDOM

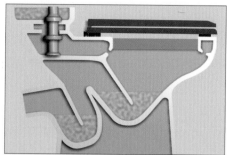

■ **A built-in toilet trap** is intentionally the most common source of blockages in a soil pipe, and is easily cleared with a plunger.

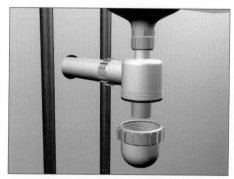

■ **Bottle traps** on sinks and basins are easily blocked. If possible, replace with a more reliable U- or P-trap.

c Using a snake

Most blockages in baths and showers are caused by a build-up of hair and soap in the trap, which responds best to a wire snake. Just wind it down through the hole and pull the blockage out.

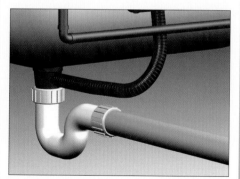

■ **Bath and shower traps** are often low-level. They may look free of blockages, but debris can collect further along the pipe.

Mending leaks in pipes

CONTAIN SMALL DRIPS *with a sponge, or a bowl or baking tray, while you gather the tools and materials needed to make a permanent repair. But if you're faced with a burst pipe, be prepared to use whatever comes to hand.*

Plan your move

Faced with a leak, your first task is to isolate the supply as close as possible to the fault and drain down the pipe (see pp. 264–65). If the pipe is accessible, aim to make a permanent repair using compression fittings (see opposite). Where the leak is hidden, consider running a new length of flexible plastic pipe between two more accessible points; these days, plastic pipe is approved for all kinds of supplies. Your buildings insurance may cover accidental damage to pipes, but not wear and tear.

Be prepared: three inexpensive items – a compression slip coupling for each pipe size, a two-part epoxy putty repair kit, and a pipe clamp – will cope with any leak or burst. For a few pounds, you could save a fortune – so buy them today!

EMERGENCY REPAIRS

The first method shown here is permanent; the others will stop the leak, but in an emergency you may have to improvise on the spot – garden hose and coat hanger wire, car body filler – anything. As a last resort, hammer the pipe flat.

a Fit a coupling

If the leak is accessible, drain down, cut through the pipe, and fit a compression slip coupling.

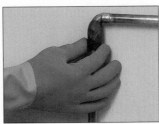

b Use epoxy putty

If the leak is partly accessible or is at a joint, patch with quick-setting epoxy putty.

c Clamp it

A pipe clamp has the advantage that you don't have to turn the water off first.

Making permanent repairs

Copper pipe and fittings can be joined using soldered, compression, or push-fit joints. Soldered joints are the cheapest and are relatively easy to make if you have the right equipment (which is cheap to buy). Otherwise, push-fit joints are the easiest – but only if you cut the pipe ends with a pipe cutter. If you have to use a hacksaw, compression joints are definitely the best option.

Aim to replace the entire damaged section of pipe between two joints if you can. If you have to cut out a damaged section of pipe, check first if there's any "give" in it. If there is, fit a push-fit or compression joint, allowing 8mm "tail" for each side of the joint; if there isn't, fit a brass universal slip coupling. As a "belt and braces" measure, wrap PTFE tape around the joint olives to seal them.

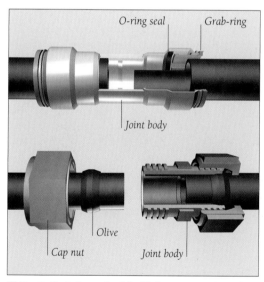

O-ring seal   Grab-ring

Joint body

Olive

Cap nut   Joint body

■ **Push-fit joints** (top) hold the pipes with grab-rings. Push the pipes firmly into the joint, then tug to engage it. Compression joints (above) rely on the olives being crimped onto the pipes by the cap nuts.

MAKING A JOINT

1 **Cut the pipe**

Cut the pipe with a junior hacksaw or pipe cutter, then smooth the cut pipe end with a half-round file or emery cloth.

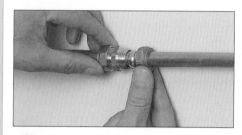

2 **Seal with PTFE**

Slide the cap nut onto the pipe, followed by the olive, leaving 8mm of pipe projecting. Seal with PTFE and repeat at the other end.

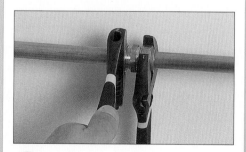

3 **Tighten the nuts**

Use a pair of spanners to tighten the cap nuts onto the joint body, about 1¼ turns past hand-tight. Then turn on the water and test.

Curing leaks in taps

A DRIPPING TAP *won't go away by itself, and if ignored for long enough can cause irreparable damage to enamel fittings. So fix those niggling tap faults before they become a major headache.*

New taps, old problems

Until the early 1980s, all taps employed a rubber washer to shut off the water flow. These inevitably wore out over time, necessitating replacement of the washer. Then came so-called "maintenance free" ceramic disc taps, which were supposed not to wear at all. This may be true, but time has since shown that the discs themselves can crack and move – with the result that taps still drip. The only way to fix a dripping ceramic disc tap is by fitting an entire new mechanism (cartridge), which costs around 100 times more than a washer. That's progress for you. You can usually spot a ceramic disc tap because it has just a quarter turn between off and full on.

Keep a mixed pack of spare tap washers in your kitchen drawer so that you can fix a leaking tap without having to visit a plumbers' merchant first. In an emergency, try reversing the old washer – it should give you enough time to buy a replacement.

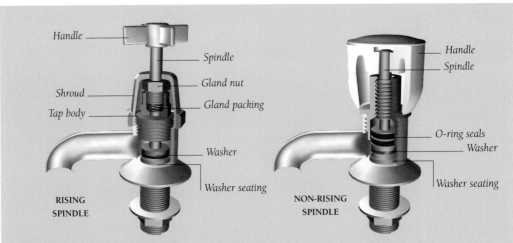

RISING SPINDLE — Handle, Spindle, Gland nut, Shroud, Tap body, Gland packing, Washer, Washer seating

NON-RISING SPINDLE — Handle, Spindle, O-ring seals, Washer, Washer seating

■ **Access to taps** *depends on whether they have rising or non-rising spindles. With non-risers, undo the screw in the head and remove it to get at the body nut; with risers, turn the tap full on and unscrew the chrome shroud. Always put the plug in the sink to prevent losing small screws.*

REPLACING A TAP WASHER

Washers vary in shape and size; some are flat, others are slightly domed. Be sure to make an exact match – otherwise the washer might not seal properly.

1 Remove mechanism

Turn off the water and remove the tap handle or head to reveal the mechanism or tap body. Unscrew this entirely to reveal the washer.

2 Remove old washer

Remove the old washer, either by prising it away from its baseplate with a small screwdriver, or by undoing its retaining nut (above).

3 Fit and run

Fit the new washer, and replace the retaining nut if fitted. Re-assemble the tap and run it fully open to clear any grit or debris from the washer seating.

CURING A LEAKING SPINDLE

A drip from the body of a non-rising spindle tap is a sign of worn seals. Rising spindle taps have greased fibre packing around the spindle, accessed via a top nut.

1 Remove circlip

Having removed the tap mechanism, hold it firmly in your hand and dig out the clip holding the spindle with a small screwdriver.

2 Remove spindle

With the circlip removed, tap the spindle head sharply on a piece of wood to free it from the mechanism and reveal the pair of O-ring seals.

3 Replace O-rings

Flick off the old seals and slide on a new pair. Smear with silicone lubricant (above), then re-assemble the mechanism and refit the circlip.

Repairing valves and toilets

FLOAT VALVES AND TOILETS FLUSHING SIPHONS *do more work than most plumbing components, so it's common for them to cause problems. Fortunately, they can be repaired with hardly any tools or specialist knowledge.*

Repairing float valves

All tanks and toilet cisterns controlled by *float valves* have an overflow/warning pipe to warn that the valve has failed. Usually, this is because the rubber washer has perished or (if the valve is very old) the washer seating has worn out. But overflows can also occur if the float itself springs a leak and fills with water. Sometimes, simply adjusting the valve will stop it leaking. On most valves there is a screw to adjust the level of water, but on some older models adjustments are made simply by bending the float arm. All types of float valve are easily dismantled with a pair of adjustable wrenches, but be sure to note how they go back together, particularly in the case

> **DEFINITION**
>
> A **float valve** – *also known as a ballcock or ball valve – rises with the water level in a tank or toilet and shuts off the water supply when the level reaches a preset limit. Designs vary in detail, but all use leverage to close a washer fixed to the float arm against the open end of the inlet.*

TYPES OF FLOAT VALVE

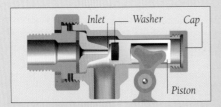

Inlet — Washer — Cap — Piston

■ **BS part 1 piston-type valve:** *this has a sliding piston that holds the washer and moves it against the seating. The float arm is attached with a split pin, and access to the piston is via a screw-on cap.*

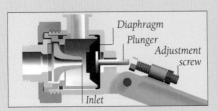

Diaphragm — Plunger — Adjustment screw — Inlet

■ **BS part 2 diaphragm valve:** *no moving parts are in contact with the flow. The washer is the centre of a flexible diaphragm, pushed onto the seating by a plunger in contact with the adjustment screw.*

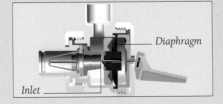

Diaphragm — Inlet

■ **Torbeck or Hushflo valve**: *the rising float arm closes the outlet in this valve, causing water pressure to close the washer against the inlet. It is suitable for toilet cisterns, but not cold storage tanks.*

of a Torbeck or Hushflo valve (the small hole in the washer is there intentionally to let water weep through and open the valve).

Don't bother trying to rewasher a very old or badly scaled float valve – it's far easier to fit a modern plastic replacement, available from any plumbers' merchant.

Toilet cistern problems

Aside from float valve problems, the most probable fault you're likely to encounter on a toilet cistern is an unreliable flushing mechanism. This will be caused by a worn or damaged siphon diaphragm. Just what work is required will depend on the syphon.

- **With a two-part siphon**, the problem can be rectified in minutes simply by removing the top section of the siphon. You won't even need to drain the cistern or turn off the water to do this.

- **With a one-part siphon** the process is more complicated. If the cistern is attached directly to the pan, you'll need to turn off the water supply and drain the cistern. The bolts holding the cistern to the pan, and the screws holding it to the wall, must also be removed. The box below describes how to make a repair from the point where the siphon has been removed from the cistern.

REPAIRING A TOILET SIPHON

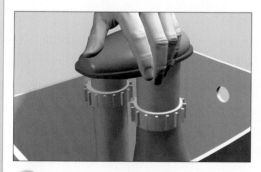

1 **Removing the siphon**

Remove the S-hook from the spindle and slide it out through the hole in the siphon bell top. Remove the washer and spring or weight. You should now be able to remove the diaphragm.

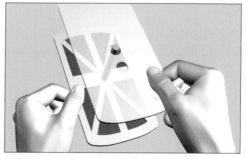

2 **Fitting a new diaphragm**

Fit the new diaphragm and cut the washer accurately so the siphon can move up and down without displacing the washer. Re-assemble the S-hook and fit the bell back in the cistern.

Replacing taps

NOTHING BRIGHTENS UP *old plumbing fittings like replacing the taps. Modern flexible tap connectors make the job a lot easier than it used to be, and you can use the same techniques when installing brand-new plumbing fittings.*

Choosing new taps

Quality taps are precision-engineered to withstand years of constant use, so buy the best you can afford. But beware of imported taps, many of which are made for high-pressure direct systems and produce no more than a trickle when connected to a UK tank-fed indirect system. Make sure that the new taps will fit the existing sink, bath, or basin: is the fitting one-hole or two-hole – and if it is two-hole, how far apart are the hole centres? Check if the holes are circular, or squares set diagonally (if they are the latter, then the new taps will need a larger base to cover the holes). Also, work out how to make the new connections (see opposite) and make sure you have all the necessary parts to hand before you start the job.

When replacing taps make sure you're comfortable. Use a pillow if you're lying down by a bath or on your back looking up under a sink. And make sure you have enough light to see the fittings.

TIPS FOR REMOVING THE OLD TAPS

This is the tricky part. At the very least, you'll need an adjustable claw wrench (which you can hire), but be prepared for some major butchery on the old taps.

a **Use a claw wrench**

Spray the nuts with lubricant, let it soak in, then loosen them with a claw wrench.

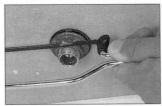

b **Saw off the old nuts**

If a nut won't shift, and there is sufficient access, saw through it with a junior hacksaw.

c **Drill and prise off**

Drill through the nut, first with a small bit, then a larger one, and prise it off.

Adapting pipework for new taps

a Brass extenders

New taps have shorter threaded tails. A brass extender should make up the difference.

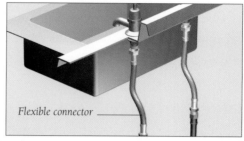

b Flexible connectors

For larger gaps and offset pipes, fit push-fit or compression jointed flexible connectors.

c Reducers for one-hole mixers

One-hole mixer tails are only 10mm in diameter. Fit reducers on the 15mm supply pipes.

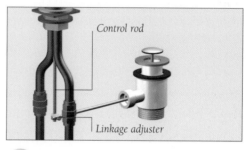

d Pop-up waste assembly

Assemble the pop-up waste mechanism, and adjust the linkage to the control rod.

Making connections

Newer mixer taps often fit through a single hole and have a backnut or screw on to a horseshoe backplate. The flexible "tails" may be threaded, which means that they have to be screwed into the tap body before the taps are mounted. Fit reducers to attach the small-bore tails to the existing pipework or to flexible tap connectors. Make sure the tap body faces the right way round; the small screw that holds the spout on should be at the back. As supplied, the hot tap goes on the left, although you can easily swap the heads around. If the mixer has a pop-up waste attachment, be prepared to shorten or make adjustments to the linkage in situ.

■ **On a single-hole mixer,** *screw the flexible tails into the tap body before mounting. Make sure you don't loosen them when attaching the pipes.*

Making alterations

TEEING INTO OR MODIFYING *existing pipework to take new or replacement fittings is seldom as daunting as it seems, but call in a plumber if you have to run a brand-new wastepipe to a stack or closed gully.*

Arranging hot and cold supplies

Small modifications are best made with flexible copper connectors using compression or push-fit joints. For larger alterations, it's quicker to use pre-soldered joints and elbows, with compression-jointed tee fittings at the source. It's a good idea to sketch the pipe runs and individual fittings before you start so that you don't get caught without a part.

Hot and cold supplies must always be run horizontally or vertically and shouldn't cross over each other. The easiest way to run them is along a wall, fixed with pipe clips at 1 metre intervals; fit the clips first, then push the pipes on to the clips and join them as you go. If a tank-fed pipe has to rise along its length, make sure it does so towards the tank or the taps on the fitting, to avoid airlocks.

Avoid having the water off for long periods by installing the pipe runs back towards the source, then tapping into the hot and cold supplies last of all.

TAPPING INTO A SUPPLY PIPE

1 Drain and cut

Turn off and drain down. Cut the pipe with a slice of pipe sized to match the pipe.

2 Fit a tee joint

If there is some "give" in the pipe, use an ordinary tee-joint. Otherwise use a slip tee.

3 Tighten the nuts

Tighten the nuts on all three sides, making sure you hold the fitting and not the pipe.

SOLDERING NEW CONNECTIONS

People often panic at the mere mention of solder, but on new pipe runs where there is sufficient access, it really is very easy – especially using pre-soldered "Yorkshire" fittings. The only other equipment you need is a jar of flux, a heat-proof mat, and a gas blowtorch. Two rules. 1: Make sure the pipe ends are absolutely clean by rubbing with a piece of fine emery cloth. 2: Make sure the pipes are completely empty.

① Apply flux

Smear a small amount of flux around each pipe end and slide on a presoldered fitting.

② Apply heat

Gently heat the joint with a gas blowtorch, protecting any surfaces around the pipe.

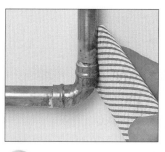

③ The magic circle

When the solder meets in a full circle, the joint is watertight. Wipe off flux while still warm.

Modifying waste pipes

Modify waste pipe runs using matching lengths of plastic pipe and compression couplings or tees. Fit brackets at 600mm intervals. Cut the pipe with a hacksaw, wrapping card round it to ensure the cut is absolutely square. Afterwards, remove any roughness inside and out with a file. Slide on the nuts, back rings, and rubber seals, then tighten one quarter turn over hand-tight. Avoid using adjustable wrenches to do this, as they can deform the pipe and cause leaks. A new waste pipe should fall 20mm per metre towards the outlet, with a minimum trap depth of 75mm at the fitting. The finished job must be passed by your local authority building inspector to make sure it complies with local regulations.

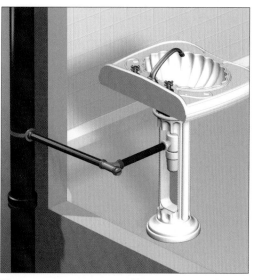

■ **New waste pipe installations** *to a stack need local authority building inspector approval, so you may prefer to leave the job to a plumber.*

Plumbing in new fittings

CHANGING A BATH OR SINK *isn't as difficult as it seems because there are never more than three connections to be made: hot supply, cold supply, and waste. The only real disruption will be to the surround decorations.*

Changing a sink

Most people these days prefer to have a sink set into the worktop, in which case cutting the hole is by far the hardest part of the job (see p. 189). If a template isn't provided, use the sink itself to mark the worktop, then draw a cutting line 10mm inside the outline. Fit the taps and waste fittings before you drop the sink into the worktop. The chances are you can use flexible copper connectors with push-fit joints to make the final connections to the existing pipework. Make the waste pipe connections once the sink is in place, using a universal multi-outlet trap.

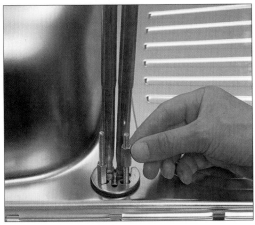

■ **When changing a sink** *fit the taps first. Tighten the backnuts by hand and make sure the tap sits squarely in the hole before final tightening.*

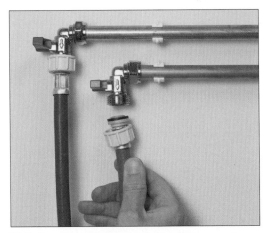

■ **Before connecting to the appliance** *make sure that the supply hoses have rubber washers at both ends for a watertight seal, and don't overtighten the nuts.*

Changing appliances

Washing machines, dishwashers, and other plumbed-in appliances should have valves on the hot and cold supplies, which makes changing them easy. If there aren't any, or they don't work, turn off the water, drain down, and fit new ones. There are two drainage options. One is to run the drain hose to a multi-outlet sink trap, making sure that the hose is higher than the trap itself to avoid back-siphonage from the sink. The other is to connect to a conventional waste outlet via a standpipe – a 750mm vertical length of waste pipe incorporating a U-bend; simply slip the drain hose into the top of the standpipe.

Changing a bath

Disconnect the old bath and clear it right out of the way. Removing an old cast iron bath can be difficult. The simplest way is to smash it up with a sledgehammer (wear eye and ear protection), but you may prefer to leave it where it is and have it professionally re-enamelled.

Make up the new bath with legs, handles, taps, and waste fittings before you position it. Work out the bath height to suit the side panel or any existing tiled splashback. On a masonry wall, cut a shallow channel in the plaster to accommodate the bath rim, using a club hammer and cold chisel, so that the bath sits tight into the wall. Once in place, the bath must be levelled on all sides by adjusting the screw feet. If the floor is chipboard, place timber boards under the feet to spread the load. After levelling, fix the bath securely to the wall to prevent movement. If you can't gain access to the wall brackets supplied, run some aerosol foam filler along the underside of the rim to hold the joint with the wall steady.

After connecting up the taps, turn your attention to the waste. If there's a limited amount of room underneath for the trap, fit a low-level bath trap instead of a standard trap. It can be turned in any direction to connect to a 40mm waste pipe, although it is easier to connect the trap and then run a new section of waste pipe, rather than trying to make the trap meet the existing pipe.

If space is really limited, fit a length of corrugated plastic waste pipe to the bath waste outlet and then fit the trap at the nearest available point further down the waste pipe run.

FITTING A BATH

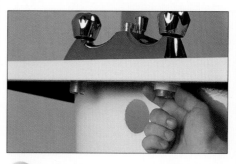

a Bath taps

Fit taps and handles to the bath before putting it in position. Supply pipes should be 22mm for tank-fed and 15mm for mains-fed.

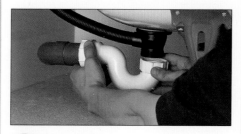

b Bath traps

If a floor joist is directly below the waste outlet, don't cut it. Fit a low-level bath trap to take the waste water away.

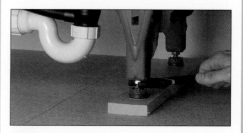

c Level fittings

The bath should be fitted level. The required fall to the plughole is built into the shape of the bath.

Shower alterations

IF THE FLOW THROUGH YOUR SHOWER is a trickle rather than a flood, then the time has come to squeeze a bit more performance out of it. Here are some simple tricks of the trade...

Improving shower performance

The easiest way to get more oomph out of your shower is to pump it. Providing it is fed indirectly from a tank and not straight off the mains, you can fit a low-voltage pump that fits on the hose from the shower to the showerhead. The box sits on the wall and the cable is so thin that you can often run it in the grout line between a row of tiles. If you don't want a pump, think about raising the cold water tank: even an extra metre will give you greatly increased pressure at the head.

In hard water areas, scale is the biggest cause of sluggishness in showers. For optimum performance, soak the shower head in descaler at least every 6 months.

FITTING A NEW SHOWER HEAD

Replacing the shower head is a quick and easy way to improve shower performance on tank-fed mixer showers. It won't do much for an electric shower, though, as the flow of water is governed by the power of the water heater.

1 Unscrew the old head

Unscrew the shower head from the hose. If the hose has collapsed, or the braiding is damaged, you might as well replace the hose as well.

2 Fit the new head

Make sure the rubber washers in the shower hose are in place. With some hoses you might have to add an extra washer to fit the new head.

Fitting an electric shower

An instantaneous electric shower has just one cold connection, run from the cold supply, and one electrical connection. The water supply can be taken from any convenient point using a tee joint in 15mm pipe. It is also advisable to fit a service valve so that the shower supply can be isolated.

In most homes, the easiest route for the supply pipe is down from the roof space, with the end of the run hidden behind the wall tiles or run in surface-mounted trunking along with the electricity cable. The pipe can also enter the shower box from the back or the underside – simply remove the appropriate panel. The supply pipe connection is often a simple push-fit joint, otherwise it will be a compression fitting.

■ **An electric shower sliding rail** *should be mounted to suit the tallest person in the house. The closer you are to the head, the less heat is lost.*

A simple summary

✓ Most blockages are easily cleared with a plunger or snake. Call an expert if a main drain is blocked.

✓ Mend leaks with anything that comes to hand, so you can take the time to make a lasting repair.

✓ Keep a spare set of washers in case a tap starts to leak.

✓ For the same reason, keep a spare float valve washer, too.

✓ When replacing an old tap, don't apply excessive force to the old fitting; saw through it instead.

✓ If in doubt about an alteration, consult on expert – especially if drains are involved.

✓ You can buy couplings to join new fittings to old pipe runs.

✓ Descale a shower head regularly if you live in a hard water area.

Chapter 22

Know your electrics

FIRST, THE BAD NEWS: don't even think about doing your own electrical work unless you understand how your home's electrical system works. Now the good news: it really isn't that complicated. Really. As long as the electricity is turned off – and in this chapter, I'll show you how to be 100 per cent sure that it is – there is no possibility of getting a shock. So read on, and prepare to be initiated into the not-so-mysterious world of cables, circuits, and fuses.

In this chapter...

✓ How power circuits work

✓ How lighting circuits work

✓ Outdoor electrics

✓ The consumer unit

✓ Troubleshooting

ALWAYS MAKE SURE THAT THE POWER IS SWITCHED OFF BEFORE WORKING ON YOUR ELECTRICS

How power circuits work

ELECTRICITY CIRCULATES *through your home via circuits of cables.*
These circuits all start at the fusebox (consumer unit), where they are protected
by fuses or circuit breakers that blow or trip in the event of a fault.

Rings and radials

The circuits that carry power to electrical sockets and fixed appliances are called power
circuits. Most homes have one power circuit per floor, plus extra circuits for a cooker
and an electrically heated shower because of their high power ratings. There may also
be a separate circuit for the kitchen, due to the large number of electrical appliances
found there, and an outdoor power circuit feeding the garage and garden.

In the more modern ring system, the cable is looped from socket to socket. This permits
a ring circuit to carry heavier loads than the older radial system, where one socket is
wired from another in a simple chain. But that's not to say that radial circuits are unsafe.
Cookers and showers always have their own separate radial circuits, and those for the
kitchen, garage, and outdoor sockets are often radial, too. The chief drawback of radial
circuits is that they can't always be extended easily. On ring circuits, you can add extra
sockets on mini-radial circuits called spurs.

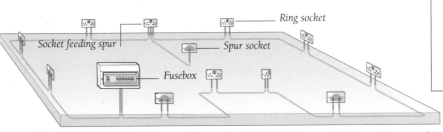

Ring socket
Socket feeding spur
Spur socket
Fusebox

■ **Socket wiring:** *red
cores go to live, black to
neutral, and
green/yellow-sleeved to
earth. A separate
length of earth cable
links the earth terminal
to a metal box.*

■ **Ring circuit:** *the cable runs from a fuse in the fusebox and is looped from socket
to socket, finally returning to the same fuse. Extra sockets may be added as spurs.*

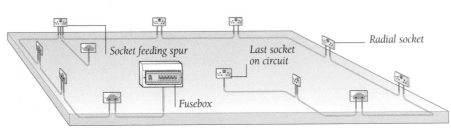

Socket feeding spur
Last socket
on circuit
Radial socket
Fusebox

■ **Radial circuit:** *the cable runs from a fuse in the fusebox and is looped from socket to
socket, ending at the last. Spur sockets may be added, but risk overloading the circuit.*

Circuit cables

Circuits are wired with PVC-sheathed copper-cored cable with cores of various sizes (measured in mm²) to suit the load the circuit is designed to carry. Most circuit cables have three cores – a red-insulated live core, a black-insulated neutral core, and a bare earth. Cables for two-way lighting circuits have four cores – red, blue, and yellow insulated plus a bare earth. Cables should not be confused with flex, which carries the power from sockets and fixed outlets to appliances. Flex has two or three cores: brown for live, blue for neutral, and – unless the appliance is double-insulated – green and yellow for earth.

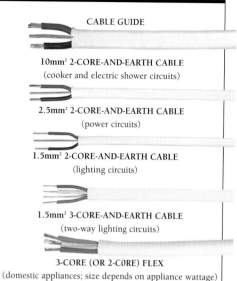

CABLE GUIDE

10mm² 2-CORE-AND-EARTH CABLE
(cooker and electric shower circuits)

2.5mm² 2-CORE-AND-EARTH CABLE
(power circuits)

1.5mm² 2-CORE-AND-EARTH CABLE
(lighting circuits)

1.5mm² 3-CORE-AND-EARTH CABLE
(two-way lighting circuits)

3-CORE (OR 2-CORE) FLEX
(domestic appliances; size depends on appliance wattage)

Safety measures

The key built-in safety measure is the earthing system, in which one core of the circuit cable is connected ultimately to the ground. In the event of a fault, the earth core transmits the excess electrical current safely to the ground, instead of melting the circuit cables or frying the unfortunate individual on the wrong end of a live wire. It is vital that this circuit is never broken. Nowadays, metal pipes are also *cross-bonded* into the earth circuit.

Extra protection comes from the fuses or circuit breakers in the fusebox. But since these don't always trip in time to prevent a shock, it's wise to fit an extra safety measure in the form of an RCD (Residual Current Device) to appliances that are especially at risk, such as power tools used outdoors.

> **DEFINITION**
>
> Electrical **cross-bonding**, in which all metal pipework is wired to the earth circuit, became mandatory on new installations in the early 1980s. Mortgage surveys often insist that older systems are brought up to scratch.

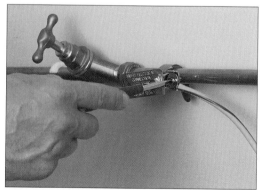

■ **Metal pipes** *must be cross-bonded to ensure a continuous earth in case a live wire touches them.*

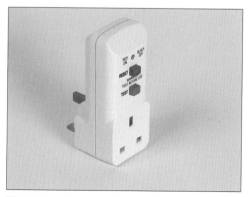

■ **RCDs** – *Residual Current Devices – provide extra protection for portable appliances.*

How lighting circuits work

LIGHTING CIRCUITS *work on the same principle as power circuits, but the addition of remote switching adds an extra complication. There are also two methods of wiring lighting circuits, and many houses use a mixture of both.*

Junction box and loop-in

As with power circuits, there is normally one lighting circuit per floor of the house, with the possibility of extra circuits for wall lights and outdoor lights. The circuit cables carry the power to the light fittings in one of two ways (see below), both of which incorporate an extra live loop between each fitting and its switch so that the light can be turned on and off. This loop is wired with the same 2-core-and-earth cable as the rest of the circuit, which is confusing, since effectively both the red and black cores are "live" when the light is on.

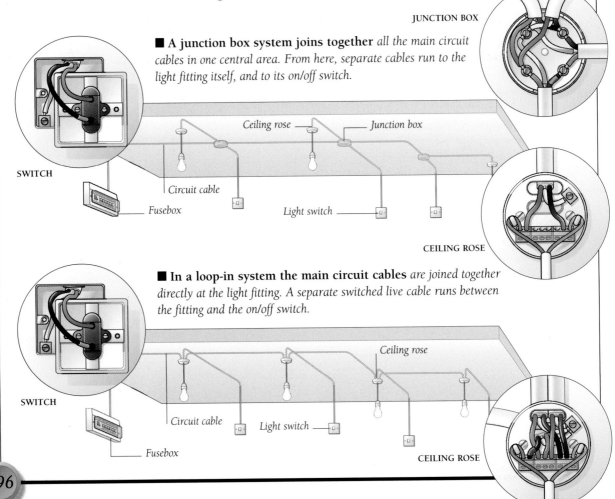

JUNCTION BOX

■ **A junction box system joins together** *all the main circuit cables in one central area. From here, separate cables run to the light fitting itself, and to its on/off switch.*

SWITCH

Ceiling rose — Junction box

Circuit cable

Fusebox — Light switch

CEILING ROSE

■ **In a loop-in system the main circuit cables** *are joined together directly at the light fitting. A separate switched live cable runs between the fitting and the on/off switch.*

SWITCH

Ceiling rose

Circuit cable — Light switch

Fusebox

CEILING ROSE

Two-way switching

Where two switches control a single light – for example in a hallway and landing – an extra 3-core-and-earth cable is run between the two switches. The yellow and blue cores of this cable add an extra loop into the existing switched live loop, allowing current to flow to the fitting irrespective of which switch is "on".

The black cores of a switched live cable should be marked with red sleeving or tape, both at the switch and at the light fitting.

Unfortunately, cables are not always marked which makes identifying each separate one very difficult and potentially dangerous. When replacing a light fitting, always make a note of where each core goes before you disconnect it.

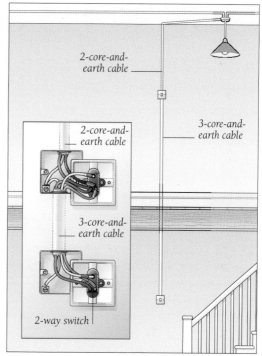

2-core-and-earth cable

2-core-and-earth cable

3-core-and-earth cable

3-core-and-earth cable

2-way switch

■ **Two-way switches:** *2-core-and-earth cable runs from the light to the first switch; 3-core-and-earth cable links the two switches.*

CIRCUIT ANOMALIES

Sometimes, usually for convenience, wall lights are wired into a power circuit via a fixed outlet (below left). Wall lights can also be wired on their own separate lighting circuit incorporating patented socket outlets (below right). Such arrangements have the advantage of being easy to isolate if the fittings need changing, and of remaining live even if the fuse in the main lighting circuit has blown.

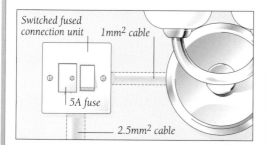

Switched fused connection unit   1mm² cable

5A fuse

2.5mm² cable

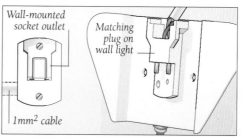

Wall-mounted socket outlet

Matching plug on wall light

1mm² cable

Outdoor electrics

A CIRCUIT TO SERVE A GARDEN OR OUTBUILDINGS may be wired directly from the fusebox, or – if there isn't room – from a separate mini-fusebox known as a switchfuse unit. New installations must also be protected by an RCD (residual current device) if they leave the bounds of the house.

Outdoor circuitry

There are three choices for running cable in the garden: along a masonry wall joined to the house (but not a fence); overhead, supported on wooden posts; or under the ground. Above-ground cable must be the grey PVC-sheathed type, as white-sheathed cable is damaged by sunlight. Buried cable must be armour-sheathed; the sheath acts as an earth and is joined at either end using brass nuts. Extra appliances or single outdoor sockets can be wired as a spur from a power circuit, switching to armoured cable via a junction box and fitting an RCD where the circuit leaves the house. Installing a circuit with fixed lighting and power sockets is best left to an electrician.

Circuit options

The first job is to decide which of these circuit options is best suited to your garden.

■ **Armoured cable** *can be run underground if protected from damage, or may be fixed to walls attached to the house. Seal plastic pipes into walls where the cable passes through them.*

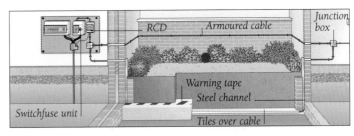

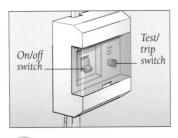

a **RCD unit**

Detects current difference in the live and neutral circuits due to a fault, and isolates the supply.

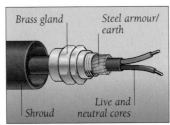

b **Armoured cable**

Requires a special brass gland at each end for making an earth connection at the junction box.

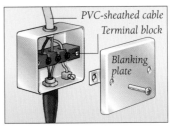

c **Junction box**

Fit at both ends of armoured cable to connect to 2-core-and-earth cable for wiring the fittings.

The consumer unit

THE CONSUMER UNIT (right) is where all circuits start, and is where you'll find the main switch to isolate the entire supply. Always turn off at the mains before doing any electrical work.

Where to turn off

The consumer unit or fusebox is where the mains supply is split into individual power and lighting circuits, each of which is protected by a circuit fuse (either replaceable wire or cartridge), or by a switch-operated miniature circuit breaker (MCB), which is more sensitive to faults. Depending on the size and age of the unit, there may be spare fuseways for adding new circuits, or it may have been extended already by means of a separate switchfuse unit.

Never mend replaceable wire fuses with anything other than fuse wire of the correct amp rating for the circuit. Cartridge fuses are different sizes for this reason.

The consumer unit is permanently connected to the electricity supply and shouldn't be meddled with. If you need a new circuit, get a professional electrician to make the final connection to the unit. If your consumer unit is the old rewirable fuse type, contact the electricity company about having it updated to the MCB type.

ISOLATING CIRCUITS

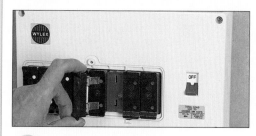

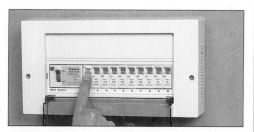

a **Isolating a fused circuit**

Remove the fuse cartridge or wire-fuseholder, then re-test the circuit to make sure it's dead.

b **Isolating a circuit breaker**

Turn off the switch or trip the button and leave a note that you've isolated the circuit.

Troubleshooting

WHEN AN ELECTRICAL APPLIANCE *doesn't work, do some detective work before the sparks start flying. Approach the job logically and you should be able to pin down the fault in no time. But if the same fuse blows twice in quick succession, it's time to call an electrician.*

What to do when the power goes off

1 **Is the power off everywhere in the house?** If it is, you've probably suffered a power cut. A phone call to your neighbours should confirm this.

2 **Is the power off on one circuit only?** Confirm this by testing other sockets or lights on the same circuit. If the answer is yes, check any RCD installed in the circuit, then move on to check the fuse or circuit breaker for that circuit in the consumer unit. Before you replace/reset, investigate the cause of the fault.

- Have you just rewired something? If you have, this is almost certainly the cause of the fault.
- Have you just switched on an appliance with a faulty flex or plug?
- Is the flex or extension lead fully extended? (If flexes are left coiled, they may start to overheat.)
- Have you just acquired the appliance secondhand?
- Is the light switch, fitting, or socket damaged in any way?
- Is there moisture anywhere near the switch or appliance that could have caused the circuit to blow?
- Is there an abnormally heavy load – for example, a high-wattage fan-heater.

3 **Is the fault confined to one socket?** If so, plug the appliance in elsewhere to check. If the fault seems to rest with the appliance, check the plug fuse by exchanging it for a fuse that you know is working and of the same rating as recommended by the appliance's manufacturer. Do the same for a fixed appliance wired to a fused connection unit (FCU). If the fault is at the socket, check that the faceplate isn't cracked and that there are no loose wires. A damaged socket or switch faceplate should be replaced as soon as possible.

4 **Is the fault confined to a single light fitting?** If so, switch off the supply and unscrew the light fitting or ceiling rose. These are the most common sources of faults, often because the packed-in wires have come adrift of their terminals, or the weight of the light fitting is supported only by the flex cores. As with sockets, check that roses, light fitting baseplates and switch faceplates aren't cracked. A metal switchplate should have a length of green and yellow sleeved earth wire running between the switch and its metal backing box.

Don't take chances!

If all household electrical systems were wired as they should be, very few of us would get an electric shock. Unfortunately, people have been known to abuse the wiring regulations, which is tantamount to leaving death-traps for those unfortunate enough to follow in their footsteps. To give you an example, it took a friend of mine several years before he discovered (by accident) that the electric cooker in his converted flat was wired into his neighbour's mains supply.

If you've just moved house or are unfamiliar with your electrical system, keep a look-out for anything that doesn't appear to make sense, or for obvious signs of "cowboy" work and bodging. Remember, too, that the life of PVC-sheathed circuit cable is about 25 years, after which the insulation becomes brittle and apt to fracture. If you spot signs of old wiring, old fittings, or a profusion of wires around the mains switch, have the system inspected by a qualified electrician – the chances are, it is long overdue for rewiring, incorporating the latest safety devices.

Trivia...

The author's only experience of an electric shock was a bad one. After removing some kitchen cabinets, I found what looked like an old cooker cable buried in the wall. I already had a cooker wired in, so I assumed the old cable was dead; it wasn't, but I could have been.

A simple summary

✓ All the power circuits in your house start at the consumer unit (fusebox), where they are protected by fuses or circuit breakers. Most homes have one power circuit per floor, plus extra circuits for the cooker and and the electrically-heated shower, where one is fitted.

✓ Always mark the black cores of a switch cable, at the switch and light fitting, with red sleeving or tape; also the blue and yellow in a two-way-switched circuit.

✓ All new outdoor electrical installations must be protected by an RCD (residual current device) once they leave the bounds of the house walls.

✓ The consumer unit is always live. Ask the electricity supply company or an electrician to make the final connections.

✓ Always replace a plug fuse with one of the correct amperage as specified by the manufacturer of the appliance.

Chapter 23

Electrical Jobs

S O NOW YOU KNOW HOW YOUR ELECTRICAL SYSTEM WORKS, it's time to put the theory into practice. Always make sure the electricity is switched off at the mains before you tamper with wiring or an electrical appliance.

In this chapter...

✓ Light fittings and switches

✓ Fitting fluorescent strip lights

✓ Fitting low-voltage lighting

✓ Adding extra sockets

✓ Wiring in appliances

✓ Fitting wall lights

✓ Fitting outdoor lights

✓ Garage door openers

NEW LIGHT FITTINGS CAN TRANSFORM A ROOM

Light fittings and switches

THEY MAY BE ECONOMICAL TO INSTALL, but ordinary pendant light fittings do very little for a room apart from throw light where it's not wanted. The answer is to replace them with something better suited to the task.

How ceiling lights are fixed

A replacement light fitting must be securely fixed to the ceiling and wired within a flame-proof enclosure. If it has an enclosed base, make the connections inside it; if not, fit a plastic or metal circular conduit box to house the connections. Some lights will fit over the base of a ceiling rose – simply connect to the flex terminals.

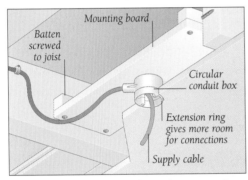

Mounting board

Batten screwed to joist

Circular conduit box

Extension ring gives more room for connections

Supply cable

■ **Support a new light** *fitting from a wooden platform screwed between the ceiling joists.*

Since you'll probably need to modify the existing fixing, ensure you have access to the ceiling cavity from above.

If you're lucky, the old rose will be mounted on a wooden platform between the joists; if not, you'll have to install one. Position it so that the connection box for the new fitting sits flush with the ceiling.

Mounting arrangements for ceiling lights

Chandeliers, spotlights, and pendants all require different mounting and fitting methods.

a **Chandelier**

Must be supported by a metal conduit box, to which the fitting's baseplate is screwed

b **Ceiling spotlight**

If the fitting has an open base, screw it to a lighter weight plastic conduit box.

c **Rise-and-fall pendant**

This, must be fitted to a conduit box. Make sure that the box mounting can take the weight.

Wiring the new fitting

All new light fittings are wired to the circuit cables via 5 amp nylon or ceramic terminal blocks, so make sure they are supplied, or that you have some handy. Check, too, that the baseplate of the new fitting matches the screw holes in your conduit box, and that you have the requisite machine screws to secure it.

Wiring-in is simply a matter of identifying the right cable cores to link to the fitting's flex cores. In a junction box system they will be red (live), black (neutral), and green and yellow sleeved (earth). In a loop-in system, they will be black, hopefully with a red tag (switched live), black (neutral), and green/yellow-sleeved (earth). Take care not to disturb wires when folding into the backing box.

CHANGING A CEILING LIGHT

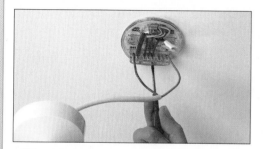

1 **Remove old rose and label wires**

Switch off the mains and unscrew the old rose. Release the cable cores from the terminal block, taping those from the same block together.

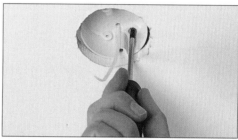

2 **Fit the new backing box**

Arrange a platform for the backing box, and if necessary enlarge the ceiling hole. Feed in the cables, then screw the box to the platform.

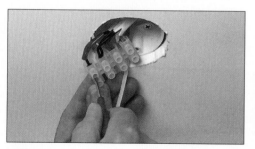

3 **Reconnect the circuit cables**

Wire each group of cable cores to a separate nylon terminal block. Test each connection for tightness before proceeding.

4 **Wire the new fitting**

Connect the flex cores in the fitting to the live, neutral, and earth terminal blocks. Then screw the new fitting to the backing box.

Changing light switches

There are several reasons why you might want to change a light switch: to fit a straight replacement, change the style, convert to a pull-cord switch, or fit a dimmer. In all cases, if you take care to label the wires, you can't go wrong.

Buying considerations

Replacement light switches can be one-way, two-way or *intermediate*, and single- or *multi-gang*. Make sure that you replace like with like, not forgetting that you may need to replace the backing box as well. If you're fitting a dimmer switch, be aware that you may need to enlarge the existing switch recess.

If you're converting a wall switch to a pull-cord, make sure you have access to run cable back from the old switch and on to the new one, Use a junction box to extend the circuit cable, if necessary.

Switches with metal faceplates need extra care. Run a length of green/yellow-sleeved cable earth core between the earth terminal on the switch faceplate and its backing box. If the existing switch isn't earthed, have the wiring inspected: it could be overdue for replacement.

■ **Dimmable lighting**: *dimmers enable you to vary light levels to suit your mood – and save electricity when the lights are low. Fitting a dimmer (inset) is simply a matter of replacing a light switch.*

Identifying switch types

Switch off the mains and unscrew the faceplate to see what kind of switch you're dealing with. Five of the most common layouts are shown on the right. A one-way type switches from one position only; two-way and intermediates enable switching from different locations.

If you encounter a faceplate where the C or COM (common) terminals are linked with short pieces of red cable core, replicate the positions on the new switch.

On multi-gang switches, follow this foolproof system to avoid getting in a muddle. First, label each switch A, B and so on, then label each cable core correspondingly. Before you remove a core, add its position on the terminal (e.g. L2) to the label so that you know exactly where to wire it on to the new switch.

ONE-GANG, ONE-WAY

ONE-GANG, TWO-WAY

ONE-GANG INTERMEDIATE

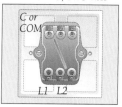

TWO-GANG

THREE-GANG

■ **Switched on:** *use these diagrams to identify what type of switch you're dealing with, so that you know what to ask for when buying a replacement.*

WIRING DIMMER SWITCHES

Wiring a dimmer switch is easy. The trickiest part of the job is enlarging the existing backing box recess to take the deeper box required by many dimmers, but even this is straightforward and in practice may not be necessary.

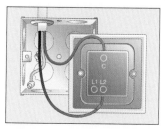

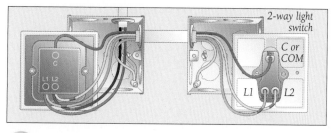

(a) **One way dimmer**

If there are three terminals, use the one marked C or COM and either of the other two.

(b) **Two-way dimmer**

In a two-way arrangement, fit the dimmer to the more used of the two switches and retain the other switch as a "slave". Do not fit pairs of dimmers to the same circuit.

Fitting fluorescent strip lights

STRIP LIGHTS ARE THE PERFECT *way to provide illumination for kitchen worktops, walk-in cupboards, and bathroom mirrors.*

DEFINITION

A fixed appliance is usually connected to the circuit cable in a **fused connection unit (FCU)**. *This does the job of a plug, incorporating a fuse of the correct rating for the appliance. It may be switched and have a flex outlet facility.*

Arranging the power

Some types of strip light have separate on-off switches. Special enclosed fittings are available for bathrooms and you can buy "skeleton" systems with separate choke units for installation in a tight space.

If you want to fit a series of strip lights, controlled by the existing ceiling light switch, take the power supply from the switched live and neutral terminals on the existing loop-in rose or junction box. If you prefer independent control, wire the lights via a switched *fused connection unit (FCU)*. Connect this as a spur from an existing power socket (see pp 312-13), or wire it via a junction into a power circuit cable. In a bathroom, use an unswitched FCU in conjunction with the pull-cord switch on the fitting itself.

■ **In a kitchen,** *it's often easier to supply the strip lights from a socket or power circuit cable and switch them via a 5 amp fused connection unit (FCU) (inset right), connected as a spur outlet.*

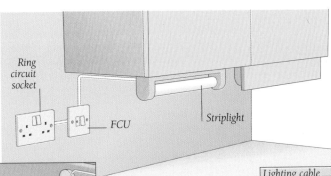

Ring circuit socket

FCU

Striplight

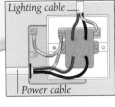

Lighting cable

Power cable

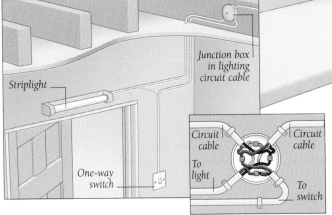

Striplight

Junction box in lighting circuit cable

One-way switch

Circuit cable

Circuit cable

To light

To switch

■ **In a walk-in cupboard,** *it may be preferable to take the power supply from a lighting circuit via a junction box (inset left) and control it from a separate switch by the cupboard door.*

Fitting low-voltage lighting

LOW-VOLTAGE LIGHTING is *attractive and easy to install, as well as being much cheaper to run than mains-powered tungsten lights.*

Planning the installation

Low-voltage lights come in spot, track, and downlighter form, and are often sold in kits complete with a mains transformer and cabling. The fact that the transformer can be fitted close to the lights allows you to cut down on new cabling, and makes it relatively easy to arrange a mains power supply. If you're replacing an existing mains circuit, you should be able to make use of the existing switches and cabling. But if you want to dim the lights as well, fit special-purpose low-voltage dimmers.

■ **Downlighter kits** *are especially popular, as the lights can often be installed without full-scale access to the floor space above.*

To avoid malfunctions, make sure the output of the transformer is matched to the total wattage of the light fittings connected to it. If a light blows, fit a replacement immediately to save the life of the others.

Low-voltage lighting equipment

Low-voltage lighting is easy to install but remember to check the wattage specifications.

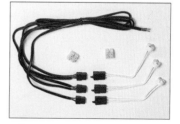

a **Low-voltage lights**

Often sold as downlighter kits, track units, or multiple spots.

b **Transformer**

Make sure it matches the total wattage of the connected lights.

c **Cable and connectors**

These must suit total wattage; often supplied with the lights.

Arranging the wiring

It's worth drawing a plan of your new set-up so that you know what materials to buy and where to site them. Once done, you will then be ready to start the wiring.

1 Individual light units are wired directly to the transformer or to a central, joist-mounted 5 amp junction box. The connections are made with special fly leads, or with two-core low-voltage cable and plastic terminal blocks. Use the existing mains cable to connect to existing switches – on the mains-voltage side of the transformer. The system does not need earthing, so simply tape back the core.

2 Take the power supply from the switched live and neutral terminals of the existing ceiling light (if you're replacing it) or from the lighting circuit cable via a 4-terminal junction box and a separate switch.

3 Site the transformer somewhere that will remain accessible – under the floor in a fitted cupboard is ideal – while providing reasonably short (and accessible) cable runs to the lights themselves. If access from above is a problem, you may be able to feed the downlighter cables through the ceiling space from their fixing holes. Track systems generally have an integral transformer, which makes fitting easier. A spot unit can be fitted in place of the existing ceiling light.

Trivia...

A "volt" is a unit of potential difference – in plain language, the "oomph" behind an electric current that causes it to flow. The word was coined by the 18th century Italian scientist Count Alessandro Volta (1745–1827), who also invented the chemical battery and the condenser.

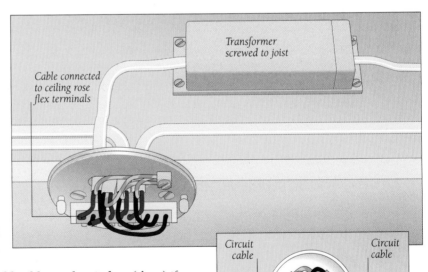

Transformer screwed to joist

Cable connected to ceiling rose flex terminals

Circuit cable

Circuit cable

Junction box

Switched feed cable to transformer

Switch cable

■ **Make use of the old cables and switches** *(above) if you're fitting the lights in place of mains-powered ceiling lights, and take the power from a junction box wired into an existing light circuit. If you want to control the lights independently, it's easier to wire them into a power circuit, switched collectively via a 5 amp fused connection unit.*

Fitting the lights

Low-voltage recessed downlighters fit invisibly from below into their circular fixing holes. Cut the holes with a padsaw or hole-saw drill attachment, and clear the area above of debris and insulation to guard against overheating. Then connect the fly lead or cable terminal block and clip the light in the hole. Track and spot systems can be screwed to the ceiling in the normal way.

Don't handle low-voltage tungsten halogen bulbs directly with your fingers, or you'll deposit grease that could cause the bulb to blow. Avoid turning low-voltage lights on and off too often, as this, too, can dramatically shorten bulb life. And don't use incorrectly rated cables; despite the low voltage, there's still a fire risk.

FITTING RECESSED CEILING LIGHTS

1 **Create the ceiling opening**

Measure the light fittings, then drill or saw openings in the ceiling to suit. Take care to avoid any joists.

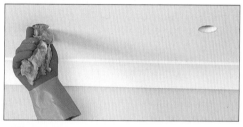

2 **Clean the opening**

Trim the edges of the plasterboard, and clear away any insulation or debris within 100mm of the hole to prevent overheating.

3 **Connect the light**

Connect the fly lead to the transformer, run through the ceiling cavity, and plug into the light fitting.

4 **Fit the light**

Press the two prongs of the fitting's spring clip together and gently push into the opening until the clip grips the plasterboard.

Adding extra sockets

IT'S EASIEST TO WIRE A NEW SOCKET as a "spur" from an existing socket, but the rules for doing so without risking overload are complicated. People have been known to flout the rules of course, but my advice is: don't. If you're in any doubt, ask an electrician's advice.

To add or not to add?

You can't add sockets to sockets that are themselves spurs, or have been spurred off. Also, it's unwise to add a socket to the end of a radial circuit. So the only way to find a source for your new spur is to switch off the supply and open up a likely-looking donor socket to see how it's wired. Only one cable means it's a spur or an end socket, so no-go; likewise three cables, which means it's a ring-circuit socket that's already been spurred off. If there are two cables, and the socket is on a ring circuit, you've got the go-ahead. But if the circuit is radial, you'll have to check neighbouring sockets to make sure that the donor isn't already feeding a spur.

While you're at it, spare a thought for where the cable to the new socket is going to run. Stud walls and wooden floors present no problem. But if the donor socket is in masonry, you'll have to cut a channel and recess for the new cable and socket with a hammer and bolster (disruptive), or else surface-mount the socket and run the cable in plastic mini-trunking (messy). Exactly the same procedure is used to determine whether or not you can wire in fixed appliances to fused connection units and so on. And remember – you can't fit sockets in a bathroom.

Checking sockets

Before starting work, unscrew the faceplate and check how many cables there are.

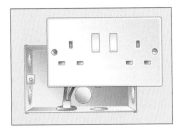

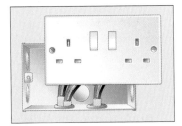

a One cable: NO

Could be an existing spur, or the end socket on a radial circuit. Either way, you can't add to it.

b Three cables: NO

This means that the socket is on a radial circuit and has already had a spur taken off it. No-go.

c Two cables: MAYBE

You could possibly add providing the socket isn't on a radial circuit and isn't already feeding a spur.

WIRING-IN THE SOCKET

1 **Open donor socket**

Switch off the supply and open the faceplate. Feed the new cable into the backing box.

2 **Connect new cable**

Strip the new cable cores and insert them alongside the same-coloured existing cores.

3 **Wire new socket**

Feed the cable through into the backing box and connect the cable cores.

Running cable

Electricians have dozens of tricks for running cables out of sight and regard cutting channels in brickwork as a last resort. Hidden cables must run either horizontally or vertically, and directly to the fitting. So before you settle for an ugly surface-mounted arrangement, do some detective work, following the guidelines set out below.

● Partition walls are the obvious route. Cut a hole in the plasterboard to accept a cavity wall backing box.

● Under wooden floors is second favourite. Feed cables along the cavities between joists by taping them to a length of oval plastic conduit. You can "fish" for them with a hook of coat-hanger wire taped to the conduit. To feed cables across joists, drill holes a minimum of 50mm below the top edge – and remember, you will have to lift floorboards to gain access. Screw down the boards afterwards, and mark them "CABLE ACCESS PANEL".

● Other routes include behind cornicing or skirting boards, and through the roof space. Cables buried in solid walls must be a minimum of 150mm from the edge of the wall, and must be enclosed in oval conduit to protect the outer insulation.

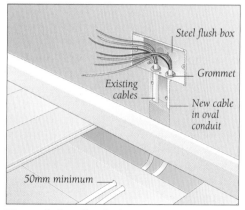

Steel flush box

Grommet

Existing cables

New cable in oval conduit

50mm minimum

■ **In solid walls,** *flush-mounting the new socket would mean chipping out a recess for the new socket and cable entry.*

Wiring in appliances

POWER SUPPLIES FOR BUILT-IN APPLIANCES *are almost always better taken from the mains than from a plug-in socket. In the kitchen, it frees up valuable sockets for other uses. In the bathroom, you have no alternative.*

In the kitchen

Depending on its power rating, an electric cooker must be wired directly to the consumer unit on its own 30 amp or 45 amp radial power circuit. The final connection is made via a cooker switch, which may also incorporate a 13 amp socket. Power supplies for other appliances are wired as spurs from the downstairs (or separate kitchen) power circuit. You have a choice of outlets (see below), depending on whether the appliance is high- or low-level, and on where the outlet is to be actually mounted. All outlets are wired to the new circuit cable in exactly the same way as a new socket.

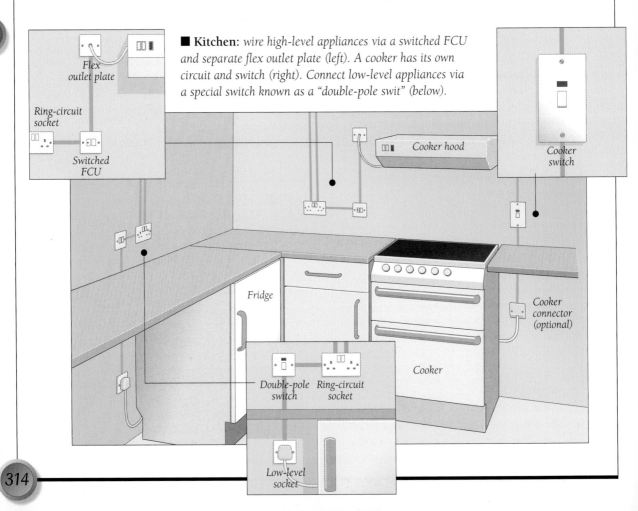

■ **Kitchen:** *wire high-level appliances via a switched FCU and separate flex outlet plate (left). A cooker has its own circuit and switch (right). Connect low-level appliances via a special switch known as a "double-pole swit" (below).*

Flex outlet plate

Ring-circuit socket

Switched FCU

Cooker hood

Cooker switch

Fridge

Cooker connector (optional)

Double-pole switch

Ring-circuit socket

Cooker

Low-level socket

In the bathroom

Electrically heated or "power" showers and immersion heaters need their own separate circuit, wired directly to the fusebox. The cable size and fuse rating will depend on the appliance's power rating. Switching can be done via a switched fused connection unit (FCU) mounted outside the room, or via an appropriately rated ceiling pull-cord switch. A shower switch must have both a neon and a mechanical on/off indicator. Other appliances, such as a wall heater or heated towel rail, can take their supply as spurs from existing sockets in other rooms. Again, if switching is needed, it can come from an FCU outside the room or from a ceiling pull-cord switch. The one exception is a shaver supply unit, which can be wired into a lighting circuit using a junction box if access is easier.

Don't be tempted to disregard the rules about no mains socket outlets in a bathroom. These rules are there for a reason – to stop wet hands accidentally causing a short circuit. Even if you're careful, spare a thought for younger members of the family.

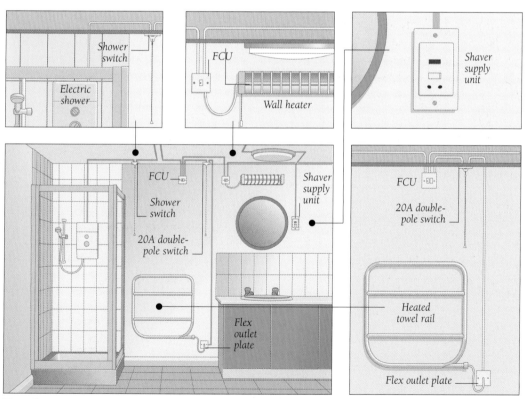

■ **Bathroom:** *switches are cord-operated. Top right: wire a low-level towel rail via a flex outlet plate. Above, left to right: a shower on its own circuit; high-level heater with integral switch; shaver supply unit.*

Fitting wall lights

WALL LIGHTS can be fitted in two different ways. They can either be wired into an existing lighting circuit via a junction box, or into a power circuit via an FCU. Either option is relatively easy to undertake; the most difficult part of the job is likely to be concealing the cables.

Planning the circuit

Take your power supply from whichever circuit is most accessible. On lighting circuits, you can break into the switched side of an existing circuit (so that the lights are operated by the ceiling light switch), or from the unswitched side (giving you independent control). It's perfectly fine to fit multiple wall lights on the same circuit – link the cables with nylon terminal blocks – but the total load, including existing fittings, should not exceed 1,150 watts, which works out at about eight fittings altogether.

If you take the supply from a power circuit, treat it as a spur: install an FCU as a master switch, then run the cable on to each fitting in turn up, to a maximum of about 20. You can also buy patented systems such as the *Luminaire Support Coupler*. Wall lights in bathrooms must have enclosed bulbs and be wired via a pull-cord switch.

> **DEFINITION**
>
> The **Luminaire Support Coupler (LSC)** *is a plug-in lighting system consisting of special sockets for wall and ceiling lights that connect to matching plugs on the fittings. These both support the fittings and make the electrical connection, thus simplifying their installation.*

WIRING INTO A LIGHTING CIRCUIT

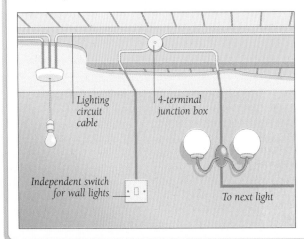

Lighting circuit cable

4-terminal junction box

Independent switch for wall lights

To next light

If you want the new lights to be operated by an existing switch, wire the supply via a junction box to the switched live supply of an existing lighting circuit. Otherwise, you will have to break into a non-switched cable and run the supply from the junction box via a separate switch. This will not affect the capability of individually controlled lights to be switched on and off.

Fitting the lights

The time to fit wall lights is before you redecorate, especially if your walls are solid and you want to cut channels for the cables. If your chosen lights don't come with an enclosed backing box, you'll need to wire them within plastic conduit boxes recessed into the wall. In this case, check that the fixing holes are the standard 51mm apart.

On solid walls, cut channels for the cable and recesses for the fittings with an electrician's bolster chisel.

■ **Wall lights** *enable the light source to be positioned in exactly the right place for the desired effect and usage.*

If you're wiring the wall lights into a lighting circuit, lift the upstairs floorboards and identify the appropriate cable. Sever it, strip back the cores, and reconnect to a "4" terminal junction box. From here you can run a new length of cable to a wall or pull-cord switch, and then run a second switched cable from the junction box to the first fitting. Wire subsequent fittings in line from this fitting. At double-insulated light fittings you'll need to connect the cable earth cores in a separate terminal block to maintain earth continuity in the circuit cable. The floor space above or below the lights will also come in handy for running the cables if you're wiring into a power circuit. Even if the new lights are individually switched, you must install a master switch (in the form of an FCU), in case the circuit needs to be isolated for maintenance or redecoration.

WIRING INTO A POWER CIRCUIT

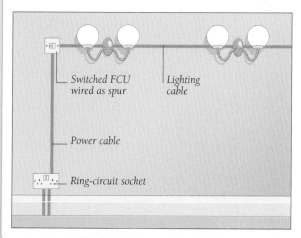

Switched FCU wired as spur

Lighting cable

Power cable

Ring-circuit socket

Wiring lights into a power circuit is better than risking overloading a lighting circuit, and means that you'll have lighting in the room even if a light circuit fuse blows. Fit an FCU as a spur from another socket using 2.5mm^2 power circuit cable, then run new 1.5mm^2 lighting cable from here to each of the new fittings in turn. Join the cable cores in each fitting using special nylon terminal blocks.

Fitting outdoor lights

OUTDOOR LIGHTING *will vastly improve the look of your garden at night, as well as performing an important security function. Choose between a mains-powered unit, or a super-safe low-voltage system.*

■ **A PIR security light** *switches on whenever it senses body heat within a certain range.*

Fitting a security light

These days, the most popular kind of outdoor light for fitting to a house wall is the PIR (passive infra-red) type. For maximum security, run the power supply directly through the wall to the fitting, either as a spur from a socket, or from the ring circuit cable using a 30 amp 3-terminal junction box. In both cases, run the cable via a switched fused connection unit (FCU), preferably the type with a built-in RCD. Mount this inside the house so that the light can be isolated for servicing.

If you have to run a mains power cable beyond the house wall, follow the same rules as for outdoor circuits. If the cable has to be buried, make sure it is the armoured type.

■ **Take the power supply** *for an outdoor light from a power circuit – either at a socket or by breaking into the circuit cable with a junction box. Run the cable directly through the wall to the fitting to prevent tampering, and seal with exterior-grade sealant.*

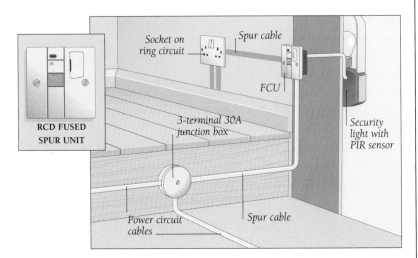

Socket on ring circuit

Spur cable

FCU

RCD FUSED SPUR UNIT

3-terminal 30A junction box

Security light with PIR sensor

Power circuit cables

Spur cable

■ **Low-voltage lights** *come in a variety of guises: for spotlighting individual features, providing background lighting and for illuminating special water features.*

Low-voltage garden lights

Low-voltage garden lights come in globe or spot form and are mounted on spikes so that you can move them around. They have the advantage that they are powered from a plug-in transformer mounted inside the house, using a single, tough, two-core cable that can safely be trailed across lawns and flower beds. The light fittings are then wired to the power cable via trailing leads employing snap-on connectors. Most types come as complete kits.

Low-voltage systems are available for various outdoor appliances, such as garden water features and powered sprinkler systems. Unless the appliance is exceptionally powerful, this is infinitely preferable to running a mains-powered outdoor circuit.

Mount the transformer on an inside wall, close to a socket, and run the cable out to the garden through a hole drilled in a door or window frame. Put the lights where you want them, run the power cable close by, then simply crimp each trailing lead to the cable using the snap-on or screw-on connectors supplied.

■ **Connect the cable** *by laying it flat across the terminals and screwing down the cap.*

Garage door openers

IF YOU HAVE AN UP-AND-OVER garage door, or are thinking of fitting one to replace the old side-hinged doors, why not add an automatic door opener as well? The latest kits have compact key-fob style remote units and can be adapted to fit just about any model of door.

Choosing a system

Most up-and-over garage doors are easily converted to automatic operation: simply measure the door, check that the garage ceiling is unobstructed behind it, and ensure that the door itself is in balance – which may mean adjusting the spring tensioners. Opener kits work by means of a remote-operated electric motor that pulls or pushes the door along a central fixed track. A pivoting attachment on the door is drawn along the track by a chain or belt, or by a geared drive mechanism.

When choosing a kit, look for the following features:
- **Reverse sensors:** these are fitted on either side of the frame and stop the door from closing on the car if you accidentally slip into reverse.
- **An outdoor light:** usually of the PIR type, this can be wired into the circuit to activate automatically as you approach the door.
- **A manual security override:** this deactivates the system from inside the garage when you go on holiday.

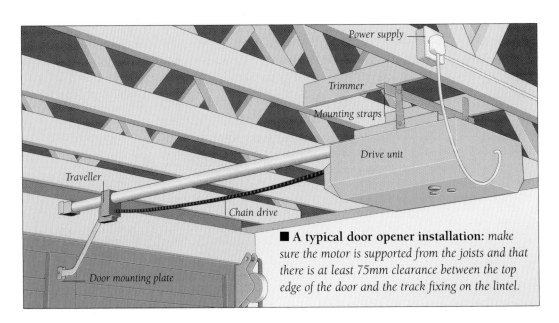

Power supply

Trimmer

Mounting straps

Drive unit

Traveller

Chain drive

Door mounting plate

■ **A typical door opener installation:** *make sure the motor is supported from the joists and that there is at least 75mm clearance between the top edge of the door and the track fixing on the lintel.*

Wiring the door

The opener kit should include all the system wiring, which is normally made with 2-core bell wire. On some systems the connections are all made at the drive unit itself; on others there is a separate connection unit that also incorporates a security override switch. Either way, the terminals should be clearly marked.

Connect the drive unit power cord to a mains power circuit (see pp. 312–13) or to an outdoor power circuit (see p. 299) via a wall-mounted switched fused connection unit (FCU). For extra safety, choose the metal-clad type, and run the circuit cable to the FCU in metal or impact-resistant conduit.

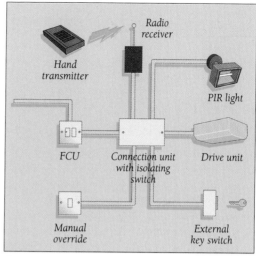

Radio receiver

Hand transmitter

PIR light

FCU

Connection unit with isolating switch

Drive unit

Manual override

External key switch

■ **Wiring layout for an automatic opener**: *in practice, connections may be made at the motor unit, or at a separate connection box.*

A simple summary

✔ When changing ceiling light fittings, bear in mind that you may need access to the floor space from above.

✔ Fit skeleton strip lights under shelves, where space is tight.

✔ Low-voltage lighting is the safest way to install extra fixed lights.

✔ The easiest way to add an extra socket is to wire it from an existing socket – but only if the socket hasn't already been extended in this way.

✔ Wiring for fixed appliances follows the same rules but uses different hardware.

✔ Wall lights are often easier to wire from a power circuit and will stay on if the lighting circuit fuses or trips.

✔ For remote lighting out-of-doors, choose a low-voltage system.

✔ The latest kits for remote-operated electric garage door openers can be adapted to fit most types of door.

More Resources

Trade Organizations

Even for someone with my experience, there are times when I have to call in the professionals. You may get by with word-of-mouth for small jobs, but when you need complex and potentially expensive work undertaken, do yourself a favour and get in touch with the relevant trade association. They offer guarantees for potential contractors, as well as insurance schemes and up-to-the-minute consumer advice.

British Security Industry Association
Security House
Barbourne Road
Worcester
WR1 1RS
01905 21464
www.bsia.co.uk

British Standards Institute
89 Chiswick High Road
London
W4 4AL
020 8996 9000
www.bsi-global.com

British Wood Preserving and Damp-proofing Association
1 Gleneagles House
Vernon Gate
Derby
DE1 1UP
01332 225100
www.bwpda.co.uk

British Woodworking Association
56–64 Leonard Street
London
EC2A 4JX
020 7608 5050
www.bwf.org.uk

CORGI (The Council for Registered Gas Installers)
1 Elmwood
Chineham Business Park
Crockford Lane
Basingstoke
RG24 8WG
Tel: 01256 37220
www.corgi-gas.com

Electrical Contractors Association
34 Palace Road
London
W2 4HY

Federation of Master Builders
14–15 Great James Street
London
WC1N 3DP
020 7242 7583
www.fmb.org.uk

Federation of Plasterers and Drywall Contractors
56–64 St Leonard Street
London
EC2A 4JX
020 7608 5092

Glass and Glazing Federation
44–48 Borough High Street
London
SE1 1XB
020 7403 7177
www.ggf.org.uk

The Guild of Master Craftsmen
166 High Street
Lewes
East Sussex
BN7 1XU
01273 478449
www.thegmcgroup.com

Heating and Ventilation Contractors' Association
Esca House
34 Palace Court
London
W2 4JG
020 7313 4900
www.hvca.org.uk

The Housebuilders Federation
56–64 Leonard Street
London
EC2A 4JX
020 7608 5100
www.hbf.co.uk

Institute of Plumbing
64 Station Lane
Hornchurch
Essex
RM12 6NB
01708 472791
www.plumbers.org.uk

Association of Plumbing and Heating Contractors
Ensign House
Ensign Business Centre
Westwood Way
Coventry
CV4 8JA
02476 470626
www.aphc.co.uk

National Federation of Builders
56–64 Leonard Street
London
EC2A 4JX
020 7608 5150
www.builders.org.uk

National Federation of Plastering Contractors
56–64 Leonard Street
London
EC2A 4JX

National Federation of Roofing Contractors
24 Weymouth Street
London
W1N 3FA
020 7436 0387
www.nfrc.co.uk

National Home Improvement Council
Carlyle House
235 Vauxhall Bridge Road
London
SW1V 1EJ
020 7828 8230
www.nhic.org.uk

National House Building Council
Buildmark House
Chiltern Avenue
Amersham
Bucks
HP6 5AP

National Inspection Council for Electrical
Installation Contracting NICEIC
Vintage House
37 Albert Embankment
London,
SE1 7UJ
020 7564 2323
www.niceic.org.uk

Magazines

There are surprisingly few skills-based DIY publications, with the modern trend in home improvements veering towards style and ideas – but all will offer you valuable consumer advice and reviews of the latest products on the market. Some of the leading DIY superstores publish their own "in-house" magazines and job-based worksheets.

Build It
Build It
Inside Communications
The Isis Building
Thames Quay
193 Marsh Wall
London
E14 9SG
www.self-build.co.uk

Homebuiding and Renovating
Ascent Publishing UK Ltd
Sugar Brook Court
Aston Road
Bromsgrove
Worcestershire
B60 3EX

Homes & Ideas
IPC Media Ltd
King's Reach Tower
Stamford Street
London
SE1 9LS
www.ipc.co.uk

Ideal Home
IPC Media Ltd
King's Reach Tower
Stamford Street
London
SE1 9LS
www.ipc.co.uk

Kitchens, Bedrooms and Bathrooms Magazine
DMG Home Interest Magazines Ltd
Equitable House
Lyon Road
Harrow
HA1 2EW
www.dmg.co.uk

Practical Householder
Nexus Media Ltd
Nexus House
Azelea Drive
Swanley
Kent
BR8 8HU
www.nexusonline.com

Practical Woodworking
Nexus Media Ltd
Nexus House
Azelea Drive
Swanley
Kent
BR8 8HU
www.nexusonline.com

Routing
Nexus Media Ltd
Nexus House
Azelea Drive
Swanley
Kent
BR8 8HU
www.nexusonline.com

Books

With books covering every conceivable area of DIY, the best starting point for the DIY beginner is one of the several excellent general purpose publications. For more specific areas, try logging on to www.amazon.com, which will give you an up-to-date guide to the latest releases, as well as featuring readers' reviews and comments.

Building Your Own Home
    Murray Armor and David Snell,
    Ebury Press, 1992

Collins Complete DIY Manual
    by Albert Jackson and David Day,
    Collins, 2001

Plumbing and Central Heating
    by Mike Lawrence,
    The Crowood Press, 1998

Reader's Digest Complete DIY Manual
    Reader's Digest Association,
    Readers Digest, 1998

Trade Secrets 2001
    by Katherine Lapworth, et al,
    Orion, 2001

The Which? Book of Wiring and Lighting
    by Mike Lawrence,
    Which? Books, 2000

Internet

Although the worldwide web is littered with sites promoting and selling DIY products, there are relatively few devoted to general advice and tips – and even some of these may require payment for full access. Also be aware of American sites where the advice given, particularly involving plumbing and electrics, may be contrary to British standards and regulations. While I can't guarantee the advice given, many sites are signed up to the Which? Webtrader Code of Practice.

www.buildituk.com
    The online arm of Build It magazine, this site is crammed with tips and worksheets for a host of DIY jobs.

www.finddiy.co.uk
    Probably your first port of call on the web, this site offers links to the best DIY sites as well as information on tools, equipment, and tradespeople.

www.homepro.com
    As well as offering innovative style ideas, this site offers legal and financial advice, and a guide to the best contractors to hire.

www.letsbuildit.co.uk
    A site dedicated to helping you find the best contractor suited to your job with advice on project-costing, contracts, and how to get the best value-for-money tools and materials.

www.referenceline.com
    A unique consumer-oriented site that contains hand-written customer references for every aspect of home improvements (as well as other services ranging from car-buying to business advice). It also provides a forum for customer complaints – and company responses.

A Simple Glossary

ABS Type of plastic used to make drain and waste pipes; cheaper and weaker than PVC.

Access eye Bolt-on plate or screw-in plug in a waste pipe that allows blockages to be cleared.

Aerator Water-saving device installed in taps and shower heads.

Aggregate Coarse stone, gravel or similar additive, mixed with cement to form concrete.

Alkyd paint Term used for oil-based paints, because most are now alkyd resin-based.

Ampere (amp) The measure of the rate at which electricity flows through a circuit.

Anchor bolt Hefty bolt that is set in concrete to form an attachment for supporting members.

Apron Sealing strip of sheet material, such as zinc, with its top edge set into a brickwork joint and its bottom edge overlapping the roof below.

Armoured cable Electrical cable wrapped with a layer of steel wires to protect it from damage in exposed situations, such as underground.

Auger Reel of flexible steel spring wire that can be fed along wastepipes to clear blockages; also a corkscrew-like drilling tool.

Backfill Loose soil, stone, or gravel used to fill the space excavated around a foundation wall.

Ballcock Float valve that controls the supply and level in a cold water storage tank or toilet cistern.

Balloon framing Construction method for timber-framed houses in which studs are run from the foundation to the roof, rather than floor to ceiling.

Baluster Turned piece of wood installed as a support for a staircase handrail.

Balustrade Collective term for the parts of a stair handrail, including newel posts and balusters.

Batten Thin wood strip used to attach panelling or to support alcove shelving.

Beam A heavy steel or wood member placed horizontally to help support the load of a building.

Bending spring Metal coil slid into, or over, copper tubing to enable it to be bent without kinking.

Bibcock Wall-mounted tap, often with a threaded outlet for attaching a hose fitting.

Blind nailing A method of nailing boards through the edges to hide the nails.

Branch Pipe connected with a tee joint into a main run of pipework to feed an appliance.

Bridging debris Soil or rendering that covers a damp-proof course and allows water to bypass it.

Building paper A vapour barrier made of reinforced bitumen sandwiched between layers of paper.

Butt joint The most basic woodworking joint, created by nailing the face of one board to the end or edge of another.

Calorific value A measurement of the heating power of fuels such as gas and oil.

Capillary joint Soldered plumbing joint in which the inside diameter of the joint fitting is very slightly larger than the pipe, causing molten solder to flow around the overlapping area.

Carriage Central board under a staircase that runs parallel to the strings to support the treads.

Casing The trim around a door or window.

Cement particle board Type of wall board made with cement, and used to finish walls in bathrooms for its water-resistant properties.

Check valve Plumbing valve that lets water flow in one direction only.

Coaxial cable Aerial and connecting cable for TV and audio equipment, with a braided anti-interference sheath around a central core wire.

Collar beam Horizontal supporting member that connects two opposing rafters.

Column Vertical supporting member, usually made of stone, concrete, or metal.

Composite board Sheet material created by layering different types of wood or wood particles, or by forming wood pieces and additives under pressure.

Conduit Plastic or metal tubing used to protect wires.

Consumer unit Electrical fitting at which the supply is divided into separate circuits, each one protected against overload by a fuse or breaker.

Convector Pipe with fins that present a large surface area for transferring heat from the hot water inside the pipe to the air in a room.

Corner trowel Trowel with an angled blade, used to seat joint tape and level compound in corners.

Crazing A defect in concrete and render in which many minute cracks appear across the surface.

Cripple stud Short vertical stud that is placed between the head plate and header or between the sill and sole plate in a timber-framed wall.

Crosscut Saw cut made across the grain of the wood.

Dado rail Decorative wood moulding installed horizontally around 900mm up from the floor.

Deadman Temporary brace used to shore up the end of a supporting member while a ceiling panel is positioned.

Dedicated circuit A circuit that runs directly to a high-wattage appliance, such as a cooker, from its own fuseway in the consumer unit.

Diverter valve Valve that diverts the water flow from bath taps to a showerhead; also a valve controlled by hot water cylinder and room thermostats to direct heating water as required.

Dragging Method of drawing a paintbrush through a thick coat of wet paint to achieve a textured effect.

Draw tape Sprung metal strip used to feed or pull cables through walls or floor cavities.

Drip groove Channel along the underside of a window sill that directs water away from the wall.

Drip mould Wood or metal moulding over a window that throws rainwater clear of the frame.

Eaves Portion of a roof at the lower end of the rafters that juts out beyond the walls of the house to create an overhang.

Efflorescence White residue, composed of salts, that leaves a stain on damp masonry walls.

Escutcheon Metal plate around a keyhole; it may be covered by a pivoting drop plate.

Expansion joint Narrow gap in a slab of concrete that is filled with treated fibreboard to relieve pressure and limit cracking; also the joint between a concrete slab and a house wall.

Face-nailing Method of driving in nails perpendicular to the surface of the wood.

False beam Hollow member created by joining three boards to create a U-shaped channel, then finishing the exterior to make it look solid. Used to cover exposed pipe runs across ceilings.

Fascia board Board nailed to the vertical ends of rafters to which guttering is attached.

Felt paper Carpet underlay that prevents dust from rising between floorboards and marking the carpet; also used for making templates for sheet flooring.

Finial Decorative piece of wood used to finish the top of a post, usually a newel post on a stair balustrade.

Fire brick Special type of brick used in fireplaces because of its ability to withstand heat.

Flap sander Drill attachment with abrasive paper strips mounted radially on a central boss.

Footing Concrete foundation used to support load-bearing walls, posts, or joists.

Framed wall Horizontal and vertical timber members sheathed with plasterboard or plywood.

Fused connection unit Electrical fitting that provides a fused outlet for direct connection of an appliance to the fixed wiring of the house.

Gable The triangular end of a pitched roof.

Galvanized Coated with zinc to prevent oxidation.

Gauge rod Board marked with regular measurements to check the height of tile or brick courses; also used to set out tiles in order to avoid fiddly cuts.

Gusset plate Triangular brace used to reinforce the corners of wooden frames.

Halving joint Joint formed by cutting away half the thickness of two pieces of same-size wood so that, when assembled, the surfaces are flush.

Handscrew Basic woodworking clamp, with wooden jaws and long, wooden screw-handles.

Hardboard Pliable sheet material formed from wood products, mainly used for lining.

Hawk Steel plate with a handle, used to hold filler, plaster, or bricklaying mortar.

Header Timber beam that provides support above the opening in a framed wall.

Head plate Top horizontal member of a framed wall, fixed to the joists above.

Hearth Stone or concrete slab that forms the base of a fireplace.

Heat gun Paint-stripping tool that uses intensely heated air to soften the paint.

Housed joint Groove cut across a board to receive the edge of another board.

Instantaneous heater Type of water heater that heats the water as it flows through the supply pipe; not efficient for high-demand households.

Ion exchange Method of softening hard water by passing it through a resin that attracts and removes the scale-forming calcium salts.

Jack post Telescopic steel post used as a temporary support for heavy structures.

Jack rafter Short rafters of varying length that make up the triangular ends of a hipped roof.

Jalousie window Window with louvered glass slats that are opened and closed via a crank.

Jamb Vertical side of any building opening.

Jointer Tool for shaping repointed mortar joints.

Joint filler Putty-like material, used to seal the joints between taper-edged sheets of plasterboard and to provide a bed for the jointing tape that covers them.

Joist Sturdy horizontal wooden member, used to support a floor, ceiling, or flat roof.

Junction box Box with screw terminals, used to join lengths of electrical cable.

Kerf The thickness of a saw cut in a piece of wood; it is greater than the thickness of the saw blade because of the set (outward angle) of the teeth, which prevents the blade from jamming in the cut.

Laminated wood Strips of wood glued together under pressure to provide extra strength and thickness.

Latex paint Generic term for water-based paints or those that can be thinned with water.

Lath Thin wooden slat or metal mesh used as a support for cement render or ceiling plaster.

Lean-to A roof that slopes in one direction only, with the upper edge supported by a higher wall.

Lintel Supporting beam over an opening in masonry, such as at a door, window, or fireplace.

Louvre vent Vent with downward-sloping slats; used to cover the end of ducting run through a wall.

Mastic Sealing compound that cures without fully hardening; used for filling gaps between different materials in buildings.

MDF (medium-density fibreboard) Fine wood particle board that is easily shaped to a smooth finish; exterior grades are water-resistant.

Mitre Corner butt joint between two pieces of same-sized moulding, formed by cutting each end to half the final joint angle.

Mortise Housing cut into wood to accommodate a tenon or a fitting such as a lock body.

Mortise-and-tenon A 90° woodworking joint in which the end of one member is reduced in area (the tenon) to fit into a housing in the other member.

Mouse Common name for a draw tape.

Muntin Central vertical frame member of a panelled door, fixed to the top and bottom rails.

Nail guard Steel plate attached to joists or studs to prevent accidental nailing through pipes or cables that are recessed into them.

Nail punch Simple tool used to drive nail heads below the surface of wood.

OSB (oriented strand board) A composite panelling material formed from random thin wafers of wood sandwiched together; for rough work only.

Pad Block of concrete that spreads the load of the structure above it, such as a lintel or column.

Particle board Sheet panelling materials created by mixing fine wood particles with resin; chipboard and MDF are common examples.

Paver Any brick, concrete or other formed piece of masonry used to pave exterior surfaces.

Penetrating oil Lubricant that is used to free seized metal parts.

Pier Thick column of masonry that is bonded into a wall to increase the wall's stability.

Pilot hole Hole drilled to prepare a piece of wood to receive a screw thread without splitting.

Plasterboard Rigid wall-surfacing material made of gypsum plaster sandwiched between layers of paper.

Plinth Moulding used to form a transition between door architraves and skirting boards, or to hide the feet of built-in cabinets.

Plumb Exactly vertical.

Pop-up waste Waste plug in a bath or basin controlled by a lever in the overflow opening or tap body.

Pre-hung door A door sold in its own frame, ready to be installed in an opening.

Pressure-treated timber Finished wooden members that have been impregnated with preservative under extreme pressure.

Profile board A board on edge nailed to stakes and set outside the foundations of a building; saw cuts or nails in the top edge mark the lines of foundations and the faces of walls.

PTFE (polytetraflourethylene) Thin sealing tape that is wrapped round threaded joints in plumbing pipework before assembly.

PVA (polyvinyl acetate) General-purpose household and building adhesive, often used as a wood glue and as a bonding agent for plaster and mortar; also known as "white glue".

PVC (polyvinyl chloride) A plastic used for cable insulation and corrugated roofing; uPVC (unplasticized PVC) is used for plumbing pipes, exterior cladding and window frames.

Radial circuit An electrical circuit that runs in a daisy chain between outlets, starting at the consumer unit and terminating at the last outlet.

Rafter Sloping roof member that runs from the eaves to the ridge and supports the roof covering.

Raft foundation Reinforced slab of concrete, often thicker at the edges, that supports a building and also forms the floor; often used in outbuildings.

RCD (residual current device) A trip switch that detects an imbalance of current in the live and neutral conductors because of an earth fault, and immediately shuts off the electricity supply.

Rebate Step-shaped recess along the edge of a piece of wood, such as in a picture-frame moulding.

Reducer Plumbing fitting that forms a joint between pipes of different sizes.

Reinforcing rods Rigid metal bars used to strengthen concrete slabs and block structures.

Ridge Horizontal board that runs along the top of a roof where opposing rafters meet.

Ring circuit An electrical circuit that runs from the consumer unit to each outlet in turn before returning to the same fuseway in the consumer unit.

Rip sawing Sawing along the grain of the wood.

Riser Vertical pipe carrying water upwards; also the vertical section of stair between two treads.

Sanitaryware Collective term for bathroom fittings made of glazed porcelain, such as toilets.

Sarking felt Sheet material made of woven fibre impregnated with bitumen that forms a secondary waterproof layer beneath roof tiles or slates.

Sash Part of a sliding window that moves.

Scarf Joint in which the ends of two pieces of wood are angled to increase the surface area of the overlap.

Service fuse The electricity company's sealed main fuse, fitted before the supply enters the meter.

Shoe Curved outlet at the base of a rainwater downpipe that directs water away from the house.

Side light Narrow non-opening window adjacent to a door, with its sill at the same level as the door sill.

Skew nailing Nailing at an angle to increase the strength of the joint.

Skim coat The final layer of plaster or surface coating on a wall; also the process of applying it.

Sleeper plate Thin strip of wood that supports flooring over a hard surface.

Sleeper wall Supporting wall of open brickwork that bears the joists in suspended timber ground floor.

Snake Common name for a plumbing auger.

Soakaway A pit dug in the ground and filled with fine stone or gravel to disperse surface rainwater.

Socket outlet Electrical fitting that allows an appliance to be plugged into the fixed house wiring.

Soffit Board nailed to the lower ends of rafters between the facia board and the house wall.

Soil stack Main vertical waste pipe, vented at the top, that carries waste from branch waste pipes to the underground drainage system.

Sole plate Bottom supporting member of a timber framed wall, nailed horizontal to the floor.

Spalling Flaking on the surface of masonry, often due to frost damage.

Spigot The end of a pipe that fits inside a socket to form a joint with an adjoining length.

Splashback Vertical panel of tiles or other waterproof material at the back of a worktop, basin, or sink.

Stile Vertical frame member of a door or window.

Strainer Perforated metal or plastic insert for a sink waste, to catch solids and prevent blockages.

String Diagonal board on a staircase that supports the treads and risers; can be 'open' – that is, revealing the sides of the steps – or 'closed'.

Strutting X-shaped metal or timber braces fixed between floor joists to give a floor extra rigidity.

Stub Length of supply pipe that sticks out through a wall and connects to a fitting.

Stud Vertical timber used in a timber framed wall.

Subfloor Wood or concrete structural floor that is covered by a semi-permanent floor surface, such as wood blocks or ceramic tiles.

Sugar soap Chemical compound used to de-grease paintwork prior to redecorating.

Swan-neck Arrangement of curved joints in a rainwater downpipe that offset the pipe back from gutter outlet to the house wall.

Sweep bend Pipe joint that curves gradually through 90°, resulting in less flow resistance than a sharp bend; similar joints are used in cable conduit.

Tack rag Sticky cloth for removing dust from a rubbed-down surface prior to finishing.

Tail Connection between a tap and its supply pipe; often threaded, but plain on monobloc taps.

Tamp To compact soil or hardcore by ramming it with a heavy piece of timber.

Tamping beam Rigid board, with a handle at each end, that is used with a chopping action across shuttering to compact and level concrete.

Tie Piece of wood or metal that links opposing members and prevents outward movement, such as the tie-beams found at the feet of rafters.

Timber connector A metal disc with teeth projecting from both faces; when bolted between two timbers, the teeth engage in both timbers and prevent them from rotating.

Torpedo level A short spirit level, sometimes with a magnetic base.

Transformer Electrical device that changes the voltage in a circuit.

Trap Plumbing fitting containing a reservoir of water that is installed directly below a waste outlet to prevent odours from the drains entering the house.

Trunking Rectangular-section duct for cables and pipes that protects them when run along wall surfaces; may be plastic or metal.

Underlay Layer of plywood or particle board applied over a rough floor to provide a smooth base for tiles or other floorcoverings; also a resilient layer of felt or foam rubber that is laid beneath carpets and woodstrip flooring.

U-value A measure of a material's resistance to heat transfer.

Valley Rainwater channel between two sloped roof sections; usually made of zinc or lead.

Veneer Thin layer of hardwood applied over a cheaper base wood to provide a decorative surface.

Volt A measure of the pressure that causes electric current to flow around a circuit.

Wainscotting Interior wood panelling covering the bottom third of a wall and capped with a dado moulding.

Wall plate Horizontal timber member fitted along the top of a wall to support, and provide attachment for, joists and rafters.

Water hammer A knocking in water supply pipes.

Water level Hosepipe with a transparent tube at each end; when filled with water, can be used to determine level over a significant distance.

Watt Measure of the power of an appliance – and therefore of the quantity of energy that it will consume per hour.

Weep hole Hole built into a wall to let water seep through; often found in garden retaining walls.

Whetstone Flat, abrasive stone, lubricated with water or oil, that is used to sharpen cutting tools.

Window board Thin shelf installed at sill level and butted against the inside of the frame.

Wood colour stick Crayon-like coloured wood putty, commonly used to disguise scratches in wood.

Index

Acknowledgments

Author's acknowledgments

I would like to thank Mike Trier, Edward Horton, Chris Peterson, Christine Heilman, Nich Hills and Judy Forvargue for their sterling support, my wife Kate for holding the children at bay during my long hours in front of the computer, and Nicki Gault and Jerry Udall for their invaluable help during the completion of the project.

Publisher's Acknowledgments

Dorling Kindersley would like to thank the following people for their contribution to this project: Neal Cobourne for jacket design, Beth Apple for jacket text, and Melanie Simmonds for picture library research.

Packager's Acknowledgments

M-Press would like to thank Mike Trier for planning and commisioning, Edward Horton for project management, Jerry Udall and Robert Bennet for design, Nicki Gault and Ieva Augustaityte for picture research, Ed Herridge, Nich Hills, David Preston, Harriet Williams, and Judy Forvargue for editiorial assistance and to Chris Peterson of Blue Steel Communications NYC for his expert consultancy. A big thank you also to Jeff Carroll and Darius Valaitis in our photographic studio, to our illustrators – Andy Green, Patrick Mulray, Peter Bull, Rob Garrard, Steve Cross, Ian Palmer, and Robert Farnworth – and to Caroline Hunt and Heather McCarry at DK.

Picture credits

key: t = top; b = bottom; l = left; r = right; c = centre

2: Houses & Interiors; 10/11: Houses & Interiors; 12: Houses & Interiors; 16: Stone; 19: Elizabeth Whiting; 20: Houses & Interiors; 22: DIY Photo Library; 24: Houses & Interiors; 26: Houses & Interiors; 27: Houses & Interiors; 28t: Elizabeth Whiting; 28b: Houses & Interiors; 29: Elizabeth Whiting; 31t: Elizabeth Whiting; 31b: Elizabeth Whiting; 34l: Elizabeth Whiting; 34c: Elizabeth Whiting; 34r: Elizabeth Whiting; 36: Houses & Interiors; 38: Elizabeth Whiting; 41: De Walt; 42: DIY Photo Library; 46: Houses & Interiors; 64: Stone; 67: Elizabeth Whiting; 81: DIY Photo Library; 84: DIY Photo Library; 96: DIY Photo Library; 108: DIY Photo Library; 110: Houses & Interiors; 115: Elizabeth Whiting; 126: Houses & Interiors; 132l: DIY Photo Library; 132r: DIY Photo Library; 136: DIY Photo Library; 144: DIY Photo Library; 150:

Stone;156: DIY Photo Library; 164: DIY Photo Library; 168: DIY Photo Library; 178l: DIY Photo Library; 178r: DIY Photo Library; 179l: DIY Photo Library; 179r: DIY Photo Library; 180: Elizabeth Whiting; 182: DIY Photo Library; 192tl: DIY Photo Library; 192tc: DIY Photo Library; 192tr: DIY Photo Library; 192bl: DIY Photo Library; 192bc: DIY Photo Library; 192br: DIY Photo Library; 194: Houses & Interiors; 210: Elizabeth Whiting; 215tl: DIY Photo Library; 215cl: DIY Photo Library; 215r: DIY Photo Library; 215bl: Artech UK Ltd; 216: Houses & Interiors; 218: Houses & Interiors; 219l: Houses & Interiors; 219c: Houses & Interiors; 219r: Houses & Interiors; 220l: DIY Photo Library; 220c: DIY Photo Library; 220r: DIY Photo Library; 221: DIY Photo Library; 222: Stone; 225l: DIY Photo Library; 225c: DIY Photo Library; 225r: DIY Photo Library; 226l: DIY Photo Library; 226c: DIY Photo Library; 226r: DIY Photo Library; 227tl: DIY Photo Library; 227tc: DIY Photo Library; 227tr: DIY Photo Library; 232: DIY Photo Library; 239tl: DIY Photo Library; 239tr: DIY Photo Library; 239cl: DIY Photo Library; 239cr: DIY Photo Library; 239bl: DIY Photo Library; 239br: DIY Photo Library; 242: Timber Decking Association: 243: Timber Decking Association; 244: DIY Photo Library; 246: DIY Photo Library; 262t: Stone; 262b: Adobe; 274: Houses & Interiors; 292: Stone; 299: Elizabeth Whiting; 302: Elizabeth Whiting; 317: Houses & Interiors; 318: DIY Photo Library

All other images and illustrations © Dorling Kindersley

For further information see: www.dkimages.com